Property of Huntsville Public Library

THE LAST BOOK ON THE LEFT

THE LAST BOOK ON THE LEFT

STORIES of MURDER and MAYHEM from HISTORY'S MOST NOTORIOUS SERIAL KILLERS

BEN KISSEL, MARCUS PARKS,
and HENRY ZEBROWSKI

with ILLUSTRATIONS by TOM NEELY

HOUGHTON MIFFLIN HARCOURT
Boston • New York
2020

Copyright © 2020 by MEGUSTALATIONS ENTERTAINMENT, LLC

All rights reserved.

For information about permission to reproduce selections from this book,
write to trade.permissions@hmhco.com or to Permissions,
Houghton Mifflin Harcourt Publishing Company,
3 Park Avenue, 19th Floor, New York, New York 10016.

hmhbooks.com

Library of Congress Cataloging-in-Publication Data
Names: Kissel, Ben, author. | Parks, Marcus, author. | Zebrowski, Henry, author. |
Neely, Tom, 1975–llustrator.
Title: The last book on the left : stories of murder and mayhem from history's most notorious
serial killers / Ben Kissel, Marcus Parks and Henry Zebrowski; illustrations by Tom Neely.
Description: Boston : Houghton Mifflin Harcourt, 2020. |
Second statement of responsibility from title page verso.
Identifiers: LCCN 2019045770 (print) | LCCN 2019045771 (ebook) |
ISBN 9781328566317 (hardback) | ISBN 9780358172284 (e-audio) | ISBN 9780358306740 (CD) |
ISBN 9781328566225 (ebook) | ISBN 9780358409809 (special edition)
Subjects: LCSH: Serial murderers—History. | Serial murderers—Humor.
Classification: LCC HV6515 .K57 2020 (print) | LCC HV6515 (ebook) |
DDC 364.152/32092273—dc23
LC record available at https://lccn.loc.gov/2019045770
LC ebook record available at https://lccn.loc.gov/2019045771

Book design by RAPHAEL GERONI
Illustrations by TOM NEELY

Clapping hands emoji on page 241 © Sudowoodo/Shutterstock.com

Printed in China

SCP 10 9 8 7 6 5 4 3 2 1

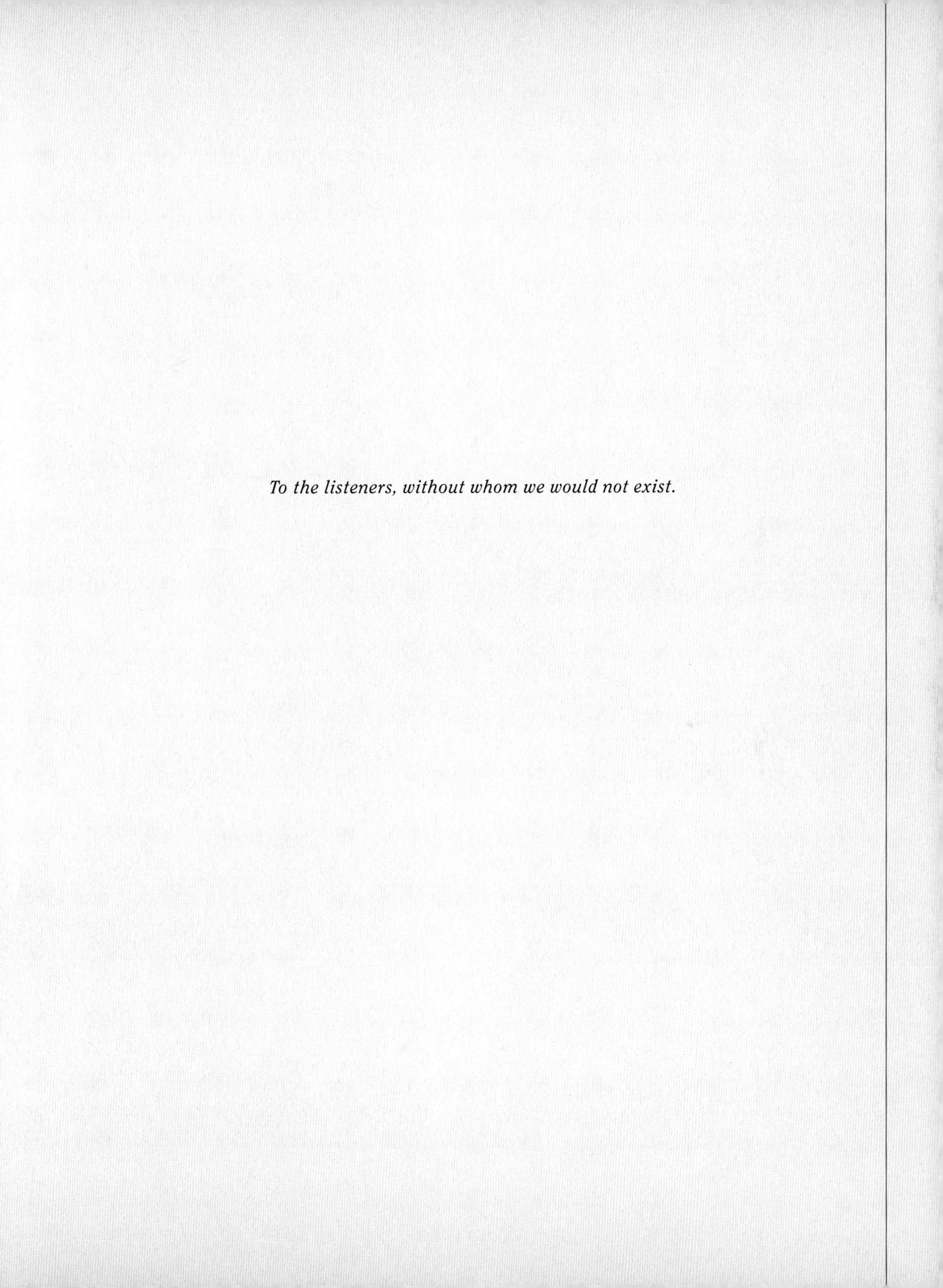

To the listeners, without whom we would not exist.

CONTENTS

GACY
ZODIAC
BTK
DAHMER
GEIN
SAY YOU LOVE SATAN
BUNDY
tomNeely '18

INTRODUCTION

This is

***THE LAST BOOK ON THE LEFT*: Stories of Murder and Mayhem from History's Most Notorious Serial Killers,**

a work thirty-seven years in the making.

IF YOU LISTEN TO THE *LAST PODCAST ON THE LEFT*, YOU ARE a person of taste and power. Thank you for your service. If you haven't heard of our podcast and just want to read about serial killers, you've come to the right place! If you haven't heard of us and you don't want to read about serial killers, put the book down, slowly back away, and go purchase a nice Dave Barry book or one of those tiny books near the cash register with a title like *100 Ways to Make Your Pet Your Child*.

The *Last Podcast on the Left* is a true crime / paranormal / all things dark and mysterious comedy podcast that was started in 2011 by three cretins in the basement of a Mexican restaurant, right next to the crates of beans. Now we are one of the most popular podcasts on the internet thanks to luck and the boredom of millions of people.

Every week we dive deep into the minds and histories of some of the most notorious serial killers the world has ever seen. Led by intrepid producer and researcher Marcus Parks, cohosts Henry Zebrowski and Ben Kissel leave no stone unturned as they examine minute details of these murderers' lives and make fun of their dimple penises and infatuation with milk. Years of researching serial killers has revealed that most of these criminals are not the monsters of nightmares they are so often portrayed to be by "true crime entertainment" but are more often huge dorks who couldn't get anything right in their lives so they turned to murder and mayhem. And we're here to pick this all apart.

Now for the *Last Podcast on the Left* roll call!

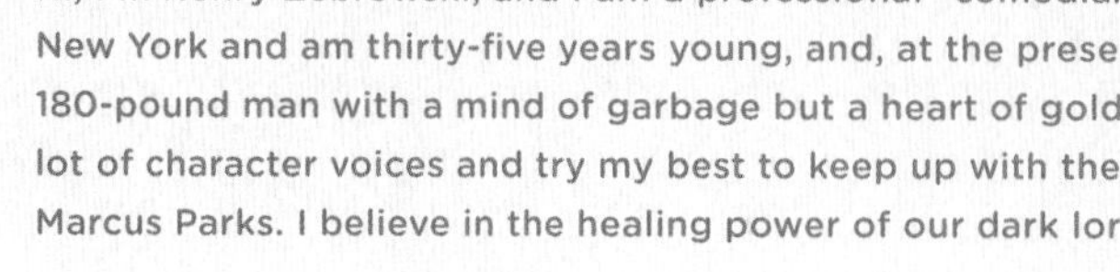

Hi, I'm Henry Zebrowski, and I am a professional "comedian." I hail from Queens, New York and am thirty-five years young, and, at the present, I'm a loose-bodied 180-pound man with a mind of garbage but a heart of gold. On *LPOTL* I do a lot of character voices and try my best to keep up with the research prowess of Marcus Parks. I believe in the healing power of our dark lord Satan.

I'm Ben Kissel! I'm a big guy from the Midwest who has always been fascinated by horror films and true crime stories. As a matter of fact, I grew up only twenty minutes from Ed Gein's grave in Plainfield, Wisconsin. My job on the podcast is to contribute levity to some of the most heinous crimes ever committed and learn right along with the audience.

He learns!

You will not see Marcus's head very often. He lurks in the shadow of his computer.

Now, what goes into the book form of a podcast? That's a good question! Each chapter is a deep dive into a serial killer, with Marcus's analysis driving the narrative and jokes interjected by Henry and Ben. We are tackling nine of the most notorious serial killers in history—most you would identify easily on the Tumblr page of a serial killer groupie—and we've addressed most of them on the show in one fashion or another, but our goal here is to look at these creatures again, with fresh eyes. You might notice Marcus's dried tears throughout as a result of these efforts. Let us be very clear: Marcus wrote most of this. Henry and Ben drank and stared at him while he was hunched over a keyboard like Jack Torrance. All we had to do was write the introduction! Which turned out to be very difficult. It's hard to write a book!

Join us as we cackle into the darkness. The only way to defeat these monsters is to laugh at them. Or put them in jail, obviously.

HAIL SATAN
HAIL GEIN
HAIL YOURSELVES
This is *The Last Book on the Left*.

ΧΩ
tom N. '19

CHAPTER 1

TED BUNDY

WHEN IT COMES TO SERIAL KILLING, ONE HESITATES TO use qualifiers like *best* or *greatest* because, for the most part, using descriptors of that sort is tasteless and disrespectful to the victims. But if one were to objectively quantify pure ability, evasion skills, and the capacity to inspire fear in the hearts of the public, Ted Bundy would come out on top. This man was so terrifying, so reprehensible, so iconic that he seemed mythical. However, when you pull back the curtain, Bundy, like all the degenerates you're going to get to know over the course of this book, was just a man.

Unfortunately, given that very few people ever actually witness a serial killer at work and live to tell the tale, we generally have to trust the most untrustworthy person in the room to create the narrative: the actual killer. The mythology that surrounds Ted Bundy is one that he helped to create, from his supposed habit of gussying up the decapitated heads of his victims with makeup to the sexual acts he allegedly performed on said heads. While there is no doubt about the heinousness of his crimes, there remains skepticism as to the veracity of some of his claims.

As a Knicks fan, I witness a serial killing every game.

They are paid millions of dollars to lose. I can relate. I am paid literally hundreds of dollars to suck on television.

Even before he got a chance to humblebrag about his crimes, Bundy was already well versed in deception. Throughout his life, he fooled those around him by combining his striking good looks with a carefully crafted aw-shucks facade that was rooted in sociopathic confidence. Outwardly, Bundy personified the old cliché: women wanted him and men wanted to be him. Inwardly, he was fueled by narcissism and rage.

Ted Bundy follows a long line of serial killers who lived double lives: during the day they were "normal," meaning they could hold a job and have relationships, but in their minds they would turn into a monster. We learned from H. H. Holmes that for serial killers, getting away with the portrayal of the "normal" part of their lives is often just as thrilling as the murders themselves. They love "getting one over" on someone else because it tickles their sense of superiority—though deep down they know they are in actuality very small and weak.

Even though Bundy's victim count likely runs well past a dozen, many were too badly decomposed when they were found for a full forensic reckoning. The true crime world, however, just couldn't help itself in filling in the blanks when building Bundy's persona and mythology. Bundy has the dubious distinction of being top of the serial killer trash pile, so he needed no help in giving his story an edge of evil. But in the pursuit of profit, crime writers and TV producers turned an admittedly deadly animal into a beast out of Revelation.

It's a common thread in true crime "entertainment": the scarier the monster portrayed, the easier it is to sell books (thank you for your purchase) and get people to watch television shows. Fear makes people buy stuff!

TED BUNDY WAS BORN THEODORE ROBERT COWELL IN Burlington, Vermont, on November 24, 1946, at the Elizabeth Lund Home for Unwed Mothers, known locally as Lizzie Lund's Home for Naughty Ladies.

Better than the original nickname, Lizzie Lund's Bastard Brasserie.

His mother, twenty-two-year-old Eleanor Louise Cowell, was a little shaky on the identity of her son's father upon Ted's birth. Originally, the man listed on Ted's birth certificate was Lloyd Marshall, reportedly a graduate of the University of Pennsylvania, an air force veteran, and a "salesman." Shortly thereafter, for reasons unknown, Louise changed the name to Jack Worthington, of whom we know nothing, save for the fact he was allegedly a sailor who impregnated Louise in Philadelphia.

Literally the most made-up name of all time since Engelbert Humperdinck.

For my money, the most made-up-sounding name I've ever heard was Dick Trickle, but who am I to correct you? (He was a race car driver—I had to look him up.)

In the definitive Ted Bundy book, *The Stranger Beside Me,* criminologist Ann Rule speculated that Bundy was the product of an incestuous relationship between Louise and her father, Samuel Cowell. While Rule provides no hard evidence to support this claim, that hasn't stopped the allegation from being bandied about as the truth for decades. It seems as if most felt that the only other option was that Bundy's father was a mysterious character out of one of the darker Tom Waits songs, perhaps even the devil himself come to the City of Brotherly Love.

People look for any sort of explanation for behavior they feel rubs against the fibers of society. An explanation is comforting and makes it feel like there is purpose or logic in our random universe. Unfortunately, a lot of these monsters are made at random. Like sharts.

Bundy's parentage is probably no more remarkable than that of any other illegitimate kid in Philly whose mother provided shore-leave entertainment and forgot to use a condom. Either way, the Cowell family—proud, upstanding Methodists one and all—decided to spare Ted the shame of illegitimacy and instead raise him as the son of Louise's parents, Eleanor and Samuel. This lie was repeated to every person who came in contact with the Cowells, from friends and family to the neighbors next door. In other words, it was a secret begging to be discovered.

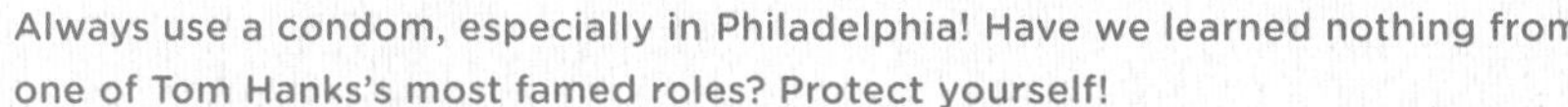

Always use a condom, especially in Philadelphia! Have we learned nothing from one of Tom Hanks's most famed roles? Protect yourself!

Technically, Ted got a lot more consideration than many other kids get. Your parents really have to give a shit about your birth to start an entire conspiracy. Ask Dick Cheney how hard it must have been to put *his* big one* together. *9/11.

Ted's grandfather, Samuel Cowell, was said to be a terrible human being in every way. Animal cruelty was a favorite pastime of his—not a cat in the neighborhood was safe from Samuel swinging them by their tails. Predictably, Samuel was violent toward his family as well; it was reported that he once threw Ted's aunt down a flight of stairs for oversleeping. Interestingly, Ted said he got along famously with his grandfather, mentioning in a 1989 interview with psychiatrist Dr. Dorothy Lewis that he had a special bond with him, even as a very young child. It's possible that the man saw something of himself in his grandson.

Whether it was his grandfather's creeping influence or the awakening of an inborn darkness, it soon became apparent that young Ted was anything but normal. His aunt Julia claimed to have awoken one day to find her then-three-year-old nephew standing at the foot of her bed, smiling. When she lifted the covers, she found that he had arranged three butcher knives around her body, all pointing inward.

Also the Origin Story of the Incredible Chef DAVID CHANG.

Whether it was this specific incident, the violent home situation, or the fear that Ted would discover the secret of his lineage as he grew older, Louise Cowell packed up her son and moved across the country to Tacoma, Washington, shortly thereafter.

Like a struggling indie band looking to make it sorta big.

Like Pavement!

In 1951, Louise met a diminutive hospital cook named Johnnie Culpepper Bundy at a Methodist get-together. Within a few months, the two were married, and five-year-old Ted Cowell was rechristened Theodore Robert Bundy. Johnnie tried to bond with his new stepson, but Ted never took to playing ball or going on fishing trips with his stepfather.

It's hard to bond with a man with *pepper* in his name. Ask Barry Pepper. Too spicy for friends.

Culpepper Bundy sounds like a tool used to clean out Uncle Eddie's sewage tank in *National Lampoon's Christmas Vacation*. "The crapper is full—hand me that Culpepper Bundy hose to drain it out!"

From a young age, Bundy begged out of father-son activities by playing sick because his stepfather was, in Bundy's words, "not too bright." He saw his stepfather as a lesser-than because he worked a blue-collar (yet entirely respectable) job. His stepfather's choice of profession and subsequent inability to provide an upper-crust lifestyle for his family grated on him; even as a young boy, he believed he deserved better.

Bundy was known to be a solitary child. His only solace came from listening to the radio. He particularly enjoyed talk radio, but not for the content. In an interview given in 1980, Bundy said he liked radio because he felt as if he were eavesdropping on other people's conversations, a hint of his budding sociopathic tendencies.

I don't want to condone supporting violent criminals, but if he had subscribed to our Patreon, I'd have accepted the money.

Last Podcast on the Left cannot be held responsible for the actions of our fans.

The other thing Bundy was apparently a freak for—even as a small child—was pornography. Supposedly, before Bundy even arrived in Washington, he had whiled away countless hours in his grandfather's shed, looking at the hard-core collection the old man kept stashed behind the garden tools. Bundy said that seeing these magazines at such a young age essentially broke his brain. Tellingly, though, when he was finally outed as a killer it was found that his masturbation material was not the stuff of torture and bondage, but rather a magazine devoted to the art of cheerleading called *Cheerleader*.

Wait, a radio fanatic who also liked smut? What's next—a professional cornhole player who also likes buckets of beer?

Are we *all* monsters? There was a period of my life when if I put two cantaloupes next to each other, I would become aroused. When I was a kid, I got most of my porn from the illegal cable box my family had, like a real millennial. I'm just trying to say the porn didn't make him bad! Oh my god, what have I done?

Once Bundy was in his teens, however, his actions began to pattern those we see in many serial killers. He was a pathological liar and an accomplished shoplifter, and he was arrested twice on suspicion of car theft and burglary. Unfortunately, the details of those crimes are lost to history because the records were shredded once he turned eighteen. But one detail we do know about his kleptomania was that he was most fond of stealing ski equipment.

Bundy was indeed a skier, but as a lower-class kid, the sport's expenses were essentially prohibitive. He said he would get sideways glances from his peers when he showed up with the latest-and-greatest ski equipment, but he learned early on that he could get away with a crime if he maintained a nonchalant attitude. In his mind, he was owed the finer things in life by dint of his very existence, and he was determined to reach that special status by any means necessary. In trying to explain his motivations to investigators, Bundy said, "I felt kind of deprived, at a disadvantage to those people who had the money, the successful parents, all the goodies."

Across the spectrum of true crime we see a theme of this "I'm actually supposed to be a very important millionaire" mentality. This is used to justify a superior attitude toward other people and help validate crimes against society. David Berkowitz had this same mentality, as did Jim Jones and L. Ron Hubbard. And a lot of people who live at the Greyhound station in West Hollywood.

Part of Bundy's desire to ascend the ranks of society led him to the University of Washington. The year was 1967, and while much of America's youth was being swept up in free love, good drugs, and some of the best music ever recorded, Bundy focused himself on two things that could not have been more diametrically opposed to the burgeoning hippie movement: skiing and China.

Both also fun words for cocaine, which I imagine was around quite a bit.

While skiing was Bundy's gateway into a more privileged social echelon, learning to speak Chinese was supposed to be his pathway to power. Once Bundy arrived at UW, he enrolled in an intensive Chinese language course—solely because he believed that the Chinese were likely going to take over the world, sooner rather than later.

This really helps me understand his love of Richard Nixon.

Throughout his middling college career, Bundy continued skiing, which eventually led him to meet Stephanie Brooks, who would turn out to be both the love of his life and his victim prototype. He'd bum rides up to the mountains with her and slowly fell in love with the beautiful brunette from a rich, stable family. While the feelings were not fully reciprocated, Stephanie certainly felt a kind of puppy love for Ted. But from her perspective, he was immature, emotional, and undependable: perfect for a college fling, but definitely not husband material. In other words, Stephanie was slumming it every time she hopped into bed with Bundy, and she knew it.

Though Bundy himself was not living a posh lifestyle, he tried his best to nuzzle into the upper class, both through these interactions and a series of part-time jobs in more monied settings, like as busboy at a yacht club. However, he didn't use his yacht club employment as an opportunity to hobnob; instead, he preferred stealing from club members. This propensity for theft, lying, and straight-up sociopathy naturally drew him to the world of politics.

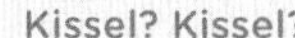

Kissel? Kissel?

Ted Bundy is the perfect poster boy for the alt-right. His politics are terrible. He dresses well. And he's constantly attempting to cover up his weird fetishes.

But unlike fellow politician-turned–serial killer John Wayne Gacy (D-Illinois), Ted Bundy was a dyed-in-the-wool lifelong Republican. These two men's motivations for getting into the game differed as well. Gacy looked at politics as a way to gain influence and inflate his ego; his brand was sleazy and local, true Chicago-style. Bundy, on the other hand, liked standing next to those in power—he was cleaner and more formal. While Gacy wanted theme parties and parades, Bundy wanted policy.

Maybe he also liked the dichotomy of knowing there was a homicidal gremlin roiling on the inside and a put-together Republican on the outside. And he gets the extra kick out of being a contrarian during a very liberal part of our history. There are so many fun ways to make white people horny!

He would support the death penalty for people who wear white after Labor Day, don't own a yacht, and don't rewind VHS rentals, like Kathleen Turner in *Serial Mom*!

In 1968, at the age of twenty-two, Bundy was appointed both the Seattle chairman and the assistant state chairman of the New Majority for Rockefeller, backing the titular Nelson Rockefeller in his third unsuccessful run for president. Bundy traveled to that year's Republican National Convention in Miami only to have his political dreams crushed when Rockefeller was destroyed at the hand of the by-then unstoppable political machine that was Richard Nixon.

And even as an adult, Bundy didn't kill as many people as Nixon! Nixon beat him at everything!

That political heartbreak was only the first of many disappointments that year for Bundy. In the fall, Stephanie Brooks, realizing more and more that Ted was a lying, scheming layabout, told him it was over. Devastated, he dropped out of the University of Washington. He eventually landed a job as a driver and bodyguard for another political candidate, Art Fletcher. Fletcher was headed for the lieutenant governor spot, but the only thing he gained from that campaign was a mention of Ted Bundy on his Wikipedia page.

How did he get hired as a bodyguard? "Yes, find me the man who most resembles an L.L.Bean model so I can feel safe."

After the Fletcher defeat, Bundy returned to Philadelphia, the city of his conception, where he enrolled at Temple University for one half-hearted, aimless semester.

Afterward, he traveled to Vermont and supposedly discovered the truth behind his parentage: his parents were his grandparents and his sister was his mother.

Disgustingly, this is an actual genre on Pornhub.

In the true crime genre, this event has been put forth time and again as the breaking point for Ted Bundy, but this claim is circumstantial at best. It may have been a catalyst, but it was by no means an immediate cause and effect, as it was another three years before he attempted his first murder. What's even more telling, though, is that multiple high school friends later reported that they clearly remember him unironically calling Louise "Mom" on multiple occasions. It's very likely that by the time he returned to Vermont, Bundy had known the truth for years.

Narcissists like Bundy always have to control their story arc. This was him putting in his own chapter headings. He saw his whole life as this dramatic tale that everyone would read about one day. Now he's being played by Zac Efron, and I'm mad because of how sick his abs are. Totally rude, sick abs.

But no matter what happened during his adventure out East, the fact remains that in the spring of 1969, Bundy returned to Washington a changed man. No longer the rudderless busboy of the past, he emerged from his experience in Philadelphia as a straight-A student. He set aside his fantasy of Chinese domination and reenrolled at the University of Washington with a major in psychology. In this, Ted seemed to have found his calling.

His psychology background also gave birth to perhaps one of the most misunderstood episodes of Bundy's life: his time as a suicide hotline volunteer. This era was well documented by Ann Rule, a former Seattle police officer turned student and the author of the aforementioned book *The Stranger Beside Me.* Rule answered phones right alongside Bundy during the summer of 1970, spending twelve hours a day with the most notorious serial killer in history.

This is the only redeeming quality of Ted Bundy's life. It's kinda in the opposite order of how Michael Vick killed dogs but now he helps them! Donate to his foundation here . . .

Bundy's time as a volunteer has been the focus of many discussions when it comes to parsing the mind of a serial killer. The notion that a sociopathic murderer would willingly save lives by working a suicide hotline naturally raises the question of his possible motivations for doing this. The answer is surprisingly mundane: working for the hotline was a work-study requirement for his psychology degree. He and Rule worked side by side as partners for months. According to her, they made a good team. He spoke to callers with patience and empathy, in a drawl that she described as almost courtly, and she considered him a close friend. For Ted, though, it was just another role to play.

But whether or not he appeared normal, there was still something vicious bubbling beneath the surface of Bundy's psyche. Around this time, he began acting in a way that was relationally sociopathic, briefly bringing his old flame Stephanie Brooks back into the mix while ensnaring a completely different woman into a decades-long thrall.

In September 1969, Bundy met and started dating a young single mother named Elizabeth Kloepfer. She wasn't as pretty or blue-blooded as Stephanie Brooks, but she was devoted to Ted and would stay by his side for a surprising length of time, even after Bundy was placed behind bars.

For the single ladies out there, when you're dating a new guy, here's a trick: place a mannequin in your bed and invite the guy over. Casually put your phone on video record behind a teddy bear and hide in the closet. If the dude comes in and immediately starts strangling the mannequin, break up with him, y'all! This has been dating advice from Henry Z.

Bundy's greatest trick was convincing Elizabeth that no matter what he did, she was lucky to have him. She was so blind to who he really was that she didn't even notice—or refused to notice—when he reconnected with Stephanie Brooks in early 1970. Since Stephanie had first dumped Ted, he'd undergone an impressive transformation. In addition to earning his psychology degree, he'd started becoming successful in politics on a state level, was admitted to two law schools, and had even saved a local toddler from drowning. To Stephanie, he had grown up, but in reality, these changes were not born of any desire to turn his life around. Instead, Ted Bundy had become a better man in order to destroy Stephanie Brooks, using his accomplishments as the cheese in the trap.

If he was Bobby Bonilla and this was about Bobby defying his father and winning at baseball, I would be rooting for him. But it's not. Also, I'm not sure about Bobby Bonilla suffering too much hardship. I think his dad might have loved him.

When Stephanie heard about Ted's shifts in personality and social standing, she was smitten. Now that he had seemingly transformed into the man she needed him to be, the two talked on the phone and visited each other as much as they could. Marriage was even discussed. However, right when he was on the verge of proposing, the manipulation began and he slowly and methodically broke her heart. Sex became perfunctory and emotionless; he'd ditch her for days on end; and a fictional ex-girlfriend who supposedly badgered Ted for an abortion was created to sow phony discord. After months of this behavior, Stephanie confronted him about his emotional 180, but his only response was a flat, "Stephanie, I have no idea what you mean." Smart enough to see the game he was playing, she never spoke to him again.

There are more red flags in this relationship than what you see in Google Maps when you search for bagel shops in Brooklyn.

This motherfucker had his psycho tendencies baked in; dude is legitimately scary. And this is *before* he started killing people!

This sequence of events has generally been described as one of the triggers that thrust Bundy down the killing path, but it's hard to say for sure. After all, he'd orchestrated the whole charade himself, and the only rejection was his own. It is worth noting, though, that in the same month that his relationship with Stephanie Brooks ended, he began following women home from bars without their knowledge. It could be that he'd been planning this all along, treating Stephanie Brooks's heartbreak as just another item in a checklist on the way to something more nefarious. But it *is* uncanny that the vast majority of Bundy's victims had long hair parted down the middle, just like Stephanie Brooks.

Even though his internal sociopathy was begging him to go further, Bundy needed one more ingredient to make the leap into violent assault: alcohol. He began drinking heavily in this era, finding that when he was drunk, the inhibitions that kept him from acting on his dark impulses were removed. In early December 1973, leaving a bar after a long night of boozing, he followed a woman home on a whim.

I don't recall seeing this trope in Bud Light commercials.

They cut it out of the American run, but it's still in the Dutch version.

As he followed this woman, Ted took a shortcut and got ahead of her. Then he grabbed a two-by-four he found next to a dumpster and waited in the shadows. But just before she crossed paths with Bundy, she took a left turn, possibly saving her life. However, instead of waking up the next morning feeling remorse, Bundy said he opened his eyes feeling both terrified and excited. He'd gotten a taste of the hunt, and the only thing that would satisfy his newfound hunger would be a successful catch.

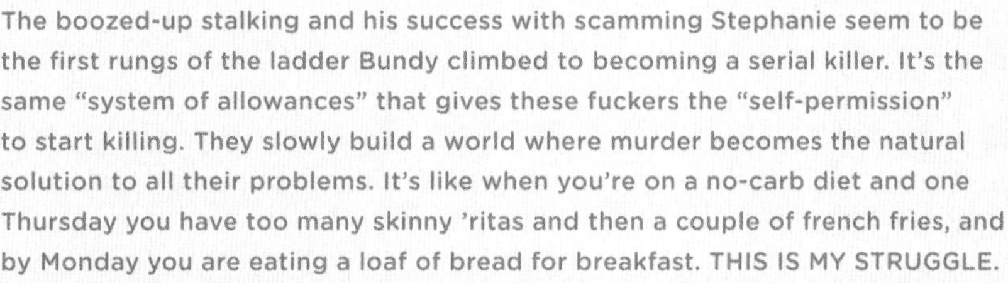

The boozed-up stalking and his success with scamming Stephanie seem to be the first rungs of the ladder Bundy climbed to becoming a serial killer. It's the same "system of allowances" that gives these fuckers the "self-permission" to start killing. They slowly build a world where murder becomes the natural solution to all their problems. It's like when you're on a no-carb diet and one Thursday you have too many skinny 'ritas and then a couple of french fries, and by Monday you are eating a loaf of bread for breakfast. THIS IS MY STRUGGLE.

Emboldened by this first venture, Bundy went out again the next few nights, seeking an opportunity to strike. Three days after the failed attempt, he came across a woman fumbling with her keys as she tried to open her car door. Sneaking up behind her, he bashed her in the head using a club, possibly the same two-by-four from his earlier effort. However, the blow wasn't enough to knock her out; instead she fell to the ground screaming, sending Bundy running off into the night.

Bundy went out on countless occasions after that, but he only found a victim who was "just right" a handful of times. Although Bundy's system was simple, serial killers are often captured when their system breaks down. As the urge to kill rises, the less patience they have when it comes to finding a victim, and less patience means more mistakes. As the infamous Ted Bundy quote goes:

> "You learn what you need to kill and take care of the details. It's like changing a tire. The first time you're careful. By the thirtieth time, you can't remember where you left the lug wrench."

Bundy claimed his urge to assault this woman coincided with the appearance of what he called the "entity." While his rational mind was supposedly battling the constant craving to attack, the entity was what got him into the streets to look for a victim. However, he said that it was not the entity itself that committed the murder—the mysterious presence was only responsible for the assaults. Bundy claimed that it was his rational self who committed the murders in order to cover up the entity's crimes.

Kinda fun fact: *The Entity* is also a horror movie starring Barbara Hershey.

Following that first assault, Bundy switched tactics and began seeking victims via window peeping. After carefully scouting for his first home invasion, he found an opportunity with Karen Sparks, who had a basement apartment near his law school. From the moment he entered her apartment on January 4, 1974, Bundy was swift, cruel, and full of wrath. He snuck into her room while she was asleep, quickly twisted a metal bar from her bed frame, and beat her unconscious. Then he sexually assaulted her with the same metal bar he'd used to beat her half to death.

Karen was found by her roommate under blood-soaked sheets the following afternoon. She had survived but was left with permanent brain damage. Bundy would ensure his next victim wouldn't even be left with that.

Just a few days after his attack on Karen Sparks, he picked Lynda Ann Healy as his next target. He stalked her for weeks, watching her every move and waiting for the perfect moment to strike. That moment came on January 31, 1974, almost one month to the day after his last conversation with Stephanie Brooks. He broke into Healy's bedroom, knocked her unconscious, wrapped her in a sheet, and carried her out to his infamous VW Bug. Taking her to a spot where he and Stephanie had occasionally gone on ski trips, Bundy proceeded to rape Lynda Ann Healy before strangling her to death.

With this murder, Bundy claimed to have moved on from amateur status to what he called his "prime" or "predator" phase. For the next seven months, there was not a coed in Seattle who was truly safe from him.

He has no business having this Eric Trump level of confidence.

Unlike many serial killers who go years between their first, second, or even third kills, Ted Bundy had, to put it in sports terms, one hell of a rookie year. Two months after Lynda Ann Healy came Donna Manson, who disappeared moments after leaving her house to go to a jazz concert. Next was Susan Rancourt, bludgeoned in the head with a tire iron while she was in the middle of doing a load of laundry. She, too, took a trip to the mountains with Ted Bundy.

After these three young women mysteriously disappeared, some members of the community came forward with reports of a suspicious handsome man with his arm in a sling driving a VW Beetle and approaching women on the street. One woman said the stranger asked her to help carry a load of books to his car, but when she noticed it was missing its front passenger seat—removed by Bundy to facilitate a quick kidnapping—her flight instinct took hold and she ran away. Other women reported similar encounters. This trick became Bundy's signature move: preying on women by pretending to be injured, and then using their kindness as an opening to attack them in a vulnerable moment.

After the first three murders, both the frequency and the brutality of the attacks escalated. Take Brenda Ball. Bundy's confession of the Brenda Ball murder included an admission to the most unnatural act known to man: necrophilia. He claimed to have met Ball when he picked her up from the side of the road as she was hitchhiking. They went to his apartment and had consensual sex, but that wasn't enough for the so-called entity. Bundy strangled Ball and claims he then had sex with the corpse. He kept the body in the closet for days, pulling it out like a favorite toy when the entity wanted more. When the smell got to be too much, Bundy took the body to his dump site in the mountains before moving on to his next victim just a week later.

Now, we don't know if this story is true, as the only evidence for it comes from Bundy himself. It's difficult to understand the motivations in his confessions. At times he was forthcoming with details of his crimes, while at others he conveyed the information entirely in third person, as if to remove himself from the situation. For example, at the age of fourteen, Bundy had a job tossing newspapers. In 1961, eight-year-old Ann Marie Burr disappeared from a location that was on his route. Her body was never recovered, but in 1989 Ted told investigator Robert Keppel that even though he had confessed to over thirty murders, there were some he would never talk about. He then switched to a third-person narrative, saying those killings included a murder, "committed at a young age, against a child victim, close to his own home."

This type of obfuscation is fairly common among highly compartmentalized killers, the ones who manage to live a "normal" life while indulging in their macabre hobby. In order to blend into society, these men have to separate themselves into different personas, and those personas rarely overlap.

For killers like Bundy, who believe they are superior to the rest of society, control is what they seek, be it with their victims or in the narrative of their crimes. Whether it's true or not that Bundy was a necrophiliac, he liked to make people feel extremely uncomfortable. It was an intrinsic part of his sexual gamesmanship. He knew he could say anything and people would believe him, and so the mythmaking became another form of power. People were quick to accept the monstrous persona that Bundy helped shape during his incarceration as truth; he, in turn, got pleasure from increasing the gap between his life as a "civilian" and his life as a serial killer. The farther away a serial killer can push his "normal" life from his "deviant" life in terms of extremism, the better the serial killer can show how capable a predator he (or she, you're welcome) is.

Now I am scared.

Less than a fortnight after the murder of Brenda Ball, Bundy embarked on the first of what would be a series of incredibly audacious crimes: the murder of Georgann Hawkins. A student at the University of Washington, her disappearance gained the most notoriety of his murders in Seattle because of the almost supernatural way in which she disappeared. She was walking back to her sorority house after visiting her boyfriend at his fraternity. The two houses were located a mere ninety feet away from each other, connected by an alleyway, and—as if we needed any more help making this feel like a slasher flick—two students saw her when she was just forty feet from home. But in those forty feet, Georgann Hawkins disappeared without a sound.

The theory as to what happened is that while Bundy was lying in wait for a victim, he'd heard one of the students at the frat house refer to Georgann using a familiar nickname: George. As she walked past Bundy's Bug, he may have whispered this name, drawing her close. Then, quick as a rattlesnake, he swung his tire iron and knocked her unconscious, killing her instantly. Georgann Hawkins is one of the few who fell victim to Ted Bundy whose body has never been found.

The fact that he didn't need much prep before abducting his victims is part of what made Bundy so deadly. So here's a tip: don't stare at your phone when you're walking at night! You could be a target! Buy a flashlight or a whip, and use THOSE instead. Whip your arms around your head like a helicopter and make cat noises. Now you're being scary AND getting in some cardio.

By June 1974, all of Washington State was on high alert, specifically young women. This presented Bundy with a problem: his old tricks would no longer work. Nobody was going to venture into a dark corner with a stranger now that these disappearances and subsequent searches were almost-daily news. To circumvent this, he changed his MO, or at least partly. Ted stuck with the injury ruse, but instead of doing it under the cover of night, he started claiming victims from a place and time where no one would expect a snatch-and-grab killer to strike: at the beach in broad daylight.

On July 14 Bundy began approaching solitary women at Lake Sammamish, twelve miles east of Seattle, where over forty thousand people were trying to cool off on a scorching day. With his arm in a cast, he charmingly asked women for assistance attaching his sailboat to his car. Many followed him off the beach, assuming they were only going to the parking lot, but once there Bundy added a second location—actually, the boat was at his parents' place up the road.

NEVER HELP ANYONE.

Woman after woman refused upon hearing this new information, but at 12:30 p.m., twenty-three-year-old Janice Ott offered to help. Bundy took her to an abandoned house, raped and terrorized her for hours, and then left her tied up, still alive. He returned to the house at around 5:00 p.m. with Denise Naslund, who had been taken in by the same ploy. She was raped while Janice watched before he proceeded to strangle them both. Their bodies were dumped only two miles away in Lake Sammamish State Park, near the bodies of Lynda Ann Healy, Brenda Ball, and Susan Rancourt.

Police were once again baffled by the disappearances, especially because they had occurred during the day. But in an act of hubris, Bundy had given his real name every time he had approached a potential victim. Police now knew they were looking for a Ted, but what they didn't have, surprisingly, was a solid sketch.

One of Bundy's greatest advantages as a serial killer was that his facial features seemed to morph and change in a way that bordered on the paranormal. He was known to be handsome, but every person who sketched the mysterious Ted could never seem to draw him with any recognizable facial features.

Every police sketch of Bundy looks like it's drawn by a talentless hack trying to get into art school to waste their parents' money.

Even so, the sketch of the man named Ted resembled him enough for coworkers, friends, and even his girlfriend, Elizabeth, to tease him for his similarities to the Sammamish Beach killer. The sketch looked just like him, the man's name was Ted, and he reportedly drove a VW Bug just like Bundy—and yet, even the remote possibility of Ted Bundy being a murderer seemed like the most ridiculous idea in the world.

How funny is that?! Ted, look, this serial rapist has the same name as you and he drives the same exact car! Isn't that funny? Ted, put down the knife!

Conveniently for Bundy, he'd already accepted an offer from the University of Utah to attend law school in Salt Lake City. Just as investigators were presented with a few promising leads about Seattle's coed killer, he left town to embark on a killing spree that would span at least five states and two coasts.

Honestly, by Salt Lake City standards, Ted Bundy is the wildest guy since Jeremy Piven from *PCU*!

But Bundy was leaving more than just victims behind; he was leaving Elizabeth as well. She doubted his promises that he would return to Seattle—but over the previous year, he'd introduced other worries into her mind, mostly concerning some of his more inexplicable possessions.

"Wait a second, you mean to tell me all the tubs that Ted brought home . . . they were not butter? I can't believe it!"

The plaster of paris and crutches were odd things for a healthy man like Bundy to keep around, but according to him, he'd stolen the plaster just for the thrill of it and was storing the crutches as a personal favor to his landlord.

COME AND GET ME, SNAKE-BOY!

The fake mustache he kept around was strange as well, especially since Bundy had no trouble growing facial hair. Then there was the meat cleaver, kept in a pinkish leather case, which was one of the few items he ensured made the trip to Utah with him.

Only serial killers and prop comedians carry around unneeded crutches. Both erode the fabric of our nation!

We had a wheelchair for our sketch group for many years and we used it to bring cases of beer from the car to the apartment. So we were a responsible part of the comedy community.

It wasn't just the objects that were suspect to Elizabeth. As Ted's killing spree continued, his behavior had become more and more erratic. He would leave in the middle of the night, giving Elizabeth no idea of where he was going, and he bought her the relatively benign book *The Joy of Sex* and used it as an excuse to incorporate near-death chokeplay and hard anal into their sex life. But weirdest of all, Elizabeth woke up in the middle of the night more than once to find Ted under the covers with a flashlight, studying every inch of her body as if she was no more than an object. At the time, she'd played it off as one of his silly peccadilloes, but as his travels and the trail of the dead converged more and more, even she could not ignore the red flags of the past.

After arriving in Utah, Bundy's old patterns of peeping, stalking, and scouting began anew almost immediately. A woman named Teresa wrote a letter to Ann Rule recounting how she vividly remembered a stranger skulking around a house that she shared with a few other young women in Salt Lake City during this era. They even got a clear look at his face one night while he was hiding behind a bush, but the sketch made then had no more of an effect in capturing Bundy than the ones in Washington had. He finally left them in peace, but not before leaving a large pile of feces under the window where they'd last seen him. When Ted Bundy was finally caught, Teresa was positive that he had been their mystery pooper.

If this was the worst thing he ever did, he'd only be guilty of being the funniest guy in the Delta House frat.

Bundy's first victim in Utah was taken from the streets of Holladay on October 2, 1974, and before his first semester of law school was over, he would go on to kill four more women. In recounting these events, Bundy revealed that he had gone as far as to apply makeup to and style the hair of two of these victims after their deaths, telling investigators, "If you've got the time, they can be anything you want them to be."

Humans are not Potato Heads, Ted. None of us care about what you learn in your fancy law school books!

I've heard law school is murder . . . Okay, I'll show myself out. Thank you!

One victim, however, was able to escape Bundy's clutches. Trading out his injury getup for a dependable fake mustache, he talked eighteen-year-old Carol DaRonch into his VW at the mall by impersonating a police officer. When she noticed he was driving in the opposite direction of the police station, she tried opening the door. Bundy responded by slapping a handcuff on her wrist, but she fought back, even after he pulled a gun on her. Amid this struggle, Carol managed to open the door and spill out onto the street, but Bundy was ready with a tire iron. Before he could land a fatal blow down upon her head, however, DaRonch kicked him in the groin and ran away to safety.

This attempt had been a horrendous failure, one that Bundy planned to rectify that very night. So he improvised, driving just a few miles to the nearby town of Bountiful. There he happened upon a school play and made the mistake of trying to talk a busy teacher into coming over to his car. After she refused twice, he left the Bug and instead lured a teenager named Debra Kent from the parking lot. But in his haste to restore what ego he'd lost in the Carol DaRonch debacle, Bundy left behind a physical clue: a key, which fell out of his car in the process of kidnapping and eventually killing Debra Kent. That key unlocked the handcuff that was still dangling from Carol's wrist when she was rescued. In addition to this, a witness had seen Bundy speeding off in his Beetle. It was now plainly obvious to the people of Utah that there was a serial killer in their midst.

While today this would be national if not worldwide news, in the seventies, even the murders of a handful of pretty young girls stayed somewhat regional. Few outside of Washington State knew the details of the Seattle killing spree, and similarly, word of Bundy's Utah murders barely spread beyond the borders of the state. The only person who noticed the connection was Lynn Banks, a close friend of Elizabeth Kloepfer.

Banks was one of the few humans whose hair stood on end in the presence of Ted Bundy. She had been flabbergasted when everyone had laughed off his similarities to Sammamish Ted, and during a family visit back home to Utah, she saw photos of the girls he'd killed there and immediately noticed how much they looked like his victims in Washington. Banks tried her best to sound the alarm in both states, but no one would take her seriously. It wasn't until authorities from Washington and Utah spoke to each other at a crime conference that a connection was made, but that didn't help in the physical capture of Ted Bundy. Seven more women would die before Ted was caught for the *first* time.

Bundy's first arrest would be far less dramatic than his last. In the wee hours of the morning on August 16, 1975, he was pulled over for reckless driving in a residential neighborhood of Granger, Utah. When the officer asked what he'd been

doing that night, Ted said he'd been to see *The Towering Inferno* at the local drive-in but had gotten lost on his way home. Knowing there had been no showing of *The Towering Inferno* that night, the officer asked Bundy to step out of the car while he searched it.

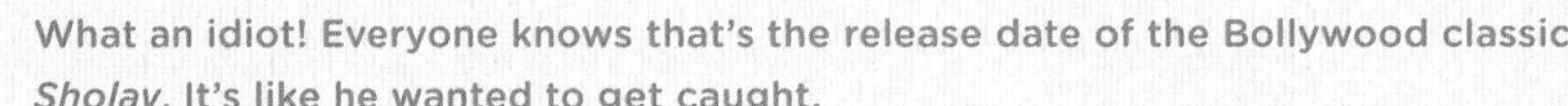

What an idiot! Everyone knows that's the release date of the Bollywood classic *Sholay*. It's like he wanted to get caught.

Someone worked with our research assistant!

Inside the trunk, the officer found a bag and pulled out Bundy's tools of the trade one by one: a ski mask, wire, an ice pick, rope, handcuffs, and the infamous tire iron. A deeper search turned up a flashlight, gloves, and a terrifying custom-made pantyhose mask. Bundy was booked on reckless driving charges and possession of burglary tools, the first time he'd been arrested as an adult. After that, things promptly started to fall apart.

He might as well have been driving Jigsaw's tricycle!

Bundy was quickly connected to the attempted abduction of Carol DaRonch and charged with aggravated kidnapping. Now that a clearly violent MO had been established, an officer in Salt Lake City remembered a call he'd gotten earlier that year from a woman in from Washington State who said she thought her friend's boyfriend may have been responsible for the rash of murders plaguing Utah. Working off that tip, authorities brought Elizabeth Kloepfer in for questioning. She recounted the strange objects and suspicious behavior she'd observed while dating Bundy, but most damning of all, she revealed that she'd done her own detective work after her friend had been so adamant about her suspicions. After cross-referencing her calendar and diary with newspaper reports, Elizabeth Kloepfer discovered that her boyfriend had been unaccounted for on every night that a girl had disappeared in Seattle in 1974.

Move over McConaughey, there's a new true detective in town.

I'd say you shouldn't track your boyfriend's life this closely, but in this case, she was completely correct to do so. Wait, do all significant others do this? I'm innocent!

While the connections to the murders in Utah were still circumstantial, the case for a crime he'd committed in Colorado was about to become concrete. Earlier that year, he had traveled to Aspen, ostensibly for a little skiing. While there, he kidnapped a woman named Caryn Campbell from the hotel she was staying at with her fiancé and his children after she left them in the lobby to go back to their room for a magazine. According to Bundy, he faked chest pains, led her to his room, and knocked her unconscious. He hadn't stalked her; his room just happened to be between Caryn's and the elevator. Witnesses had seen her get off the elevator on her floor, and since the magazine was still in her room, it's likely the abduction unfolded in minutes, if not seconds. Nobody saw him load Caryn into his VW Bug, but when he removed her, she left behind a single hair. The hair was found after he was arrested, and it was eventually traced back to her disappearance.

If only I left behind *one* hair when I left somewhere. : (

But before he was to face that murder charge, he still had to contend with the crime of aggravated kidnapping in the case of Carol DaRonch. Thinking a year of law school qualified him to defend a felony case, he decided to represent himself. Bundy's overconfidence earned him a fifteen-year sentence.

He should've asked for Kuby like the Big Lebowski did!

Then it was on to Colorado to face murder charges. Ted hadn't learned his lesson and decided to give self-lawyering a second shot. This outwardly idiotic move may

have caused his jailers to underestimate his intelligence—something he would take full advantage of as soon as the moment was right.

My father always taught me if you want to get out of responsibilities, you do something badly and no one asks you to do it again.

Since Bundy was representing himself, he had near-unlimited private access to the county law library. On the day of the hearing to determine whether the prosecution was going to pursue the death penalty, he requested a little alone time to do a last-minute review. With the door closed and the window open, Bundy, wearing his court clothes, leaped twenty-five feet down from the second floor of the library and simply walked away, blending into the world as just another Aspen yuppie.

He Jackie Chan'd his way out of prison! This is a dangerous motherfucker. I can't imagine how police reacted. "He jumped out the goddamn window? We need a tank, fellas."

He knew he didn't have much time before all the roads would be sealed off, but he'd gained another advantage in acting as his own attorney. The prosecution was using a map of the area as evidence to detail the exact spot where his Colorado victim had been found, and Bundy had acquired this information in discovery. For a full week, he wandered the outskirts of Aspen from one unoccupied house to another, barely ahead of the cops, scavenging what he could.

The people of Aspen, while terrified, seemed to revel in the horror. According to Ann Rule, souvenir T-shirts almost immediately began to appear with slogans like "Ted Bundy Is a One Night Stand" and, less cleverly, "Bundy's Free—You Can Bet Your Aspen on It!"

I love novelty T-shirts, but even this is a stretch for me.

Bundy's week in the wilderness left him exhausted and frail, so when a last-ditch effort was made to drive a stolen car out west to freedom, he didn't have the strength to control it. He was pulled over on suspicion of drunk driving and was back in jail by the end of the night. But he wouldn't stay there for long—he was about to disappear from Colorado altogether, never to return. His second prison break and subsequent actions would ensure his place in the imaginations of humans the world over as one of the most terrifying Americans to ever exist.

If this was the 1400s, this guy would be like Vlad the Impaler. What we learned from covering Rasputin and Jim Jones on *LPOTL* is that if you are brazen enough to put all standards and self-preservation to the side to live your life in a specific arc, you can get away with murder and become a larger-than-life real monster. It would be really inspiring if it didn't lead to so much homicide.

Bundy knew his next escape would have to be more complicated than just simply jumping out of a window. So after months of studying the movements and habits of his jailers, Bundy cut a twelve-by-twelve-inch hole in the ceiling of his cell using a hacksaw smuggled in by a person whose identity he never revealed.

I'm just praying it wasn't *the* Hacksaw, Hacksaw Jim Duggan. Hey, I made a wrestling reference!

You want a cookie?

Bundy prepped for his escape by skipping breakfast every day, which served two purposes: he needed to drop weight if he was going to fit through that hole, and if he trained the guards not to interact with him until lunch, he'd be hours ahead of the authorities before they realized he was gone.

Amazingly, in the two weeks prior to his second escape, he left his cell through the hole again and again. Each time he scouted the layout of the building and would go a little farther, looking for the perfect way out. He finally found it in the jailer's apartment while sitting in the rafters, listening to the jailer and his wife having a conversation over dinner.

Bundy waited for a night when he knew the couple was out of the apartment, then crawled out of his escape hole. He walked through the rafters to the jailer's closet, dropped down, and walked through the front door. After stealing a car, he started making his way to the Aspen bus station, but a foot and a half of snow had fallen earlier that day and he hadn't chosen the right vehicle for the weather. In a snap decision, he flagged down a passing motorist and feigned panic, saying his wife had gone into labor in Denver.

Bundy was raced to the bus station, where another layer of his devious genius came into play. Since he had represented himself in his case, he'd been given a credit card to make long-distance phone calls. This county convenience was used to buy a bus ticket to Denver, and from the bus station in Denver, he caught a cab to the airport. By the time the jailers noticed that Bundy was no longer in his cell, seventeen hours had passed and he was over a thousand miles away, in downtown Chicago.

With a new lease on life, Bundy decided he'd start over: no more stealing, no more raping, and especially no more murdering. And with this fresh start came a new location. He remembered how much he'd loved Florida when he attended the Republican National Convention in 1968, but Miami wasn't his style. Ted Bundy was a college boy. He looked to the University of Florida at Gainesville but, according to him, it "didn't look right on the map." No, the place where Ted Bundy would travel for his final spree would be the same place our very own Henry Zebrowski would attend college decades later: Tallahassee.

Cut to Henry getting thrown out of every party for joking about Ted Bundy while wearing a dashiki!

It's true! The Greek community didn't enjoy me but the Greek RESTAURANT community loved me! I was three hundred pounds, super into Ornette Coleman, and had a dorm room covered in Area 51–themed merch. A college town is a great place to hide out in plain sight as a serial killer.

Ted arrived in Tallahassee on a manic high. Gone was Theodore Robert Bundy, thief, rapist, killer, necrophiliac. Enter Kenneth Misner, Tallahassee layabout. Bundy may have been on the FBI's Most Wanted list, but he figured as long as he kept his nose clean and didn't cause any trouble, he could live out the rest of his life in the Florida sun. In reality, he wouldn't last two weeks.

Bundy spent his first few days in Tallahassee wandering about and drinking, promising himself that tomorrow would be the day he'd go out and get a job. When it became obvious that a job wouldn't magically materialize, the small allowances began. He stole a bike, then a TV, then a racquetball set. Next came wallets and cars. After the thefts, the peeping returned. In just two weeks, Bundy had gone from starting over to repeating his entire criminal evolution. And naturally, he couldn't just stop without going all the way. On January 14, 1978, the devil came to Chi Omega.

Earlier that night, Bundy had been drinking in a popular disco named Sherrod's, next door to the Chi Omega sorority house. There, he danced with a sorority girl named Mary Ann Piccano. Mary Ann said she'd had no real reason to fear the man who had asked her to dance but the vibe he gave off was eerie, as if Bundy's aura was telegraphing the evil he was about to commit. Luckily for Mary Ann, she would not bear the brunt of it, though some of her sorority sisters would not be so fortunate.

At 2:45 a.m., Bundy broke into the Chi Omega house and walked into the room of Lisa Levy, wielding a piece of firewood that he'd picked up on his way inside. He raised the club and swung it down on Levy's head as she slept, knocking her out. In a frenzied rage, he began biting into her flesh, ripping off one of her nipples and sinking his teeth into her buttocks so hard that they left an identifiable print. But this was just his opening act. He then walked from room to room, bringing the same terror and cruelty to three more sorority sisters. Two would survive, but Margaret Bowman's head was struck so hard that her skull shattered. He also choked her so forcefully with a nylon stocking that he reshaped her neck, giving her body the appearance of a macabre hourglass.

The murders of Margaret Bowman and Lisa Levy and the attempted murders of two more of their sisters had taken no more than fifteen minutes. But still, even after four victims that night, Bundy wasn't done. His last victim of the evening lived in a duplex eight blocks away. She survived, but he struck her so hard that her dreams of being a ballerina were ended by a permanent loss of equilibrium.

While one would think that he might want to leave town as soon as possible after this vicious spree, he stuck around, continuing to steal until the entity demanded one more sacrifice. On February 9, Bundy drove to Lake City, Florida, where he inexplicably changed up his MO, signature, and victim profile. Instead of using his charm and wit to lull a young woman into a false sense of security, Bundy forced a twelve-year-old girl named Kimberly Leach into a stolen van parked outside her junior high school. He drove her thirty-five miles to an abandoned pig shed where, instead of strangling her as he had most of his victims, he stabbed her to death. Leach's body would not be found for another eight weeks, but police strongly suspected that this disappearance was connected to the Tallahassee slayings.

Ultimately, Bundy didn't leave Tallahassee because of the heat his crimes would inevitably bring—he left because he owed his landlord $320 and didn't have the cash to pay. On February 12, Bundy packed up what little of a life he'd built during his month there and stole another VW Bug, one last hurrah with his favorite model.

If you want to be a fake cop, you've got to smell like one.
POLICE
BUNDY
COLOGNE

Two days later, Pensacola police officer David Lee became suspicious when he spotted Ted's Bug pulling out from an alleyway behind a restaurant that had been closed for hours. When the officer called in the plates and the car came back as stolen, he turned on his siren. Bundy stepped on the gas, and after about a mile of speeding through the streets, he abruptly pulled over. Lee walked up to the car with his gun drawn and ordered Bundy outside. He'd snapped only one cuff on Bundy when Bundy kicked Lee's legs out from under him and took off. Lee fired a shot and Bundy dropped, but when Lee got to Bundy, he put up a fight, almost wresting the gun away from the officer. Finally, Lee overpowered Bundy and snapped on the other cuff, putting an end to a killing spree that had spanned five years and at least four states. When Lee booked Bundy into the station that night, Ted allegedly said, "I'm the most cold-blooded son of a bitch you'll ever meet."

Um, sorry, Bundy, but the most cold-blooded SOB is Stone Cold Steve Austin.

Bundy's trial for the Chi Omega murders was a farce, as could be expected, because he once again chose to represent himself. In fact, he was so confident in his own abilities that he rejected a pretrial plea deal that would have waived the death penalty. Instead, his own arrogance got him killed.

He has so many of the official traits of a true psychopath according to the Hare Psychopathy Checklist:

glib and superficial charm X
grandiose (exaggeratedly high) estimation of self X
need for stimulation X
pathological lying X
cunningness and manipulativeness X
lack of remorse or guilt X
shallow affect (superficial emotional responsiveness) X
callousness and lack of empathy X
parasitic lifestyle X
poor behavioral controls X
early behavior problems X
lack of realistic long-term goals X
impulsivity X
irresponsibility X
failure to accept responsibility for own actions X
juvenile delinquency X
criminal versatility X

Ted Bundy's trial was among the first to be broadcast into the living rooms of Americans. At times, Bundy appeared almost competent, possibly even innocent. It was only when it came time to discuss the murders in the Chi Omega house that it became painfully obvious to the jury and to all of America that the perpetrator of the killing spree was standing right before their eyes. In the defense proceedings, Bundy called up a responding officer to the scene, seemingly just to ask for a recounting of the gruesome details. He asked the witness what condition the bodies had been found in, what position, and what sorts of wounds they had suffered. Then, when he'd gotten his fill of the particulars, he dismissed the witness without any follow-up, both baffling and chilling viewers at home and in court.

After seven hours of deliberation, the jury found Bundy guilty on all charges. He maintained his innocence even after the ruling, though, refusing to plead for his life. He said, "It is absurd to ask for mercy for something I did not do." The sentence quickly came back as death.

The same verdict and sentence came the next year after the murder trial of Kimberly Leach, Bundy's last victim. He remained seated and silent as he was sentenced to the electric chair for the second time, but when the jury began filing out of the box, he suddenly stood. Tracking his eyes from the judge to the jury, Bundy, abruptly raising his voice as he spoke, said, "I just want to tell the jury THAT THEY ARE WRONG!"

Eleven years later, after a myriad of appeals, confessions, and even a failed attempt to help the FBI Behavioral Science Unit catch the Green River Killer, Ted Bundy met his doom strapped to the electric chair at Florida State Prison. Hundreds gathered outside the prison and celebrated his death, as if the devil himself was being sent back into the maw of hell, hopefully never to return.

USA! USA! USA! But we should think about the innocent people on death row as well!

So, as we now see, no myths needed to be created when it came to Ted Bundy. The incestuous ancestry and dramatized character building can be tossed away like the Hollywood nonsense that it is. When it comes to the most feared serial killer in history, the truth is more than enough for a thousand nightmares.

I'M A ROCKEFELLER REPUBLICAN

by Ted Bundy

Like most sexy, hip, in-the-know young men in the 1960s, I was a staunch supporter of the Republican Party. I especially admired Nelson Rockefeller. When people think of Nelson Rockefeller, they think of the three simple words "try, try, try," and that's what I've done my entire career. Mr. Rockefeller ran for the highest office in the land in 1960, 1964, and 1968 and served as vice president under Gerald Ford. I wish Ford had been killed like Kennedy so our nation could've been blessed with the presidency of the single greatest American in her history. It makes me so mad he didn't win, I could just freak out and strangle someone, ha ha! Oh, man, did I mention he had a great sense of humor?

A lot of Republicans didn't like Rockefeller's more progressive political views. He was considered a moderate—just like me. His policies were as slick as his hair and his vision as strong as the prescription of his snazzy glasses. It was the honor of my life to be a delegate at the 1968 Republican Convention in Miami after working for him in Seattle. That said, I didn't really care for Miami; there were a lot of men who seemed to really enjoy one another's company, like a *weird* amount. I didn't always feel comfortable in the pool shower, but man, the guys at the Republican Convention love their group showers! Anyway, I was there to focus on work and that's what I did. I spent the days stabbing campaign pins on the blouses of young ladies. That was a thrill; I just love buttons because they're like patches with little knives.

1968 was a tough year for me. After the small-minded hicks at the Miami convention didn't nominate the obvious choice and decided to support the decrepit Richard Nixon, I was so upset I had to let off some steam in Atlantic City. And I don't mean gambling! Let's just say I had my own little Treaty on Fifth Avenue down on the boardwalk.

I was always drawn to Mr. Rockefeller's eyes. They spoke to me urgently, like a scream—a muted scream, a scream struggling to be heard. When he looked at you, it felt like when you put your hand over someone's mouth and they look at you like "please don't kill me," and then you let them breathe again and they're super grateful and happy to be alive. Yes, his eyes are just like that.

Did you know he was appointed by Harry Truman to be chairman of the International Development Advisory Board? Isn't that cool? I mean, Truman is the guy who dropped the bomb that killed over two hundred thousand people! That's pretty awesome. I'll be lucky if I can kill over twenty, LOL!

Following his appointment by Truman, Rockefeller ran for governor of New York. Despite the fact that Democrats were winning elections across the nation, he came out of nowhere and unseated the Democratic incumbent W. Averell Harriman. No one saw Rockefeller coming! It was like he was slowly stalking his prey, hiding in the shadows and waiting for the right time to strike. During his time in office, Rockefeller expanded the state university system in New York, and later in Florida. I love the university system in Florida. It's so big you can sneak under the radar and not be noticed at all. Rockefeller was also one of the first governors to grant student aid to disenfranchised coeds! This was really beneficial for me at FSU. Without his programs there'd be fewer sororities, and that would be horrible for my career . . . as a suicide hotline counselor.

So thank you, Mr. Rockefeller. Without you there would be no Ted Bundy.

MAC FRIES
MAC FRIES
tomN.
after KEANE

CHAPTER 2

RICHARD CHASE

MENTAL HEALTH BREAKDOWNS RUN A BROAD GAMUT. THE more common examples involve a period of depressive haze spent in one's own bed, or a manic binge of unprotected sex. Fortunately, when it comes to the world of mental breaks, these scenarios and most others are not violent in any way. But there are exceptions.

While it is true that those of us with mental illness are far more likely to be the victims of violent crime than the perpetrators—ten times more likely than the general population, according to the Department of Health and Human Services—untreated mental illness can conceivably lead to tragedy on a scale so savage that the brain struggles to comprehend it. When it comes to not taking your medication, that worst-case scenario was named Richard Chase.

Under "worst-case scenario" in the encyclopedia, it's 1) no TP in the stadium bathroom, 2) a Mike Pence presidency, 3) Richard Chase. This man was a grenade ready to explode, and not a Bruno Mars grenade. A very serious grenade that would damage Sacramento for years to come.

Richard Chase would make a great Scientologist! I could totally see him jumping on Oprah's couch and screaming about thetans.

Richard Chase—aka the Vampire of Sacramento—claimed the lives of six people over the span of just one month during the winter of 1978. Fueled by his largely unchecked schizophrenia, Chase believed in the power of drinking blood to sustain his health and killed his victims in order to satiate that foul urge. Chase's belief had its roots in two conditions: haematodipsia and Renfield syndrome. The former is a sexual fetish that is almost par for the course in the world of the serial killer; haematodipsiacs are sexually aroused by blood, just as podophiliacs get their pleasure from feet.

And a Parrot Head loves Jimmy Buffett. Richard just had an intense fandom for spurting blood.

Renfield syndrome is not exclusively sexual in nature, although there is some debate as to whether it is an expression of schizophrenia rather than a syndrome unto itself. But supposing that it is a legitimate illness, a person suffering from Renfield syndrome considers the consumption of blood a basic need to sustain their existence, just as Dracula's Renfield devoured insects in an attempt to absorb their life force.

Renfield is my dream role. I hope to play him in the eventual CW teen drama about his life.

I knew a kid who ate bugs in middle school, but he just ended up ostracized for half a year until we became friends after realizing we both really liked heavy metal.

The syndrome has three stages, beginning with experimental self-harm when the afflicted tests the waters by opening a wound and consuming their own blood. Next comes the consumption of animal blood from a living specimen, known as zoophagia. Finally, the afflicted will decide, as Richard Chase did one afternoon, that the only source of power strong enough to keep them alive is his or her fellow humans, often with tragic results.

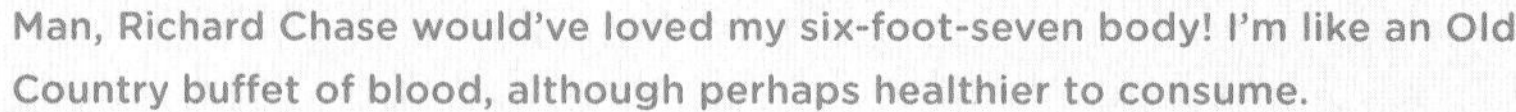

Man, Richard Chase would've loved my six-foot-seven body! I'm like an Old Country buffet of blood, although perhaps healthier to consume.

Oh my god, he'd love your clots. It's like when you find big chunks of dark chocolate in vanilla ice cream. A decadent delight!

It's worth clarifying that Chase was not a serial killer *because* he suffered from schizophrenia. Rather, his mental illness only guaranteed that his serial killing would manifest itself in some of the more hellish crime scenes in history.

RICHARD TRENTON CHASE WAS BORN IN SANTA CLARA County, California, in 1950, the younger of two children. While some sources contend that Chase endured numerous childhood beatings from his father, Ray Biondi, the man who helped capture Chase and who wrote the definitive book on his life, maintains that his father was no more than your average strict disciplinarian. That being said, it's undeniable that his parents made grave mistakes concerning little Ricky's dire need for regular medication and hospitalization. In fact, there had been signs for decades that something was very wrong with their son, but the Chases chose to ignore them all.

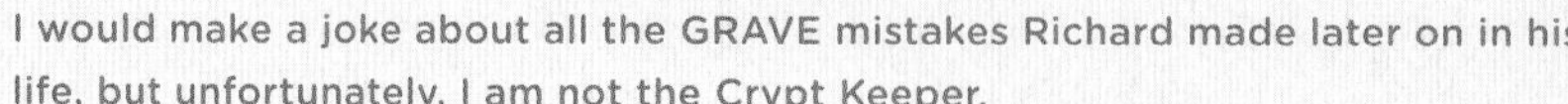

I would make a joke about all the GRAVE mistakes Richard made later on in his life, but unfortunately, I am not the Crypt Keeper.

It's hard for a parent to comprehend that their son might be a vampire, sort of like when a kid from Wisconsin comes out as a Chicago Bears fan in a Green Bay Packers house.

Not much is known about Richard Chase's early years, but in 1960, when Chase was ten years old, his mother confided to a neighbor that she had found a dead cat buried in her flower boxes and that she had no idea where it came from. While the neighbor listened sympathetically, she later told Biondi that several cats had gone missing in their neighborhood while the Chase family lived there. Once they left town, the mysterious disappearances stopped.

This calls for Heathcliff and the gang to protect the neighborhood! There's a cat vamp on the loose, for crying out loud!

Richard Chase is the poster child for animal mutilation, like an experimental chef without the tat sleeve. And what is a chef without a tat sleeve? Just another chubby ginger with a felony on their record. Richard Chase would never funnel his "curiosity about nature" into anything remotely constructive.

Chase started showing other signs of aberrant behavior specific to serial killer development years before his mental illness had even manifested. Young Richard had a penchant for starting fires, petty thievery, and lying. Taken separately, these behaviors are fairly common in adolescents, but when both are present during a child's development, they can be a strong indicator of future antisocial behavior. Richard's parents viewed it as boys being boys.

Richard showed no outward signs of schizophrenia during his middle and high school years. According to his former classmates, he was successful both socially and romantically. The problems only came when he tried taking the romance to the next level.

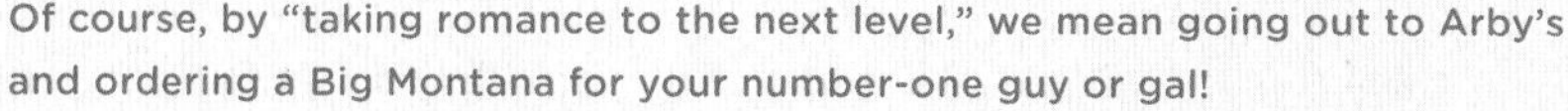

Of course, by "taking romance to the next level," we mean going out to Arby's and ordering a Big Montana for your number-one guy or gal!

I would have loved to see his Tinder profile.

Both girls with whom Chase attempted sexual encounters in high school reported that he had problems sustaining an erection. This embarrassing setback would be devastating to any teenager, but to a boy whose mind was already beginning to fracture, this inability to become erect became the foothold his schizophrenic delusions needed to firmly establish themselves.

If this was 2020, he would've realized you gotta get good at the cunnilingus and keep yourself in the game! Except he probably would've been real bitey, and I don't need *Cosmo* to tell me women don't enjoy a man playing Hungry Hungry Hippos with their genitals.

To his credit, Richard saw a psychiatrist about his impotence, although it seems his burgeoning schizophrenia was either ignored or glossed over completely by the professional who spoke with him. Rather, he was told that the most common cause of impotence in teenagers is suppressed anger, specifically anger toward women. Richard brushed it off; he wasn't interested in the cause, only the cure. He decided that he'd find another way to solve his problem, without the trouble of trying to unpack his inner rage. He had read in health class that a penis becomes engorged by filling with blood, and his schizoid brain reasoned that his impotence had a simple solution: more blood. If he were to find and drink enough blood, he reasoned, his sexual organs would be just as functional as any other boy's in his class.

I can already see Alex Jones selling "male vitality blood pills" to his target audience of incels.

The first victim to fall prey to this reasoning was a kitten Chase stole from his girlfriend's house and started raising at his own home, unbeknownst to her. The next victim was a neighbor's dog, named Sabbath. Richard shot Sabbath with a .22 pistol and collected its blood in a Dixie cup that he pressed up to the bullet holes, as if he were casually refilling a soda at McDonald's.

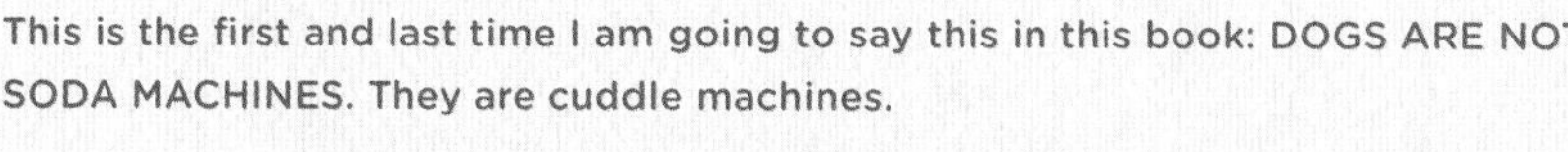

This is the first and last time I am going to say this in this book: DOGS ARE NOT SODA MACHINES. They are cuddle machines.

Remember mixing all the fountain sodas together at fast-food restaurants?! It has nothing to do with draining blood from a dog, but it was kinda fun, and this is how I'm coping with this information!

Although he wasn't diagnosed until years later, it's obvious from Richard's behavior that his schizophrenia worsened after high school, as it often does when the afflicted matures from adolescence. A two-year stint at a local junior college proved largely unremarkable, but when he moved out on his own at the age of twenty, things started falling apart.

Chase lived with two women, one of whom he knew from high school and one he'd met since graduating. While things seemed fine at first, Richard's mental state quickly began to deteriorate. This was only exacerbated by the era in which he lived—it was the seventies, which meant the casual use of weed, acid, and speed was the norm in their household.

Hell yeah! Oh wait, that's bad.

Richard's brain was already expanded farther than Chris Christie's baseball pants, so I don't think he needed any hallucinogens.

Spurred by mind-altering substances and increasing paranoid delusions, he stopped showering and refused to wash his clothes. One night he boarded up his bedroom door, locked himself in the closet, and boarded that up from the inside as

well. When his friends managed to extricate him from this makeshift fortress and asked him why he'd done it, Chase said it was because "People were sneaking up on me from the inside." On another occasion, he strolled out of his room nude and joined some friends in the living room, jabbering complete nonsense. His behavior at a party a few weeks later was equally alarming when he spent the whole night wriggling on the floor, moaning and making strange noises.

Is it possible Chase was like "It's cool when Iggy Pop does it, so let me charm the pants off these folks!"? I'm just asking questions!

One by one, Richard's friends abandoned him for more stable companions. His circle of acquaintances dwindled to almost nothing, then became nonexistent after an incident at one of his remaining friends' apartment. It was a small gathering and Richard was left alone with a stranger while the other two guests whom he knew left on a beer run. As soon as they were out the door, he began grabbing at the girl, following her around the room as she attempted to fend him off. When the two men returned, the girl immediately told them what had just transpired. Richard met this accusation with his own unique rebuttal, amplifying his soft, high-pitched voice to a screaming falsetto and saying that nobody had any right to tell him what to do or where to go. Inexplicably, they listened to Chase scream for an hour before he finally decided to leave.

Richard might have been the scariest sovereign citizen of all.

It's possible that word of this incident got back to his roommates, as he was kicked off the lease of his apartment soon afterward. At twenty-one, Richard was friendless and living with his mother after his parents' divorce. Left to his own thoughts, another of his motivators for killing came to the forefront: extreme hypochondria. His supposed health problems were not possible but he believed in them vehemently, going as far as to tell his mother that his heart would stop momentarily, his stomach was turned around backward, and that bones were growing out of the back of his head.

Jeez, sounds like he thought he was Pumpkinhead!

For some reason, this is what really scares me. When I used to have panic attacks, I would have long episodes where I convinced myself I could no longer unconsciously breathe. That was unbearable; at one point, I even went to an emergency room. The pain, confusion, and fear Richard lived with must have been very intense. But seeing his x-rays must have been fun!

All of this made Chase a very difficult person to live with, so after bouncing back and forth between his mother's and father's homes, he was sent from Sacramento to Los Angeles to live with his grandmother. Here he spent what we assume was a fairly uneventful year driving a bus full of developmentally disabled kids to the school where his grandmother worked. Nothing is known about the specifics of what transpired during this time, but Richard was back in Sacramento in less than a year.

Hold on a second! He drove a bus full of children? This is more dangerous than *Nightmare on Elm Street 2*, when Freddy was driving the bus over a cliff!

Shortly after his return, Richard's imagined health problems worsened, prompting call after call to emergency services. Finally, a paramedic who refused to treat him suggested that his condition might all be in his head. He suggested to his mother that she get him professional help, and after she checked him into the American River Hospital, Richard received real mental health treatment for the first time in his life and was diagnosed as schizophrenic. Doctors recommended inpatient treatment and care, but ultimately deemed him safe enough for the streets. His mother took him home and they resumed the status quo of their living arrangement, ignoring the doctors' recommendation for a treatment plan.

Essentially, they sent him home with an "Ain't no crime in being creative!"

Consequently, his delusions only worsened, to the point where Richard believed his mother was poisoning his food and controlling his mind. His parents must have known their son wasn't mentally fit, but instead of encouraging intensive treatment or even at-home care, they decided the best cure for their son's schizophrenia was independence. He was squirreled away in his own apartment across town, given an allowance, and left to his own devices.

I think I read that somewhere: the best care for the deeply mentally disturbed is a CREDIT CARD AND AN APARTMENT.

Oh my! Richard needed more independence like the Food Network needs another Guy Fieri show! (Actually, there's never enough Fieri, but it's still a fun joke.)

Richard spent the first period of his newfound freedom riding his bike back and forth to a local rabbit farm. He would buy a rabbit, bring it home, butcher it, and eat its entrails raw. If he had the time, he would drink the blood separately, but if not, the entrails and blood would be dumped in a blender and consumed in a chunky half-liquefied concoction.

At some point in my life, I'll end up paying twenty-five dollars for this at a very fancy restaurant.

This is why we need to take *Of Mice and Men* out of schools immediately!

Lennie didn't eat the rabbits! I think he just had sex with the rabbits? I don't know. Every time I tried to read the book in high school, I just stared at the pages and thought about Fairuza Balk.

Chase engaged in this disgusting practice because he believed his heart was shrinking and the only thing that would keep it from disappearing altogether was buckets and buckets of blood. In more technical terms, he was displaying signs of Cotard's syndrome. Cotard's has three iterations: the patient believes they are a walking corpse, the patient believes they are alive but rotting from the inside, or the patient believes they are missing essential pieces of their anatomy such as blood or organs.

Fucking metal! But also incredibly scary. THESE GUYS JUST WALK AROUND LIKE THIS. THERE IS ONE IN YOUR NEIGHBORHOOD.

After months of consuming raw rabbit, Chase discovered that his supposed cures were actually making him sick. One night, his father walked into the apartment to find his son sitting on the couch wearing only shorts, as white as the rabbits he'd been eating. After giving his father a quick rundown of his recent culinary habits, Richard told him that one of the rabbits had gone bad and he most likely had food poisoning.

Yeah, it's the FOOD that's the problem.

That's like blaming the road for you crashing your car while drunk.

Doctors found that Richard was indeed sick, but not in the way he'd thought. Rather, it was blood poisoning, brought on because he'd moved from gulping down bunny cocktails to mainlining the ingredients. Richard claimed he'd eaten a rabbit contaminated with battery acid, and that the acid had seeped through the walls of his stomach into his flesh. He had convinced himself that the only thing that would cure the influx of bad blood would be an injection of clean blood straight into his system.

So he's dabbing animal blood? Believe me, I love meat and I love blood-based foods (looking at you, Scotland), but you'd think just the SOUNDS coming from his room would have called somebody's attention to the situation. Like how terrifying is it to be this man's neighbor? Rabbits' death screams, him rolling back and forth across the floor doing his haunted burrito dance. This guy . . . he's a little weird!

After this, Richard's father could no longer ignore his son's mental problems. Chase was committed to a mental institution, but it only took two days for him to escape by running out the front door. He was soon brought back and transferred to a more secure facility, where he earned the nickname "Dracula" from the hospital staff because he only talked about blood and killing animals. This reputation was further bolstered when he emerged from his room one day with blood smeared on his face. When the orderlies checked his quarters, they looked out the window and found two birds with broken necks lying on the ground.

He's like Hannibal Lecter, if instead of brains he enjoyed treating birds like juice boxes and drinking their blood.

But if he found himself in the kitchen of one of the many locavore restaurants dotting the landscape of this hungry country of ours, we could be looking at a possible James Beard Award winner!

Richard was released from the hospital on September 29, 1976, much to the strong disapproval of the entire staff minus his personal doctor. He alone found that Richard had developed "good socialization" with a "realistic view" of his problems.

There's a good chance his doctor was Dr. Satan from *House of 1000 Corpses*.

Oh yeah, he's totally good. Anybody who talks about blood 24-7 who isn't a BLOOD DOCTOR is just fine!

To be fair, Richard was medicated upon release, and his parents were granted a temporary conservatorship to watch over his behavior in the short term. Almost immediately, though, his mother resumed her lifelong denial of her son's problems and weaned him off his medication, saying he didn't need it. Richard's parents then allowed the conservatorship to expire after thirty days, leaving him on his own once again and opening the door for the carnage that followed.

The 1970s: The decade where taking mental health medication was more stigmatized than drinking the blood of cats!

I'm starting to think Richard's parents just really hated cats.

On August 3, 1977, tribal police were called to Pyramid Lake in Nevada on a report of an abandoned car. They arrived to find a 1966 Ford Ranchero stuck in the sand with a bumper sticker that read "I'd Rather Be Flying."

Inside, they found a loaded .30–30 rifle and a .22 rifle, both stained with blood. Next to the guns was a pair of bloody tennis shoes and a blood-soaked pile of clothes. The floorboards held an even more disturbing discovery: a fresh liver marinating in a bucket of blood.

Using their binoculars to scan the area, the police spotted a nude Richard Chase perched on a large rock about a half mile away. When the cops approached him, he took off through the desert but was quickly apprehended by an officer on an ATV.

"Holy shit, Officer Gorski . . . is that Wayne Coyne?"

When they approached him, Chase had blood smeared across his chest and face, under his armpits, and in his ears. When the cops asked him about the source of the blood, he replied, "It's seeping—from me." When it was discovered that the liver had come from a cow and not a human, Chase was let go once more, escaping all charges, including a public indecency rap for roaming the desert naked.

An insight gained from my father being a cop: I can pretty much guarantee that the reason why they let Chase go is they didn't want to get blood all over the back seat of the squad car.

I feel like they could've charged him with a little something just to let him know it's not okay to be naked, covered in blood, and running around the desert like you're on the world's smelliest vision quest.

Four months after the incident in the desert, for reasons known only to him, Chase's violent behavior escalated into the realm of attempted murder. On December 27, 1977, at 6:30 p.m., Dorothy Polenske was doing the dishes in her kitchen when she heard a sharp pop followed by breaking glass and felt a streak of heat pass right above her skull. Chase had fired his newly—and legally obtained—.22 pistol from his Ranchero as he drove by her house, choosing it randomly. The bullet had passed through the tight bun atop Dorothy's head and lodged itself in the back of an open kitchen cabinet. No one had seen the person who fired the bullet that almost took Mrs. Polenske's life, so the police were at a loss, but they would find a bullet that matched the gun at a much more serious crime scene the next day, when Chase once again took his .22 to the streets of Sacramento.

Man, I wish his car wasn't called "Ranchero" because now all I can think about is huevos rancheros, and I can't be mixing any thoughts of brunch into this!

As Richard was driving a few blocks from his apartment, he spotted fifty-one-year-old Ambrose Griffin unloading groceries from the trunk of his car. Griffin's wife heard two loud pops, turned around, and watched her husband slump to the ground. While the first bullet had missed, the second hit Ambrose directly in the chest. His wife was so shocked that she never saw Richard Chase's car speeding away.

Now that he had taken a human life, Chase's bloodlust intensified. Over the next month, a neighbor, Dawn Larson, witnessed him carrying two dogs and a cat into his apartment on different occasions. As she never saw him walking the dogs, she could only guess at what he'd done with his new pets, but she didn't think it important enough to report at the time.

Well, I guess there are two options regarding what Chase did with the pets: 1) He found them nice homes and they grew up happy, or 2) He killed them and drank their blood like Augustus Gloop drank the chocolate river in *Willy Wonka and the Chocolate Factory*.

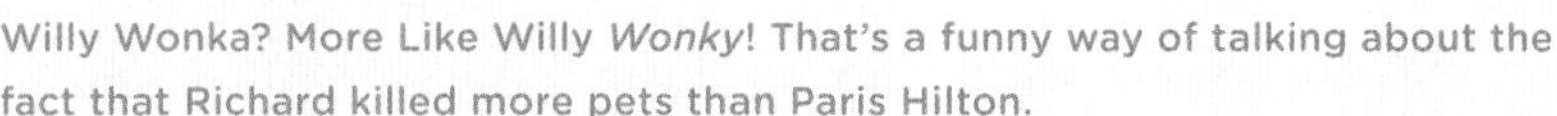

Willy Wonka? More Like Willy *Wonky*! That's a funny way of talking about the fact that Richard killed more pets than Paris Hilton.

It was becoming apparent to Richard that animal blood wasn't making him feel any better, so on January 23, 1978, he switched up his strategy and had his first up-close-and-personal encounter with a human victim. He first tried his luck at 2909 Burnece Street, walking up to the patio door of a woman named Jeanne Layton, and the only thing that prevented her encounter with Chase that day was the law of the vampyr. Richard would later tell FBI profiler Robert Ressler that he had only one rule when he left the house for murder: the homes of his victims had to be unlocked. It was his belief that a locked house meant that he was "not welcome." One wonders if Richard Chase knew this or if it was only a coincidence, but his one and only principle does indeed echo the old folk belief that vampires can only enter a residence if they're invited.

Remind me to get a "not welcome" sign on my door immediately!

It wouldn't work, Kissel. A mat you purchase at Michaels has no power over the vampyr.

Initially, Richard found Jeanne Layton's front door locked. Still trying to find an invitation into the home, he moved on to the windows, which were locked as well. Finally, he tried the back door, where he found Layton staring out through the glass. Layton was disturbed but called the police only after she'd heard about what occurred later that afternoon. In describing what happened, she said Chase had stared at her with no emotion, as if he were looking at a car he was thinking about buying. He then lit a cigarette and walked away through her backyard.

He did the Deal with It meme in the middle of a murder spree.

Oh man, he looked at her like Wayne looked at the Excalibur guitar in *Wayne's World*.

Thirty minutes later, he entered the unlocked home of Robert and Barbara Edwards. The couple had been out on a quick trip to the grocery store, and when they opened their front door, they found a filthy, scraggly Chase standing in their hallway. He scampered from room to room, evading the rightful homeowners at every turn until he finally escaped back through the front door.

Like Benny Hill but covered in blood and shit. So like Benny Hill off camera.

When the Edwardses searched the house afterward, they found a bag containing items that Richard had planned to take, including rings, a tape player, a decorative dagger, and a stethoscope. Then they walked into their baby's bedroom, where they found that he had soaked their baby's clothes with urine and defecated on the very spot where their child slept.

The escape from the Edwardses' home had worked up a thirst in Chase so he went to the very same grocery store they had just left for a refreshing orange soda. While searching for the drink, he ran into a high school classmate, Nancy Holden. Walking up to her, he asked, apropos of nothing, "Were you on the motorcycle when Kurt was killed?"

> This line is so bad that I wouldn't be surprised if even Mystery, that pickup artist from that horrible VH1 show, disapproves of it!

Nancy had in fact dated a kid named Kurt who had died in a motorcycle accident when they were teenagers, but she barely recognized Richard. Dressed in a bright-orange ski parka, Richard was filthy, smelly, and skinnier than usual.

The two made small talk, or at least what passable version Richard could manage, until Nancy tried to break free from the conversation. Richard followed her outside, asking for a ride, but she got in her car, started the engine, and drove off just as Richard was about to open the passenger-side door. His intentions toward Nancy Holden remain a mystery.

> It's a meet-cute!

Foiled by Nancy's vigilance, Richard returned to the neighborhood from whence he had come and, after wandering for a short period of time, focused on 2360 Tioga Way, the home of Teresa Wallin. His motive as he approached the house is unclear. The only explanation, if there is one, is that he may have recognized Teresa's van from his earlier trip to the grocery store, as Teresa had been there too. Schizophrenics are known to sometimes make connections where none exist, so it is possible that Richard Chase confused coincidence for destiny.

He walked up to Teresa Wallin's door, took his handgun from his leather shoulder holster, ejected a bullet, and placed it in her mailbox. Checking the door to ensure it was unlocked, Richard opened it to find Teresa on her way outside with a bag of garbage. As he raised the gun, she dropped the bag and then, just as he fired, held her hand out in defense. The bullet entered her palm, traveled through her arm, exited at her elbow, and nicked her neck. Richard fired again. The second bullet entered the top of Teresa's skull, dropping her to the ground. The last shot was fired into her temple from six inches away, a mercy considering what was still to come.

Picking up Teresa's body by the shoulders, Chase dragged her to the bedroom, leaving a long, dark streak of blood on the floor. After he'd laid her down on the bed, he walked back to the kitchen, found a knife, and picked up an empty yogurt container from the pile of spilled garbage in the hallway on his way back to the bedroom. There, knife in hand, Chase began his vile work.

He began stabbing the body with such force that he split open the sternum. He then sliced the left side of the belly, reached inside the wound, and pulled out the intestines. Richard proceeded to stab the corpse eight more times, taking care to avoid the kidneys. That's when the yogurt container came into play. Like a field-worker dipping a cup into a water barrel on a hot day, Chase dunked his receptacle into the open stomach cavity and filled it to the brim before bringing it to his lips for his first taste of another human's blood. The cup was filled again, but this time he took it to the bathroom and smeared it on his face and hands as if it were soap. The final indignation came when Chase walked outside in broad daylight, still covered in his victim's blood, and picked up a pile of dog feces from the yard and shoved it into the corpse's mouth. Worst of all, when the autopsy was performed, it was discovered that Teresa Wallin was three months pregnant.

This story is more disturbing than the toilet scene in *Trainspotting*!

Thank you, Kissel—you are truly easing the tension.

The Sacramento Police Department had no immediate leads when it came to the graphic butchering of Teresa Wallin. The only clues police had were a set of footprints in a pool of her blood, the bullet that had ended her life, and a series of crimson rings near the body that appeared to be from a bucket or pot that had been set on the floor. Alone, those clues wouldn't be enough, and Richard Chase would go on to claim four more victims in a single day before police even knew his name.

Unlike the seemingly impulsive decision to target Teresa Wallin, it's thought that his search for his next victims began three days prior to the eventual quadruple murder. On January 24, 1978, Richard went door to door in a Sacramento neighborhood, asking for back issues of *Mad Magazine* and *Cosmopolitan*. Whether he was casing houses for his next crime or acting on some schizophrenic impulse is unknown, but his behavior was strange enough that he was reported to the police as a suspicious person.

I guess this has taught us that California is where the Venn diagram of *Cosmo* and *Mad Magazine* readers overlap.

This story reads like a true-life horror movie. Richard has no discernable motive—he moves to a wind that no one else can feel—and yet everything has a terrible amount of symbolic meaning to him alone. Every chance encounter is *fate* telling him what to do. You can't reason with that, so he can strike anywhere and at any time.

On January 25, a couple in the same neighborhood where Richard was looking for magazines made a disturbing discovery on their back patio: one of their Labrador puppies had died from a gunshot wound and its stomach had been ripped open. When police asked them if they'd seen any strange characters, they told police of a terrible-smelling man wearing a dirty orange parka who had visited their house days before and had left with two of their puppies. This caught the attention of Ray Biondi, the lead detective in the Teresa Wallin murder and eventual author of *The Dracula Killer.* The reports of the magazine hunter had piqued his curiosity, but when violence was attached to a man with the same description, Biondi ordered an autopsy on the poor pup. They only found fragments from a .22 bullet, which wasn't enough for a match with the bullets found at the Wallin scene, but Biondi was thankful for any clue, no matter how small.

No fault of the Sacramento Police Department, two days later Richard would escalate from animals to humans once more, in what would prove to be one of the bloodiest and cruelest mass murders in modern American history. Evelyn Miroth was a thirty-eight-year-old single mother living with her two sons, Vernon, thirteen, and Jason, six, in the Country Club Centre neighborhood of Sacramento. On January 27, 1978, Evelyn was at home with Jason and her sister-in-law's twenty-month-old toddler. The plan was to send Jason on a playdate with a neighbor to the foot of the Sierra Nevada mountains, but sadly the boy would not leave the house alive.

At 9:05 a.m., Evelyn's friend Danny Meredith came over to the divorcée's house on a friendly social visit, just to say hello. It's a cruel twist of fate that he showed up when he did. Evelyn had neglected to rent snowshoes for her son's trip so she asked Meredith to run the errand; had she gone out, it's possible the bloodshed would've been avoided. Fate was cruel, though, and after Meredith left, Richard Chase entered the house through the unlocked back door and walked to the bathroom where she was enjoying a soak in the tub. He quickly shot her in the head, killing her instantly.

This is the first Gold Star moment in our book. Proceed with caution.

While we don't know exactly what happened next, it is presumed that Jason heard the shot and walked toward the bathroom in the bedroom to see what had happened. The boy was quickly killed by two shots to the head at close range, his body left next to the bed where it fell. Richard then turned back to Evelyn's body, removed it from the tub, and dragged it to the bed. His plan was to repeat the actions of the Teresa Wallin murder, but first he'd need a knife. He went to the kitchen to choose the appropriate tool, but the front door opened as he searched; it was Danny Meredith returning with the snowshoes. Pulling his .22 from his shoulder holster,

Chase met Danny in the hall and shot him between the eyes. The gunshot triggered a noise from the next room—the cries of a toddler. To end it, he walked into the room, pointed his gun at the toddler's head, and pulled the trigger.

Returning to the bedroom with two carving knives in hand, Richard began the same depraved blood ritual he had performed on the corpse of Teresa Wallin. The stomach was cut open from sternum to navel, then cut again across the belly, exposing the intestines, which he pulled out. He then began stabbing at specific organs, once again leaving the kidneys unscathed. The liver, however, was given no such distinction; he removed it, carved off a piece, and ate it. The rest of the organs were pulled out and discarded, unimportant. The ultimate prize was the blood that had pooled in the corpse's stomach cavity. Using a bucket, Chase collected as much as he could carry.

Because of the movie *Se7en,* I never ask what's in a box, and now I'll never inquire about what's contained in a bucket.

Then, with horrifying cruelty, he took it even further, rolling the body onto its stomach and stabbing the anus six times before sodomizing the wound. He then rolled the body back over, sliced open the neck, and carefully cut out one of its eyes.

And here is where I tap out like Kurt Angle tapped to Chris Jericho.

Would it make it worse if he hadn't done it carefully? I submit that it would not!

After finishing with Evelyn Miroth's body, Chase returned to the toddler's room and brought that body to the bathroom. He split the head open above the bathtub and began removing the brains from the skull, a hellish spectacle that was interrupted by a knock at the front door. Jason was now hours late for his playdate to the Sierras, and his friend had been sent to make sure everything was all right. It is a great mercy that Richard did not open the door. Instead, he waited until the little girl left, took the keys to Danny Meredith's station wagon from the corpse's pocket, and escaped undetected, a bucket of blood and the body of the twenty-month-old in hand.

Thirty minutes later, the crime scene was discovered when a worried neighbor opened the same back door that Chase had and saw Meredith's corpse. She immediately ran home and called the police, saving herself from fully witnessing the most gruesome crime scene Sacramento had ever played host to.

You have to wonder what was going on in Chase's head for him to perpetrate these types of heinous crimes. On some level, he had an order to things, some sort of inner ritual. His actions are very purposeful, each part of the murder meaning something very deep to him. But this is something we can only begin to speculate about after it's all pieced together in sequence by the police. Imagine what it would be like to encounter this scene for the first time, then have to compose yourself and collect as much evidence as possible.

The police were at a total loss for motive, although it was obvious that the same person who had killed Teresa Wallin had also committed the mass murder on that cold winter morning. The same rings were found next to the body, the same footprints tracked through the blood, and the bullets had come from the same gun. But Chase, in a telling move that spoke volumes about his sense of right and wrong, had worn rubber gloves, so no fingerprints were left behind. Danny Meredith's car was found the next day, but there was nothing inside to link it to the killer. It was only after Chase's capture that the police would discover he had abandoned the car just a hundred yards from his apartment complex.

With no leads to speak of, Lieutenant Biondi tried a new technique he'd learned two years earlier at an FBI seminar: psychological profiling. Using this strategy along with crime scene evidence, he was able to make the following assumptions: since no witnesses in this skittish white suburban neighborhood had remembered seeing any minorities recently— remember, this was the late seventies, so people would have noticed—Biondi assumed that the killer was white. The only suspicious white man who had shown up in recent local police reports was the filthy stranger in the orange parka. He also surmised that the perp was most likely schizophrenic. The attacks were disorganized, occurring in broad daylight with—aside from the gloves—no real effort to cover the crimes and no concern about any witnesses. Biondi took this to mean that the killer had completely broken with reality. Extrapolating further, he assumed the murderer was probably an out-of-work, unmarried loner, partly because the killings had occurred during regular business hours. Any person capable of the Wallin and Miroth murders would not only be unemployable, but a complete social outcast.

OR A CHEF!

Biondi therefore inferred that the murderer's social skills would be limited. All evidence pointed toward the killer having no prolonged interaction with the victims while they were alive; he would have pulled the trigger as quickly as possible to gain immediate control over the situation. Finally, the detective thought that the perpetrator had probably spent time in a mental institution, possibly in the very recent past. The profile fit Chase almost perfectly.

To this day the FBI often holds up the Chase case as the gold standard of the "disorganized" killer profile, and they take quite a bit of credit for his capture. The problem with this claim is that the FBI was not involved in this case in the least bit. While the method of profiling certainly helped once the clues started to come together, the actual work of Richard Chase's capture was performed by the men and women of the Sacramento Police Department.

Sacramento, man! It has smart cops, really good tacos, and it's warmer than San Francisco, so it's better than San Francisco.

At the height of the investigation, there were over fifty police officers canvasing various Sacramento-area neighborhoods to inquire about suspicious persons. Again and again, the same tall, skinny, filthy fellow in his twenties wearing an orange parka was mentioned. But according to Biondi, this wasn't very helpful in the search, as this was Sacramento in 1978. There were a lot of tall, skinny, dirty guys wandering the town. What was most helpful was the composite sketch that emerged from the people who had seen the man himself.

Witness: "He had a screaming face, it was . . . screaming. He certainly had less blood than he should have had, because he kept saying he had less blood than he should have had."

The case broke wide open when Richard's high school classmate Nancy Holden recognized him from the sketch that came out a few days after the Miroth massacre and told her police officer father-in-law about the attempted kidnapping at the grocery store. From there, Biondi delved into Chase's past and found a concealed weapon arrest on record for a .22, records of a stay in a mental institution in which Chase was described as a violent patient with a penchant for blood, and the report of the naked-and-caked-in-blood incident at Pyramid Lake.

With this information in hand, detectives drove to Chase's address and knocked on the door. There was no answer but they could hear him rummaging around inside. Not wanting to compromise things by entering without a warrant, and still not knowing whether the toddler missing from the Miroth crime scene was alive or not, the officers put on a little play in front of the apartment. They greatly oversold their intentions to leave and come back later, then waited for Richard to emerge. Sure enough, just a few minutes later, Chase walked out carrying a cardboard box. Swiftly, the cops ran him down and wrestled him to the ground, and after a tense confrontation during which he almost reached the .22 in his shoulder holster, handcuffs were snapped on the Vampire of Sacramento.

This is why I've always said cops need to carry a crucifix, a wooden spike, and holy water on their utility belts!

This moreover demonstrates the police's need for a Foley artist to create realistic soundscapes. It takes a village to be a police officer.

When the police frisked Chase, they found Danny Meredith's wallet in his back pocket and photos of Jason and Evelyn Miroth that Richard had inexplicably taken from their house after the murder.

So fucking creepy.

A search warrant for Richard's apartment was quickly obtained, and cops discovered a scene just as disturbing as they'd expected. Almost every surface was stained with either fresh or dried blood, down to a loaf of french bread that was sitting on the couch next to his bloody sleeping bag. Small bits of bone were scattered about the kitchen, and the blender smelled of rot. In the fridge they found animals' body parts on dishes and human brain tissue stored in a container. It was assumed the tissue belonged to the missing toddler.

Whoever the sick cop was who was like, "Hey, I bet these are baby brains!" was weirdly essential to this investigation.

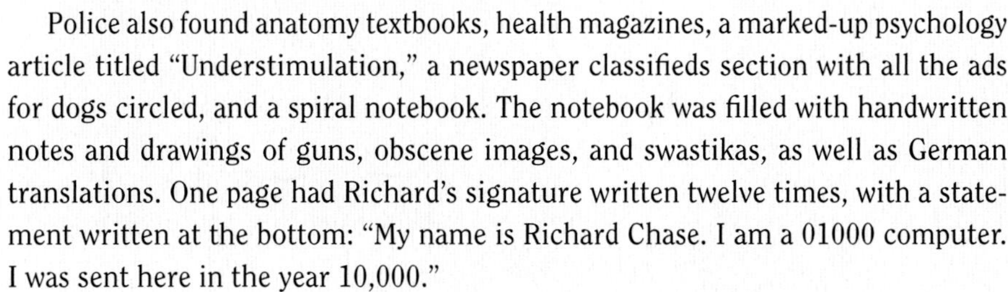

Police also found anatomy textbooks, health magazines, a marked-up psychology article titled "Understimulation," a newspaper classifieds section with all the ads for dogs circled, and a spiral notebook. The notebook was filled with handwritten notes and drawings of guns, obscene images, and swastikas, as well as German translations. One page had Richard's signature written twelve times, with a statement written at the bottom: "My name is Richard Chase. I am a 01000 computer. I was sent here in the year 10,000."

Amid all the gore and carnage, police found perhaps the most frightening object of all: a calendar. The word "Today" was written on the dates of the Wallin and Miroth murders. That same word was written on forty-four more dates over the coming year.

Charged with six counts of murder, Chase's trial had to be moved 120 miles south to Santa Clara County because of the (well-deserved) local outrage concerning his crimes. It still wasn't enough to save him. His insanity defense was rejected after only five hours of deliberation, and Richard Trenton Chase was sentenced to death on May 8, 1979. But Chase would not meet his end in the gas chamber as the state had intended. On the day after Christmas, 1980, egged on by his fellow inmates, Richard took a handful of antidepressants he'd been hoarding from his daily dose and died of toxic ingestion on death row.

We will never know what sort of life Richard Chase would have led had his family not lived in denial about his mental illness. It is true that it probably would not have been one of charity and kindness, as he was undoubtedly a sociopath in addition to being schizophrenic. However, had the right medication and treatment made its way to him, it is likely that Sacramento would never have experienced mental health's worst-case scenario.

Marcus, I just want to thank you for getting help and not killing Henry and me!

Don't provoke him!

RICHARD CHASE'S PERFECT THREE-COURSE MEAL

Hello there! My name is Richard Chase, aka the Vampire of Sacramento, and I want to welcome you to the most unique dining experience of your meaningless life. I curated this menu after years of experiencing the most intensely satisfying cuisine this world has to offer. I've eaten rabbits, cats, dogs, and, yes, even the flesh of humans. I hope you enjoy this escapade of food so dangerous it could only be served to you by the Dracula Killer!

CHOOSE 1 APPETIZER

Rabbit Brain Soup

Soup served with homemade croutons. It's possible that these croutons are toasted pieces of my own flesh, but you'll never know!

Cat Foie Gras

This delish feline dish is covered in chunky brown sauce and served with artisanal bread that would stuff the gullet of Garfield.

BBQ Human Leg Shank

Not for the weak of heart but certainly for the strong of ass, our shanks are marinated in barbecue sauce and served with fries. We searched Instagram to find the largest legs out there to make this the perfect way to start off your dinner on the right foot.

CHOOSE 1 SPECIALTY DISH

Actual-Baby-Back Ribs with Broccoli Rabe

This deliciously tender dish will add years to your life because it's from a real baby! Sure, Arby's has the meats, but do they have the baby meats? I don't think so.

Lips and Assholes Sausage

How does this differ from a normal hot dog? Well, the sausage is made up of football tailgaters after they've been eating and drinking beer for hours. These sausages would have Jeffrey Dahmer demanding to know the recipe!

CHOOSE 1 DESSERT

Head Cheesecake with Fresh Strawberries

Although usually a savory dish, our take on headcheese is as unique as a unicorn and bigfoot wedding. This succulent cheesecake will satisfy even the most sophisticated palate.

Blood-Swirl Pound Cake with Lady Fingers and Male Toes

In what can only be described as a match made in hell, this bloody good dessert will have you wanting to nibble off your own toes and fingers, just so you can savor the flavor combinations provided here.

Double-Dookie Bundt Cake with Ganache Glaze

Look away from this dish if you are watching your weight! This rich double-dookie cake will make you happier than a pig in space. I call it the "double dookie" because it's loaded with only my finest feces. Enjoy!

BY LAW I MUST ADD THIS TO THE MENU, BUT I THINK IT'S HORSESHIT!

Consuming raw or undercooked meats, poultry, seafood, shellfish, or eggs may increase your risk of foodborne illness.

MOTHER
AUGUSTA W. G
1878 19

CHAPTER 3

ED GEIN

OF ALL THE KILLERS WE'VE COVERED OVER THE YEARS, it's arguable that none have had a greater impact on American pop culture, particularly in the world of horror, than Ed Gein. Gein's crimes have inspired countless works of fiction, but only a few were able to truly capture the essence of his depravity. *Psycho* covered his psychotic mother fixation, *The Texas Chain Saw Massacre* took care of his bone-laden home decor, and *The Silence of the Lambs* illustrated some of his more disturbing creative projects. But although Gein's spirit lived on in those films, the realities of his life and crimes were far more gruesome than even those films were able to convey.

On November 16, 1957, police officers in Plainfield, Wisconsin, discovered the mutilated remains of a local storekeeper alongside dozens of objects crafted from the bodies of middle-aged women unearthed from local cemeteries. Among the macabre creations, they found soup bowls made from skullcaps, a shade-pull fashioned from a woman's lips, and a shoebox full of noses. Ed Gein became a worldwide sensation almost immediately, bringing press from as far away as Japan to this isolated community. While the rest of the planet looked upon his crimes with morbid fascination, the small-town folk of Plainfield were dumbfounded that a person born and raised among them could be capable of such actions. But while the Midwest in the late fifties is often associated with ideas of plaintive formality, it was actually a wildly violent place.

Crimes like these normally happened in the big cities, like Dubuque.

Gein also inspired the great Blind Melon song "Skinned," making him the greatest muse in the arts ever!

The true crime stories birthed from this part of the country during this time period are the stuff of legend—from Charles Starkweather and Caril Ann Fugate's ten-person spree kill in Nebraska to the Clutter massacre in Holcomb, Kansas. Even the area in central Wisconsin where Ed Gein robbed graves was cursed with a rash of mysterious disappearances that had nothing to do with Gein himself. Even still, every time one of these tragedies occurred, the townsfolk were heard to say, "These things just don't happen here."

"I am the chief of police here in La Crosse, and I'll tell ya what. Four or five more children go missing and we're gonna launch a full investigation."

Okay, before you malign my home state further, I'd like to point out we also give a free beer backer for every Bloody Mary! Also, the name "Bloody Mary" was probably inspired by Ed Gein.

To be pedantic, Ed's official body count technically disqualifies him from the accepted definition of a serial killer, which the FBI defines as three or more murders committed with a cooling-off period between each. But Gein is a special case. He may not have had the numbers of Andrei Chikatilo or John Wayne Gacy, but when you consider the heights of depravity he eventually reached, there's no question that he deserves a spot alongside the others.

LIKE A TWISTED, TRAGIC EPISODE OF *LITTLE HOUSE ON THE* *Prairie*, the Gein family legacy is a homespun tale of poverty, misery, and death. When Ed's father, George, was just a little boy in 1879, his parents and siblings were swept away in a flood as the family crossed the Mississippi, leaving the three-year-old George as the sole survivor.

Wait. His dad's family died like the bad guys in *O Brother, Where Art Thou*? That's pretty cool!

Conventional sources indicate that George was soon adopted by his maternal grandparents, but our research into Wisconsin adoption records revealed another possibility. We found that a child named George Gee was taken in around this time by a family with the last name Dingledine.

The only name worse than Dingledine is that of a former Twins baseball player, Rusty Kuntz. That's a real name; look it up!

Dingledine sounds like the name of an app you use to find dick and a free dinner.

We can't confirm or deny that this George Gee is Ed's father, but it isn't much of a stretch to imagine that Gee was combined with Dingledine to create the surname Gein. If this was indeed the case, it seems that George Gein had been adopted not for love but for free farm labor. The 1900 census marks the poor kid down as nothing more than "servant," completely separate from all the other children in the Dingledine household.

The elder Gein left the farm in the late 1890s and moved to La Crosse, Wisconsin, quickly developing a drinking problem that would persist until the day he died. Famously lazy, George never settled on a career, but he certainly settled when it came to his choice of a spouse, the exhausting Augusta Gein.

I like the idea of "developing" a drinking problem, like he's the Elon Musk of alcoholics. Perhaps he was the first to perfect the butt chug!

No man can wait to meet his Augusta. Nothing like a person whose name sounds like noises you make when lifting farm equipment.

Thickset, nasty, and difficult, Augusta Gein sounds closer to a storybook goblin than the kind, loving woman depicted in Ed Gein's later recollections. Raised in a strict German household by a father who beat his judgmental religious beliefs into her with his fists, she took his lead and berated whoever would listen.

I don't think you need to say "strict" before "German household." I think it's implied when you're raised by the people that replaced Santa Claus with Krampus!

Augusta was never afraid to speak her mind and incessantly preached to the neighbors about how the rot of moral turpitude was eating away at the foundations of early twentieth-century Wisconsin society. According to her, the sexual urges and actions of men had a large part to play in this, but she also believed women shared just as much (if not more) of the blame for turning the world into an open-air whorehouse.

Parents can really set the tone for a child's entire existence.

Nothing in this world was more repulsive to Augusta than sex, as she considered it the evilest of necessities and the root of everything that was wrong with man's earth. That belief, combined with George's habit of spending his paycheck on the drink, made for a fantastically unhappy marriage.

I would love to see Augusta's Facebook feed! The Christian memes alone would be worth signing up for that dreadful platform!

Sometimes the hatred they shared would boil over into vicious beatings, with George raining his fists down on Augusta while she continued insulting him and openly praying for his early death.

It's like if *The King of Queens* was directed by Harmony Korine.

It was into this chaotic environment that the Gein brothers were born. Henry came first, in 1902, although based on what Augusta told Ed, she never cared much for her firstborn son. She believed that her maternal instincts would bloom upon the birth of her next child, who was, God willing, sure to be a girl and open to being remade in her mother's image.

Always good to have a burner kid. Remember Larry Spock's child-rearing book *First Kids Don't Count*?

She should've stopped having kids and started collecting corgis. Only the power of corgi could warm her cold, cold heart!

Edward Theodore Gein, born in 1906, was certainly not a girl, so, upon his birth, Augusta made a decree that if it was God's will that she be cursed with sons, they would be pure, righteous, and resistant to the fleshly transgressions perpetrated by the common man. In attempting to do so, Augusta Gein created possibly the kinkiest creature to ever walk the earth.

With his small eyes and his weird smile, Ed Gein is the guy who *actually* shows up to swingers' night.

I think it's safe to say the kinkiest person ever created was J. Edgar Hoover, but Eddie is a close second.

Despite Ed's weepy-eyed insistence that his mother was a saint among sinners, his childhood with Augusta was not the stuff of kindness and compassion. Rather, her behavior oscillated between terrorizing her sons and being overly protective of them. Gein's earliest recollection of Augusta was of her roughly yanking him away from the top of a flight of stairs. He said she shook his little body and screamed at him, but she never made clear just exactly what he did wrong. It didn't quite matter, though, as that incident started him on a path of both fear and near-total reliance on his mother's guidance. And despite his devotion, nothing seemed to keep the beast of his mother's expectations fed.

This is the beginning of a really fucked-up Snickers commercial.

When Ed was seven, Augusta sent him to the store to buy bread. Somehow, along the way, he lost the coins she had given him to pay. He said that when he returned with only a wet face covered in remorseful tears, his mother told him, "You dreadful child, only a mother could love you."

Even a broken clock is right twice a day!

You only learned what that saying meant for the book, Kissel!

And according to the people of La Crosse, only a son could love Augusta Gein. She was profoundly unpopular, mostly due to her ability to find fault and alienate practically anyone almost immediately. But Ed couldn't even speak of his mother in later years without sinking into a sentimental blubber, saying, "She was like nobody else in the world."

What? Augusta Gein wasn't popular? Built like a Jeep Wrangler with the personality of Ed Asner if he doesn't get his pills on time? Marcus, stop belittling this woman!

Despite their unpopularity in town, the Geins opened a general store in La Crosse. When George proved to be just as lazy working for himself as he was working for others, Augusta demoted her husband to stock boy and ran the place all on her own. Eventually, even a town as small as La Crosse (population thirty-one thousand) was too much of a harlot-filled snake pit for a good Christian woman like Augusta, so in 1914, the Geins purchased a 195-acre farm six miles outside Plainfield. Augusta believed the boys were safe from any transgressive influences on their isolated farm compound, but since boys will be boys, Ed didn't need help from the outside world to discover his own body—and with that discovery came predictably disastrous developmental results.

When Ed was twelve his mother caught him in the middle of a perfectly normal bathtub masturbation session. But instead of leaving in embarrassment and never speaking of it again, as is American custom, Augusta punished him by reaching down into the water and clutching his genitals, scolding him for falling prey to what she called "the curse of man." It was a statement that would stay with Ed forever, warping an already fragile developing sexuality.

Gein's father was no comfort, either. His loathing for his own lot in life swelled and festered as the years went by, manifesting in beatings so powerful that Ed's ears would ring for days afterward. Despite this toxic family environment, Augusta and George never considered divorce, accepting their situation so completely that they rarely left the farm. As a result, Ed Gein never learned how to properly fit into society. Whenever his social instincts would kick in during his childhood, Augusta quickly shut them down.

RuPaul has a better chance of fitting in at a religious-right political conference than Ed had at fitting into society.

If Ed tried making a friend at school, Augusta would reject the very notion by stating that the child was wicked, usually because of their sinner parents. Because Ed always trusted his mother implicitly, he would avoid that child from that day forward, refusing to speak to them ever again. From there, his lack of socializing only spiraled.

With any luck, he'd discover he has the same powers as Powder!

People in Ed Gein's classes said that he rarely made eye contact with others and often wore an unsettling grin. Those who were able to engage him in conversation found that he would mimic their mannerisms and laugh at inappropriate times, as if he was only taking wild stabs at normal human behavior. And as far as interacting with the opposite sex went, he could barely bring himself to even speak to a woman, instead staring at them to the point of vague violation.

So not only did Ed inspire copious films and songs, he also invented the male gaze!

As if being a social misfit wasn't enough, Ed had physical disadvantages as well. A growth over his left eyelid caused it to droop permanently, which inevitably attracted jeers from other children about his "saggy, baggy eye." Even if he did have it within himself to construct some sort of witty retort, a lesion on his tongue had given him a speech impediment that made him sound like he had a slight mental handicap, so he would burst into tears instead. In other words, Ed was what Midwesterners call an oddball. The constant bullying he endured, compounded by comments from his peers about sex and other morally repugnant acts, seemed to confirm what his mother had always told him: that the world outside the Gein farm and Mother's protection was unkind and sinful.

The only thing kinder than a Wisconsin farm in the middle of winter is literally hell.

Unsurprisingly, entertainment in the Gein household was generally limited to Augusta reading only the choicest selections from the Bible, with a special eye toward passages that focus on the filthiness of women. Through the good book, she painted a picture of the world in which the only good woman was the one sitting right in front of them. And to take this family bonding time a step further, she would sometimes instruct her sons in the ways of masturbation, as she said even the sin of Onan was preferable to the touch of a woman.

Nothing gets me randier for jack-off lessons than sitting back with my brother and getting Bible readings from my huge mommy. Ed was set for life.

Hello, Mrs. Robinson!

By the mid-1930s, George Gein's drinking habit caught up to him and he became an invalid, ignored in his own home by a family that couldn't stand him. He finally died in 1937, and although no specific cause was given for his death, Augusta declared that he had died from weakness, making sure to follow that with a proclamation that her late husband was currently swimming in the lake of fire with all the other sinners.

So she inspired The Meat Puppets' "Lake of Fire"! The Geins were unwittingly music industry royalty!

In researching this story, I forgot that George and Augusta were our age while raising Ed. The fact that there are people in their thirties living like that to this day makes my chest hurt. I could have graduated high school with an Augusta Gein! And, according to the Facebook posts of some people from my class, I did.

After the death of his father, Henry became a little more adventurous, working as a foreman for road construction crews throughout the 1940s. Meanwhile, Ed found a career that you might expect to be a bad match for the town oddball: the trusted local babysitter. As it turns out, Ed Gein, one of the most feared ghouls in Wisconsin history, was great with kids. While shifty and anxious around adults, the take-you-as-you-are nature of children put him at ease. Consequently, he became one of Plainfield's most dependable babysitters and spent years looking after children. Even if he was slightly off-kilter, Ed was known as a good-natured, trustworthy character. The only thing that gave people pause was the inexplicable devotion he gave to a woman who didn't have an ounce of compassion for him: his mother.

The subject of Augusta also became a point of contention between the Gein brothers, although the conflict came bizarrely late in life. Henry and Ed were in their late thirties when the older sibling brought up the possibility that perhaps his younger brother was just a little *too* devoted to Mother. The notion completely blindsided Ed, who saw Augusta as a modern-day saint. It was the only crack in Henry and Ed's relationship—and it quite possibly led to both Ed's first mental break and his first possible murder.

"Owen loves his momma, Owen loves his momma!" That's a *Throw Momma from the Train* reference. You get it!

The conditions surrounding Henry Gein's likely murder were, to say the least, obscured. On the night of May 16, 1944, Ed showed up in Plainfield in a panic, saying that Henry had gone missing after a fire they'd started had gotten out of control. According to Ed, the two had split up when the fire threatened to take out the pine trees on the edge of a field they were clearing. Ed got his bearings and fled to safety, but he said it was too dark to look for Henry on his own so he'd come to town for help. The search party expected to look all night for Henry, but to their great surprise, once they got to the field, Ed managed to lead them directly to his brother's body. When asked how he was able to find the body so quickly, he just shrugged and casually replied, "Funny how that works."

It really *is* funny how that works. It's so funny how you can kill your brother and, in the most half-assed way possible, hide his body and create a flimsy alibi, and then be able to take people to his grave the instant they ask. Yep, super funny. Jimmy Fallon–level funny.

No evidence exists to prove definitively that Ed Gein murdered his brother, but the circumstances are suspicious, even beyond Ed leading the search party directly to the corpse. Although Henry was found on a section of scorched earth, his clothes and flesh were completely unburned, and furthermore, his head was badly bruised. These would usually be red flags when investigating a suspicious death, but the people of Plainfield believed Ed to be so harmless that they never considered him a suspect. All Ed knew was that the Gein family now consisted of the only ones that mattered: just him and Mother, all alone in an isolated farmhouse with no running water or electricity. It wouldn't be long, though, before this mother's-boy paradise came crashing down.

"Mother's Boy Paradise" sounds like one of those magazines you had to sell over the phone in the nineties.

Coming between Ed and his mother is like coming between John Candy and a porterhouse—you're gonna get killed!

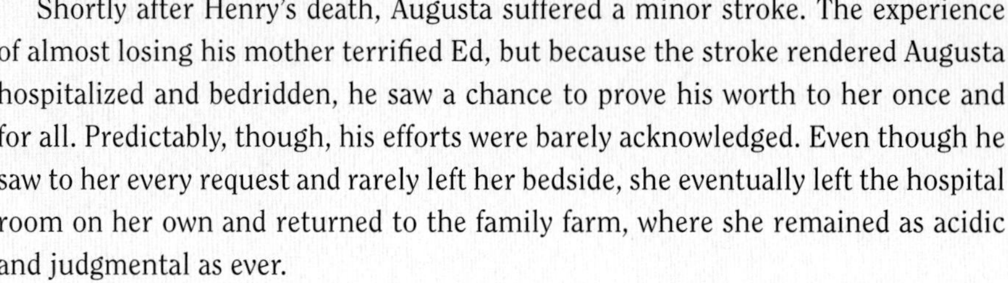

Shortly after Henry's death, Augusta suffered a minor stroke. The experience of almost losing his mother terrified Ed, but because the stroke rendered Augusta hospitalized and bedridden, he saw a chance to prove his worth to her once and for all. Predictably, though, his efforts were barely acknowledged. Even though he saw to her every request and rarely left her bedside, she eventually left the hospital room on her own and returned to the family farm, where she remained as acidic and judgmental as ever.

You really have to watch how much salt you eat, no matter how many times you watch your son masturbate.

Hate is the greatest fountain of youth there is. Just ask James Woods!

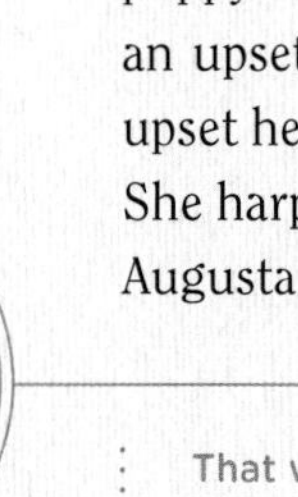

Near the end of 1945, Augusta and Ed drove to a neighbor's house to purchase straw for their livestock. They arrived to find the neighbor in question beating a puppy to death while his live-in girlfriend screamed for him to stop. Though it's an upsetting image, it wasn't the animal cruelty that disturbed Augusta—what upset her the most was that the neighbor was living with a woman out of wedlock. She harped on their immorality for a week, until a blood vessel burst in her brain. Augusta Gein dropped dead of a second stroke at the age of sixty-seven.

That will be how I die, but it'll be in the middle of screaming about the *Dune* remake.

Augusta's funeral was sparsely attended. While both Henry and George had received heartfelt obituaries in the local newspaper, she received no more than a death notice to let the townsfolk know that the local busybody was finally out of everyone's hair. With no one to witness his sorrow, Ed gave himself permission to fall apart at his mother's funeral. When he did manage to compose himself enough to say a few words, he stood in front of the congregation, his face covered in tears and snot, and said, "She was too good . . . just much too good for all that suffering."

What I wouldn't give to see footage of Ed Gein singing "Amazing Grace" at this funeral. But Augusta would have disapproved because Grace sounds like a real hooker.

It's hard to determine whether Augusta's death was the cause of Ed's extreme deviancy, or whether it was just the catalyst for something that had simmered below the surface for years. Whatever the cause, after his mother was dead and buried, Ed Gein embarked on a dark journey of depravity. Inspired by the more gruesome activities perpetrated by the worst of Hitler's concentration camp guards, Gein began to fantasize about the more creative ways that a dead body could be used. He was specifically fascinated by the depravity of Ilse Koch, commonly known as "The Bitch of Buchenwald."

It's never good when your artistic inspiration is, in fact, not an artist but rather a war criminal who possibly skinned more people than Pinhead from *Hellraiser*.

It was widely reported that Koch had saved the tattooed skins of concentration camp victims and used them to make decorative lampshades. No definitive proof of such objects was ever found, but the very concept captivated Gein to the point where he would eventually create his own little Buchenwald on the plains of Wisconsin.

"Little Buchenwald" sounds like a fun family vacation place, like if Colonial Williamsburg was set in hell instead of Virginia.

Oddly enough, Augusta had been a stabilizing force in the Gein household. Ed's entire life had been his mother; essentially, he belonged to a two-person cult. When she died, his daily activities must have been thrown into total disarray. Normally serial killers need to "give themselves permission" to start their crimes; in Gein's case, the lack of natural authority in the household allowed him to slip into madness. You know, like the old saying, "When the cat's away, the mice cover themselves in the skins of the deceased."

Gein was a voracious reader, spending hours each night poring over books by candlelight in his bedroom. In addition to his obsession with Ilse Koch, he was also enamored by stories of eighteenth-century medical students who robbed graves so they could sell the corpses to medical schools. Gein also owned a well-loved copy of *Gray's Anatomy*, although the only chapters that had gotten any use were those concerning the human head and the female reproductive organs. Ed later told one of his psychiatrists that his interest in bodies was of a completely scientific nature.

Yeah, so was Mengele's!

At least Mengele went to school for it!

Gein told authorities post-arrest that he wanted to be a doctor, just like the medical students in his stories. While that may have been partly true, it certainly doesn't explain the arts-and-crafts projects for which he gained so much infamy.

If God didn't want skulls to be used as ashtrays, then why'd she make them so perfect for it, huh?

He's having fun with it! He can't always be clinical—he needed some flair!

Despite what was happening at home in the years following Augusta's death, in the eyes of the townsfolk, Ed's behavior barely changed. He still greeted people with the same lopsided grin, and when he helped out on local farms he was still considered an industrious worker. He was generally accepted by the Plainfield community, but his socially awkward ways did occasionally give people pause, like the time he was told of a local tragedy in which a man was horribly mutilated by a combine. According to some of the men he worked with, Ed giggled uncontrollably instead of showing the least bit of empathy. Everyone liked Ed Gein—they just wouldn't want him marrying their daughter.

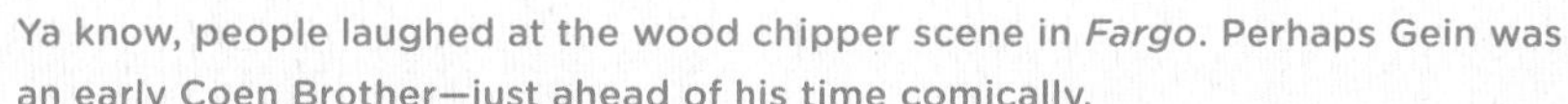

Ya know, people laughed at the wood chipper scene in *Fargo*. Perhaps Gein was an early Coen Brother—just ahead of his time comically.

Further putting a wedge between himself and the citizens of Plainfield, Ed would often jabber on for as long as you'd let him about people getting maimed or murdered. These stories often came from his extensive collection of true crime magazines—a collection that would rival even my own, if I must say so.

More information that gives me pause regarding my friendship with Marcus . . .

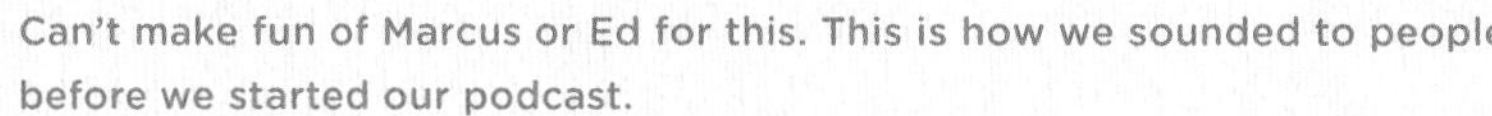

Can't make fun of Marcus or Ed for this. This is how we sounded to people before we started our podcast.

While he may have appeared to be stable to the average townsperson, Ed started to demonstrate clear signs of schizophrenic behavior about a year after his mother's death. He claimed he began hearing his mother's voice as he drifted off to sleep, and that was followed by visual hallucinations. One such incident found him staring at a tree that he believed was covered in hundreds of vultures dripping with blood and viscera. Other times, Ed would see human faces staring at him from piles of yellow leaves.

Honestly, this is kinda fun!

Ed was living a metal god's dream.

During this period, whatever desires Augusta had kept at bay for decades began to surge in ways that Ed never thought possible. He felt the need to see a woman's body but not, he claimed, for sexual purposes. But since he had no clue about how to even begin a conversation with a member of the opposite sex—they humored him at best—and paying for a woman's services would be contributing to the wickedness of the world, Ed decided the road least sinful was the graveyard.

ARE YOU MY MOTHER?
YOU'RE SEEING THINGS, ED.

Jesus, buddy, just sign up for one of those bring-your-own-wine figure drawing classes. It's so much easier and you don't need a shovel!

Definitely less sinful than having a girlfriend.

Two years after his mother passed away, Ed found himself drawn to local graveyards when the moon was full. He later recalled that he'd made about forty visits to Plainfield, Hancock, and Spiritland cemeteries over a five-year period. Those visits, however, were preceded by repeated attempts to raise his mother from the grave. Traveling to Augusta's headstone and mustering every bit of willpower he had, he tried using his misguided love as a conduit for resurrection.

Even though Ed's attempts to restore his mother never made it past the wishing stage, the myth persists that he dug up her corpse and installed it in the home they'd formerly shared, à la Norman Bates. That said, it *can* be confirmed that Ed's first excavation occurred at the grave next to Augusta's: that of local townswoman Eleanor Adams. Adams, who was only fifty-one when she died, had always reminded Ed of his mother, although he never spoke to her personally. So, not daring to disturb his mother's grave, Ed settled on a replacement. On the first night Eleanor's body spent in the ground, Ed went to the cemetery and plunged his shovel into the freshly laid soil. He opened the front half of Eleanor's coffin, slipped her out, and took her home. The only thing he left behind was the crowbar he'd used to open the lid.

C'mon, Eddy! Ya gotta pick up after yourself, like Augusta taught you to do!

Not to make light of how creepy this all is, but it must take a lot of core strength to pull a dead body out of a casket.

After successfully robbing Eleanor's grave, Ed began reading obituaries in the way that others might look at the "free" section in the classifieds. He specifically looked for notices involving middle-aged women, waiting until the night after the funeral to exhume their corpses. Ed claimed that he could occasionally pray away the desire to rob graves, but most of the time, it wasn't enough. Only once did he come out of what he termed his "haze" in the middle of a robbery, after which he immediately stopped and put the grave back just as he'd found it.

In many ways, Ed must have been scared of his own damn self. If we take his word for it, can you imagine the true horror of being in a haze of illness and WAKING UP in the middle of exhuming a grave, covered in dirt and looking at a dead woman? Like looking at the scale after the holidays. ACK!

To make it all the creepier, the victims of Ed's graveyard visits were not strangers. Plainfield was a small community and so some of these women were people that he knew well. In this way, the personal relationships to these victims—because they *are* victims, whether these acts were committed after they left this earthly plane or not—and to the two people he murdered, set Ed Gein even further apart from the serial killer prototype because male serial killers almost never murder people they know personally.

It's almost as if Ed had that quintessential small-town America neighborly attitude.

Mr. Rogers' Neighborhood, but when he comes in the house to say hello to the kids, he puts on a sweater made of breasts.

This proximity to his victims could be why Ed sometimes felt a tinge of guilt about his actions. In a few cases, he returned body parts for which he had no use to the graves where he had found them. In the case of Mabel Everson, he dug the grave back up and tossed her jaw, part of her skull, part of her leg, a scrap of clothing, and her gold wedding band on top of her coffin before covering it all again.

Eventually, Ed amended his technique to take only the body parts he needed. When he was only after the head, he would work it back and forth until the spinal cord snapped, enabling him to rip it free. He also took trips to harvest skin. In one case, he said he opened the coffin, flipped the body over, and cut strips from the corpse's back before leaving the grave the same way he left the rest, in what he called "apple-pie order." He claimed that he was almost caught only once, when he heard two lovers wandering the cemetery at night as he was knee-deep in a grave.

I'm just happy some people were in love in Plainfield, because so far it seems like the town was full of the cast from *Deadwood*.

He found the Plainfield goths! I bet they would have LOVED to go grave robbing with him—unless they were poseurs!

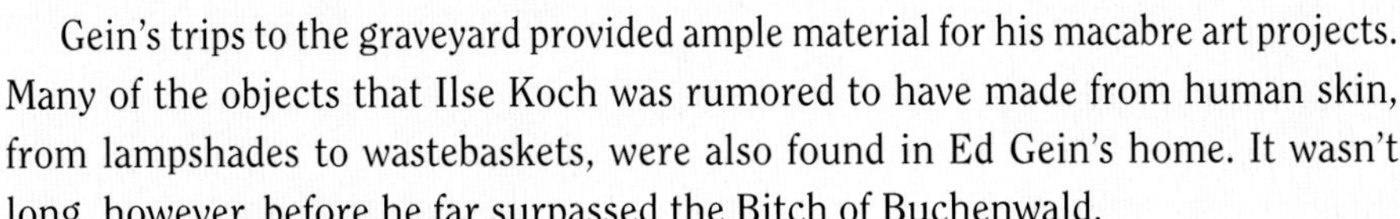

Gein's trips to the graveyard provided ample material for his macabre art projects. Many of the objects that Ilse Koch was rumored to have made from human skin, from lampshades to wastebaskets, were also found in Ed Gein's home. It wasn't long, however, before he far surpassed the Bitch of Buchenwald.

That's American ingenuity!

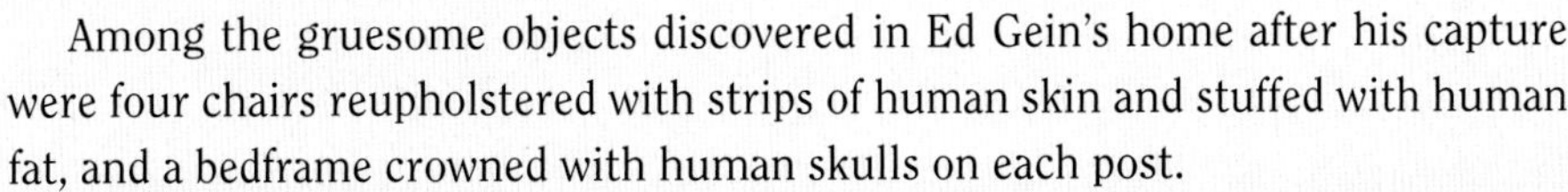

Among the gruesome objects discovered in Ed Gein's home after his capture were four chairs reupholstered with strips of human skin and stuffed with human fat, and a bedframe crowned with human skulls on each post.

Wow, and all this done before Google, so he couldn't even search "how to sleep like a supervillain."

There were other objects that he merely collected, such as the nine vulvas he stored in a box. Despite the sexual implications of this, Gein swore that he never had sex with any of the corpses, saying they "smelled too bad." Nevertheless, his final use for these bodies was undoubtedly a gross violation.

This is what I say to Ed: "LEAVE 'em ALONE!"

In the early fifties, Ed became obsessed with the story of Christine Jorgensen, who was the first widely known male-to-female recipient of sexual reassignment surgery and one of the earliest activists of the trans movement. But when that was filtered through Ed Gein's schizophrenic brain, the results were a predictable malformation of a true yearning. According to what he told a psychiatrist many years later, the truth was that ever since he was a little boy, he'd kept a secret desire hidden within his heart: Ed had always wondered what it was like to be a girl, and now that he had the skins of almost a dozen women at his disposal, he figured he'd give it a shot.

He might have suffered from gender dysmorphia, or it could have just been interest in Jorgensen's particular story. Is it possible that Augusta's demonizing of women throughout his life actually made him curious, in a roundabout way, about what it would be like to *be* one of these evil temptresses? We can't be sure.

Gein made leggings from his victims' skin and fashioned a tanned vest out of a woman's upper torso, breasts and all. He would slip on the leggings, suspend the vest from his neck with a cord and fasten it around his own torso with leather straps, and then don gloves made from human skin. On full moons, he would flaunt this look around the house, impressing no one but himself, before ending the night with an impromptu concert in his front yard with a drum made from human skin and a jawbone mallet. It's worth noting that his creations were durable, as Ed said he would sometimes wear parts of his suit during grave-robbing expeditions.

Now, while this may all seem extreme and unnecessary, and some people would even call this behavior a little *weird*, it's delightful that he could really experiment with his gender and creativity in the comfort of his home. That being said . . . what a monster—I will never stop screaming.

If Gein gave that performance today, I'm sure he'd sell out Carnegie Hall.

There was only one accessory Ed needed to finish his ghastly ensemble: masks made from the faces of the desecrated. He kept four hanging on the wall, stuffed with paper or sawdust to give them a more lifelike appearance; a few even retained the lipstick applied by the mortician before they'd gone into the ground. When Ed was asked during his confession if he ever wore the faces, he stated matter-of-factly, "That I did."

That's how you respond when your roommate asks if you picked up milk on the way home, not about a bunch of SKIN MASKS YOU HAVE IN YOUR LIVING ROOM.

CHECK, PLEASE!

Besides the masks, four additional noses were found in a box in Ed Gein's house, bringing the total number of the disinterred to thirteen. One face, however, was never removed from the skull and therefore didn't make it into Ed's prop closet. That one belonged to his first confirmed murder victim, Mary Hogan.

So he had spare noses just hanging around, like how IKEA sends you bonus screws in case you lose one? All right.

Mary Hogan was Augusta Gein's opposite when it came to how they approached the world. Although they both owned their own businesses and spoke with thick German accents, Hogan ran the local bar, the Pine Grove Tavern, and was rumored to have enjoyed a life of decadence prior to her time in Plainfield. It was said that she had been everything from a mob-connected criminal to a big-city madam. The rumors made sense to the people of Plainfield, as Mary Hogan was a brassy woman with a foul mouth, but she was always sweet to Ed Gein.

You can hear his R. Crumb fantasies churning in his farm-dog brain!

Even though Gein's father had been an alcoholic, Ed was able to keep his drinking under control, only stopping by the Pine Grove every now and then to sip a beer and stare at the bawdy bartender. What she didn't know while she was serving a Schlitz to this lonely farmer was that Gein's schizophrenic psyche was seething with something dark. There was something about Mary Hogan that made Ed Gein's brain twitch: in addition to sharing business sensibilities and accents, Mary Hogan bore a striking physical resemblance to Augusta Gein. The two seemed to be mirror images of each other, the biggest difference being that while the woman who was "good in every way" was dead, the lusty bartender contributing to the wickedness of the world was standing right in front of him, telling dirty jokes.

Aw man, Mary sounds like Jackie Zebrowski, which makes me love her but also feel sad because she lived in an era before podcasting.

Mary was a hustler, making it work as a single woman in Wisconsin. She's busting her rump, serving beers and slinging one-liners, and all Ed does is stare at her and wonder what her insides look like. Tough gig!

On December 8, 1954, Ed decided to rectify the injustice. The details are scarce, but at some point while Hogan was closing up shop, Ed pulled out his .32 revolver and shot her dead. Though he claims not to have remembered a moment of it, he eventually confessed to the murder after police discovered Mary's head in his home.

Yeah, it's pretty hard to pull the "how did this get here?" card when a human head is found in your house. It's a more intense version of when a kid lies about eating a chocolate chip cookie despite having chocolate smeared on his face.

Not a single lead in the murder was found at the time besides a pool of blood and missing stack of cash. As a result, Plainfield police threw up their hands and added her to the list of people who had disappeared in the area over the previous few years. But had anyone taken Ed Gein seriously, Plainfield's nightmare could have ended with that first death. The subject of Mary's disappearance had come up during a conversation with a few other farmers, including one Elmo Ueeck. Elmo, knowing that Ed had spent a fair amount of time staring at Hogan at her tavern, joked that if he'd spent more time courting and less time gawking, she might've been cooking him a meal instead of closing up that night. In response, Ed just smiled and said, "She's not missing. She's at the house right now."

Who is this guy, Steven Wright?

Elmo and the others just laughed this off as one of Ed's trademark bad jokes. But even after that, anytime someone mentioned Mary Hogan, Ed would flat-out say, "She's at the farm right now. I went and got her in my pickup truck and took her home."

Ed is hilarious; he's got great one-liners. His prop comedy can be a little abrasive however.

I guess it's true what they say: "First they ignore you, then they laugh at you, then they fight, and then you win." Except winning in this case means collecting human skin.

There were other signs as well. A local boy named Bob Hill, said by some to be the closest thing Ed had to a true friend, said that Ed had shown him a pair of preserved human heads he'd claimed came from a cousin who had picked them up in the Philippines during World War II. Amazingly, Hill's parents fully accepted that Ed owned human heads, so the incident was brushed off. To them, that was just the type of thing that oddball would have in his house.

This sounds like a really macabre episode of *King of the Hill*.

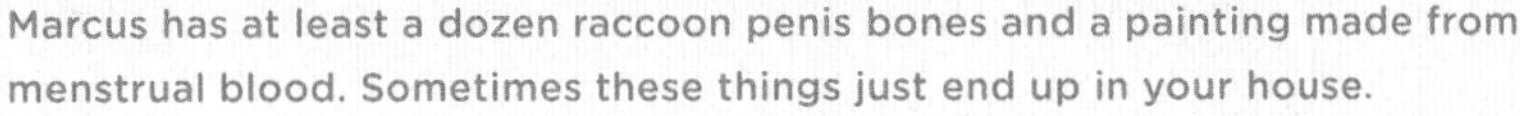

Marcus has at least a dozen raccoon penis bones and a painting made from menstrual blood. Sometimes these things just end up in your house.

Ed's predilection toward macabre objects even turned into a local joke. Once, when he was showing his house to a young couple who were thinking of buying the place, the woman pointed to a room and asked if that was where he kept his shrunken heads. Ed just smiled, pointed in another direction, and said, "No, they're in this room over here."

That is something to know about comedians. If you are friends with or date one, everything they joke about, they also mean completely seriously. When they react to something you do with a joke and then you get upset and they say, "I'm only joking!" they are, in fact, never joking.

Even though the people of Plainfield generally placated Ed and nervously laughed whenever he made a "joke," he later maintained that none of the horrible things that he did would have happened if his neighbors had shown a little more interest in his life. As it was, there was nothing stopping Ed Gein from shorting out one more time and killing another woman who reminded him of his mother.

Bernice Worden had come to dread seeing Ed Gein walk through the door of her hardware shop. In the months leading up to her murder, Ed had become a nuisance, hanging around and bugging Bernice to go to the movies or come "try out the floor" at the new skating rink the next town over. Ed later insisted that he'd again only been joking, but the suggestions had been bothersome enough for Bernice to

mention it to her son, Frank. Unfortunately for Bernice, Ed Gein's obsession went far beyond the sphere of dating.

If *Ed Gein* can ask someone out on a date, no one has an excuse not to ever again.

Good lord, he's like David Letterman's stalker, Margaret Mary Ray. Remember when that happened? Man, I'm getting old!

Like Mary Hogan, Bernice Worden physically resembled Augusta Gein. Unlike his beloved mother, though, Worden had a bit of immorality on her side, as a few years earlier she'd stolen her future husband from another woman who subsequently killed herself over the affair. In Ed's twisted mind, this meant that Bernice had to go. Once again, sin was alive, while the woman "like no one else in the world" was dead in the ground.

Plainfield was deserted on the morning of November 16, 1957, because it was opening day of deer hunting season. Just about every man had taken the day off to bag a buck, so Bernice was left all alone minding the store. Ed knew this for certain because he'd made sure to ask her son, Frank, the day before if he was planning to head out into the woods. Gein claimed that he'd never been interested in deer, insisting he never killed anything bigger than a squirrel because too much blood made him pass out. But as the day's events illustrated, Ed's knowledge of killing and butchering went far beyond the level of the red squirrel.

Ed showed up at Worden's store at 8:00 a.m. with an empty jar in hand. He said he'd seen she was having a sale on antifreeze so he figured he'd come in for a refill. Bernice obliged and wrote his name on a receipt, possibly hoping that this would be the extent of their interaction that day, but Ed asked for one more thing. He said he was in the market for a new rifle, so he asked if he could inspect a Marlin on display behind the counter.

NEVER LET THE WEIRD GUY IN THE NEIGHBORHOOD TRY THE GUNS.

After Bernice handed him the Marlin, she turned around, looked out the window at a car parked in front of the gas station across the street, and said, "I do not like Chevrolets." Unbeknownst to her, these would be her last words. While she was gazing out the window, Ed reached into his pocket and loaded the rifle with a .22 bullet he'd brought with him. Then, while her back was still turned, he pointed the rifle at her head and killed Bernice Worden with a single shot.

She's right about Chevies! Ya know what Chevy stands for: "Can Hear Every Valve Yell." I'll be here all week!

Better than a Ford, or, as I like to say, "Fixed Or Repaired Daily"! . . . How sad have we become?

Ed initially alleged that the whole thing had been an accident. He told police that he'd loaded the bullet to ensure that the gun took his preferred length of shell, then, as he was testing the sights, it went off, killing Bernice. The evidence told a different story, though. When the crime scene was discovered that afternoon, witnesses were met with a massive pool of blood behind the counter, far more than a .22 bullet to the skull would have produced. Instead, some of the cops, experienced deer hunters all, believed that Ed had followed hunting procedure. After the initial shot, they believed that he'd knelt and slit Bernice's throat right there behind the counter of her own store. According to them, a deer hunter will instinctively cut a deer's throat to improve the taste of the meat.

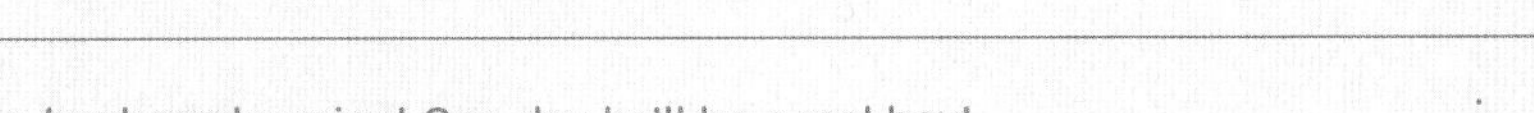

You see—he *has* been learning! One day he'll be a real boy!

Ed's behavior right after the act itself, however, betrays the cool sense of premeditation implied by the scene. Agitated and not knowing what to do, he locked the door, dragged Bernice's body and the cash register behind the store, and loaded them both into the Wordens' truck before taking off down the road. After getting out of town, he left the truck behind and walked back to Plainfield to get his own. Then he transferred Bernice's body to his vehicle and made his way back to the Gein farm, speeding past his friend Elmo on the way. The summer kitchen was waiting.

For a person as sick as Ed was, it's astounding how well he planned this crime. He was totally mired in the fog of insanity but also somehow knew that what he was doing was wrong and tried covering it up. The human mind is capable of so many things! . . . I don't know why I went all Carl Sagan on this point.

Large old houses like Ed's sometimes had sheds that provided a relatively cool environment for cooking during the warm summer months. That day, Ed used his summer kitchen as a slaughterhouse. While most other men in Plainfield were sitting in deer blinds, enjoying the afternoon sun while waiting for their prey to appear, Ed was dragging Bernice Worden's body into the dark one-room structure to do his vile work. Once he got her inside, he undressed her, slit the skin on her ankles, and inserted a sharpened three-and-a-half-foot-long wooden rod through her Achilles tendons. The rod was then tied to a rope that Ed used to hoist the body to the ceiling, after which he wrapped ropes around each wrist and tied them taut to the crossbeam. Once the body was suspended and secure, the butchery began.

Again, the core strength is incredible.

If Ed followed deer-dressing procedure, as many believed he did, it's most likely that he began by removing the head, cutting it off at the shoulders. He then moved upward, carving out the vagina as well as a chunk of the anus, removing it all in one piece. That cut then extended down from the crotch to the sternum. After making that incision, Ed reached inside, emptied the body of all viscera, and drained it of all its blood. Finally, he cleaned the cavity, wiping away any excess liquid. He claims to remember none of it.

At five o'clock that afternoon, Frank Worden used his spare key to open the family hardware store. What he found was a pool of blood and the clue to her abduction sitting right on the counter: the receipt for antifreeze bearing the name of the man who'd been bothering his mother for months.

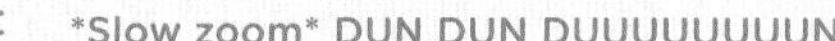

Slow zoom DUN DUN DUUUUUUUUN!

That will teach him to never get a receipt again!

Meanwhile, Ed was enjoying a dinner of pork chops, macaroni, and pickles over at his young friend Bob Hill's house. Earlier that day, Bob and his sister Darlene had gone over to Ed's to see if he could help them with some car trouble, only to find him emerging from the house with his hands covered in blood. He said they'd just caught him in the middle of butchering a deer, but he'd be happy to help with whatever they needed.

"Uhhh thanks, Ed, but maybe could you wash your hands first? I don't want deer blood on my car unless I'm puttin' it there."

He followed them back to their house, changed their car battery, and took them up on an offer to stay for dinner. Ed and the family were watching *I Love Lucy* when Bob's brother-in-law burst through the door and told them about the commotion up at Worden's Hardware. Excited by the news of a violent crime, Bob and Ed jumped into Ed's truck to head downtown for a look, but as they were waiting for the truck to warm up, traffic officer Dan Chase and deputy Poke Spees pulled into the driveway. The two walked over to Ed's vehicle, asked him to come with them, and put him in the back of their police car. Right there in front of the Hills' home, they questioned Ed about what he'd been doing that day twice over. When the two stories didn't match up, Chase called him out. Although no one had mentioned Bernice Worden yet, without prompting, Ed blurted, "Somebody framed me."

He's as calm under pressure as Chris Webber was when he called a time-out Michigan didn't have and lost the NCAA championship game.

What was his other story?

WELL, FIRST I HAD LUNCH WITH MY BEST FRIEND CARMEN ELECTRA, THEN ME AND HER HEADED OVER TO THE PIGGLY WIGGLY TO MEET MY BUDDY WALNUT THE TALKING MANATEE AND WE ALL WENT TO A BATTING CAGE FOR EIGHT OR NINE HOURS, AND THEN...

At the same time Gein was being questioned, officers had been searching his home. Again, the Gein farm had no electricity, so officers had only flashlights with which to see. So it was only after a police officer lost in the darkness brushed up against Bernice Worden's pale, blood-drained corpse that it was found. Further searches into the home revealed that Ed had scattered Bernice's parts across multiple rooms. Her entrails, wrapped in newspaper and folded inside an old suit, were still steaming with heat when officers unwrapped the ghoulish package.

I totally get how that happens. You know when you're high or drunk and you accidentally put your car keys in the freezer?

The location of her heart, along with the manner in which Ed had murdered and butchered her, inspired myths of cannibalism that persist to this day. It is highly unlikely that he actually ate any of his victims, but Bernice Worden's heart was found in a plastic bag in front of the potbellied stove, which only helped to stoke the rumors of possible anthropophagy.

Ed Gein flossing his teeth seems highly unlikely but eating human flesh is at least, kinda, definitely plausible. 'Cuz HE'S A MURDERING GRAVE ROBBER!

Investigators had just one more body part to find: the head. That was discovered in a burlap sack between two old mattresses. It seemed that Ed was trying something different with Bernice than he had with his other victims. In each ear was a bent tenpenny nail, each tied to a separate piece of twine for hanging purposes. Bernice's head was intended to be a trophy.

A trophy for least improved!

It's not great when a human head is a person's version of the Stanley Cup.

As much as investigators hoped they were done, though, they'd forgotten about one missing piece. The last thing they found was Bernice Worden's anus and vagina, still attached to one another, thrown in a box with the disembodied vulvas of nine other women. The only difference was that he'd tied a red ribbon around this particular chunk of anatomy to set it apart from the rest.

Oh, great.

Further searches that night solved a second case as well. Three years after she'd gone missing, Mary Hogan's head was found stuffed in a sack behind the door of Ed Gein's bedroom. One shudders to think what purpose it was serving there.

Dozens more ghoulish items were soon discovered, from the skullcaps he used to eat baked beans out of to his infamous nipple belt, which used the nipples of every single one of his victims save the one whose skin became Ed's vest. When investigators came upon a boarded-up room, they assumed they were about to enter the low circle of the hell they'd suddenly found themselves immersed in. But when they pried off the two-by-fours, they found the only clean area in the house: the room where Augusta had lived. Ed had left everything exactly as it had been when she'd died, the thick layer of dust that covered every surface demonstrating to investigators that no one had been inside in years.

Cut to the host of *My Lottery Dream Home* saying, "And here is the master."

This is the most fascinating part to me. He completely exteriorized his insanity by making the entire house a tribute to his dark interests, but he kept his mom's room unsullied. She never witnessed Ed being his "true self," which must have brought him great shame. I wonder if he wished Augusta could have seen him "blossom" into the Martha Stewart of Vlad Dracul's court. Or did he never go into her room because he didn't want his dirty secrets to seep into the sanctity of his mother's memory? Never going in there meant she would remain frozen in time, the only perfect person to live in her son's mind.

But Ed's obsession with his mother was the least of his worries. While we now know the origin of his gruesome possessions, cops poking around in the dark had no idea that most of them had come from disinterred corpses. After adding up all the parts they'd found that night and the next day, the Plainfield police figured they had at least eleven murders on their hands. It wasn't until thirty hours into Ed's arrest that he finally came clean and told them just where most of the parts had come from.

He had no problem talking about his ghastly projects, answering questions about whether he sometimes placed the vaginas over his own penis with a casual, "I believe that's true." But when it came to the murders, Ed Gein claimed to remember none of it. However, after the hell he'd put the people of Plainfield through, they weren't buying his excuses.

His "jokes" aren't so funny now, are they? He's sorta like O. J. Simpson in that sense.

Besides the murder of two beloved residents and the violation of their dead, Ed Gein had turned Plainfield, Wisconsin, into the ghoul capital of America. Reporters the world over swarmed the village to get every angle they could on the true crime story of the decade. The Gein case was covered so extensively that stories were published with incendiary headlines such as "300 POUND MAN RECALLS PINCH AND REMARK BY GEIN." As funny as that is, very few people in Plainfield were amused.

C'mon, Plainfield, you really could have used the publicity. What an incredible move it would've been to get an Ed Gein–themed restaurant with a bunch of rib-sticking meals on the menu. You guys could have gotten the Olympics!

Eventually, Ed was diagnosed as schizophrenic by a panel of doctors and was found unfit to stand trial. According to the state of Wisconsin, he'd been suffering from a mental disease when he committed his crimes and therefore lacked the capacity to conform his conduct to the requirements of the law. He died in a mental institution in 1984 at the age of seventy-eight, a model prisoner to the end. When he was asked by a reporter how he liked life at Central State Hospital, he replied, "I'm happy here. It's a good place. Some of the people here are pretty disturbed, though."

It's Ed Gein's world, baby, and we just live in it!

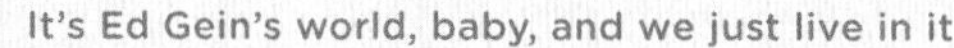

Sounds like Ed needs to have a "man in the mirror" moment and try to make a change.

The people of Plainfield never bought Ed's insanity defense and never forgave him for what he did. The night before his house was set to go to auction, the townsfolk burned it to the ground rather than let it become the shrine to the macabre that it was destined to be.

They should've leaned in and made it a tourist attraction to bilk people of their money, like what the people of Seattle did with Batsquatch.

Like anywhere else, the Midwest didn't want to be known for the crimes that had occurred in their lonelier areas. Sometimes, though, suppressing a fact can only make it stronger. Despite the best efforts of that region, Ed Gein still stands as one of the creators of America's modern macabre imagination. And although we don't condone his crimes in any way whatsoever, that may be why we end every show with a small tip of the hat.

Hail Gein.

He said it!

Dear Abby,

I'm a mother of two and a devout believer who has raised my two sons to be good Christian boys. Lately, however, I've been very disturbed by the behavior of my younger son, Edward.

Over the last couple of weeks, he's been behaving erratically. He's been staying out late—we're talking well past 4:30 p.m. I've told him many times that nothing good happens in the late afternoon. After 5:00 p.m., godless women come out and start shaking their legs on the streets, and the bars fill with drunkards who sin against our Lord and Savior Jesus Christ.

I don't want to see my boy go down the same path as his father. My husband was consumed with perverted thoughts about kissing me and being "romantic," and when I scolded him for his carnal actions he would drink himself to sleep, much like a hobo on a train car. I can't lose my boy to the sins of this earth, and I feel him slipping away.

You wouldn't believe how the women of Plainfield are given to debauchery these days. They're wearing dresses that barely cover their knees, and their shoulders are fully exposed. I'm surprised the boys can even contain their urges when they see these floozies walking around basically nude! I'm worried they've got their witch claws into my boy!

Over the past year or so, Edward has changed completely. For example, he knows I need my feet rubbed for exactly one hour every Monday or the skin on my heels cracks. He was always happy to oblige me when I demanded he rub my corns and bunions. Sometimes, he would get so happy that I could see his little Edward pop up under his pants, so naturally I would punish him physically until his body returned to God! But recently he told me he no longer wants to rub my feet, and he's stopped kissing me altogether! Now, I know you might think I'm just being a typical overly concerned mother, but I promise you something is not right!

Edward has always been dedicated to me. Since his brother, Henry, died in a fire, it's been just the two of us. I know he was sad when Henry died—he told me that he still thinks about his brother burning to death, but then he gets a little smile on his face when he remembers he has me all to himself. If it weren't for me, he'd be more depressed than a Wisconsin buck without antlers.

How do I get my little boy back before he falls victim to the sins of this earthly plane? He's only forty-two years old and he doesn't understand the ways of the world yet.

Sincerely,

Frustrated Wisconsin Mother

Dear Frustrated Wisconsin Mother,

Upon reading your letter I must say you seem a little overbearing and perhaps need to relax a bit. It's possible to be too doting, which can lead your "little boy" not to mature properly. Also, I'm worried you consider Edward to be a boy when he is forty-two years old. It's time to let your boy mature so he can find a girlfriend and maybe even start a family of his own. It's hard to see your children grow up, but he'll always be your little guy no matter what! As the saying goes, "If you love someone, set them free, if they return it was meant to be," and I'm sure you and Edward are meant to be.

Abby

Dear Abby,

You're nothing more than another tramp!

Sincerely,

Still Frustrated Wisconsin Mother

KISS MY ASS
KFC
HI I'M POGO
LEAD ME TO YOUR TAKER
KFC
TOM NEELY 19

CHAPTER 4

JOHN WAYNE GACY

SERIAL KILLERS UTILIZE A WIDE ARRAY OF WEAPONS IN THE process of accomplishing their goals. Knives, guns, ligatures, and bare hands are certainly effective for ending a life, but there is another, more abstract tool that for some is even more essential. Used both to lure victims and evade capture, the skill of manipulation is paramount for having a long career in serial killing—and no one was more adept with it than John Wayne Gacy.

John Wayne Gacy is one of the twentieth century's best-known monsters, a nightmare of a man whose mere surname is on par with Hitler's when it comes to its associations with evil. From 1972 until 1979, Gacy killed at least thirty-three young men and boys, either burying them in the crawl space beneath his North Side Chicago home or dumping the bodies into the Des Plaines River. If the testimonies of those who survived their encounters with Gacy are accurate, the young men who fell victim to the so-called Killer Clown died terrifyingly violent, prolonged deaths in the rumpus room of his suburban home. And while the sheer brutality of these crimes is legend enough, what makes them all the more chilling is that Gacy perpetrated these acts while posing as a respectable community leader who often dressed as a clown to entertain sick children.

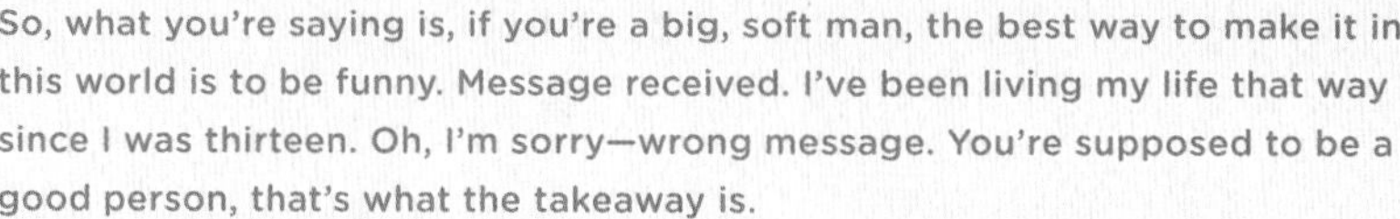

So, what you're saying is, if you're a big, soft man, the best way to make it in this world is to be funny. Message received. I've been living my life that way since I was thirteen. Oh, I'm sorry—wrong message. You're supposed to be a good person, that's what the takeaway is.

The only scarier clown than Gacy is Jerry Lewis in *The Day the Clown Cried*.

Many of Gacy's victims could be described as what criminologist Steven A. Egger called "the less dead," meaning members of society who slip through the cracks. While sex workers easily take the number-one spot on the less-dead roster, there is another group that takes a close second: homosexual men. Although gay acceptance has taken great strides in recent years, it wasn't so long ago that it was acceptable for crimes to be outright ignored if they involved a homosexual act of any kind. This meant that investigations that could have led to the discovery of other crimes ended the moment a policeman felt uncomfortable. Furthermore, many gay victims of violent sexual acts would refuse to report the crime, lest their secret become public knowledge.

Countless criminals took advantage of society's homophobia, but there was no serial killer who took it to the level of John Wayne Gacy.

Gay dudes deserve a superhero of their own, and Aquaman doesn't count!

For a while, it seemed that police officers viewed the gay lifestyle as entirely deviant—essentially a sea of orgies, drugs, and anonymous hookups. But from what I have observed, most homosexual lifestyles involve going to work, making dinner, watching *Top Chef*, and going to sleep. Wait a second, that's *my* lifestyle—am I so gay I'm married to a woman?

That's not to say all his victims were gay; some were merely poor and bereft of the sort of social currency that a man like Gacy was able to accrue. Others were employees of his construction business, young boys easily written off as runaways. But because of the latent homophobia inherent to policing at the time, during John Wayne Gacy's active serial killing years, five reports were made against him for sexually assaulting men—three in Chicago alone—before he was ever seriously investigated. Admittedly, the last report, submitted halfway through his murder spree, did result in an arrest. But after listening to both Gacy and the teenage victim, an assistant state's attorney chose to believe Gacy. The brutal encounter involving an oversize dildo and a game of Russian roulette was deemed consensual, or, at the very least, deemed to be of no concern to the police. Gacy was released and, as a result, fifteen more boys lost their lives before he was arrested again.

Despite fully admitting to the police that he participated in homosexual S&M, at no point in his life did John Wayne Gacy consider himself gay. He had no problem admitting to being bisexual, but even the mere suggestion that he might be fully gay would tilt Gacy into unspeakable anger. His talent for manipulation was so strong that he could apply it to himself, twisting his own sexual nature into an acceptable dichotomy: he made love to women, but men were reserved for what he called "animal sex." It just so happened that "animal sex" made up the vast majority of his sexual experiences.

Hmm, same as me and the "animal style" burger at In-N-Out. Are there normal cheeseburgers?

I would rather think of Chris Christie having sex than JWG. I'm sorry for putting this thought into the world.

The source of Gacy's self-hatred was no secret. As it is with many people uncomfortable with their sexuality, his fear of himself began with an extremely homophobic and possibly closeted father.

This is a nice change of pace from serial killers with mommy issues. Fathers can ruin lives, too, dammit!

When John Wayne Gacy was brought into this world on March 17, 1942, the future killer clown was mid-defecation. Despite the fact that this was evidence of a life-threatening condition, John Stanley Gacy saw the birth of a weak child as nothing more than the first disappointment of many. Stanley Gacy was a World War I veteran who worked as a machinist in Chicago after the war. Masculine to a fault, he expected the same of his son, going so far as to name him after the pinnacle of American masculinity at the time: movie star John Wayne.

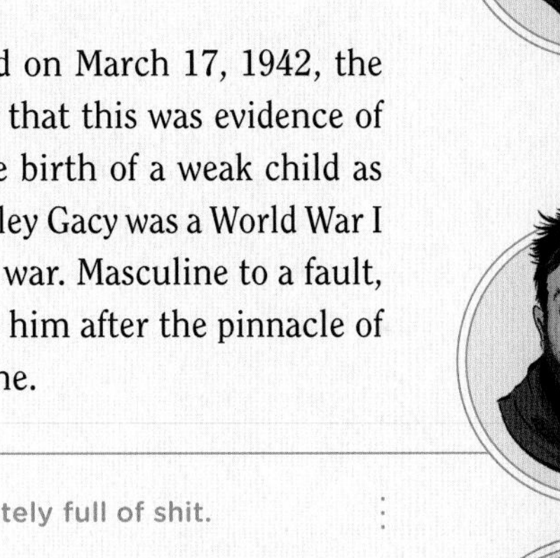

I guess it makes sense that John Wayne was also completely full of shit.

John Stanley Gacy was so masculine, he never shit once.

Young Gacy was born with an enlarged bottleneck heart, which made it impossible for him to play sports or engage in the type of childhood roughhousing Stanley expected of a son. His father started taking out his frustration on him physically when he was only four, whipping him savagely amid a torrential storm of emasculating insults after he muddled up a pile of engine parts in the garage. This set a precedent for beatings that would continue until John finally left home at the age of twenty.

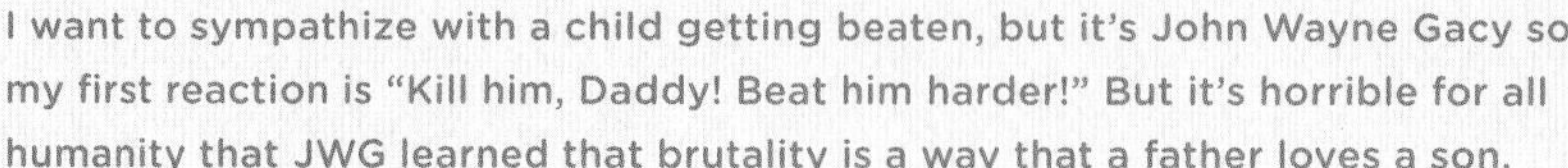

I want to sympathize with a child getting beaten, but it's John Wayne Gacy so my first reaction is "Kill him, Daddy! Beat him harder!" But it's horrible for all humanity that JWG learned that brutality is a way that a father loves a son.

Beating your child doesn't make him stronger; it just makes him listen to nu metal and become a militant Best Buy manager.

That irrational, unguided anger was not just reserved for John. Gacy's mother, Marion, bore the brunt of her husband's violence in an incident that occurred when John was only two years old. As the family was eating a silent dinner one night, Stanley, without provocation, became lost in a private rage and hurled a plate full of food at his wife's face hard enough to knock out the bridge in her teeth. He then stormed to the back of the house, grabbed his gun, and left. Marion left, too, with the kids in tow, but when she returned days later, she found Stanley had left the food he'd thrown still caked to the kitchen walls. Understanding what was expected of her, Marion cleaned up, cooked her husband's favorite meal, and waited for him to come home. That night, they ate dinner again in silence as if the whole incident had happened to someone else.

In another life, Stanley would've made a great gutter punk!

The fifties were fun for families. Stanley'd had a tough day at work. He's so straight and masculine, and he'd been forced to watch all those men in their sweaty clothes at the factory, their shirts made skintight by the sweat clinging to their lithe bodies. Boys and men grunting and lifting things, butts in the air, and he's so straight, he can only watch. He can't help them take their dirty clothes off. And then he has to go home to his family!

Like many people involved in abusive relationships, Marion tried to rationalize Stanley's behavior, blaming his rage on a benign tumor that pressed on his brain. Doctors had told them that it had no effect on his behavior in and of itself, but Marion believed that when Stanley drank, the blood vessels in his brain swelled and crowded the tumor, causing everything from casual violence to verbal abuse. It was a poor excuse for her husband being a mean drunk, but the justification kept Marion by his side until his death.

Despite these many shortcomings, Gacy Jr. swore to his dying day that he had nothing but love for his father. In a break from typical serial killer psychology, his relationship with his mother was almost completely normal and placid. As far as we know, the worst thing she did, according to Gacy, was make him wear a pair of panties that he stole when he was twelve.

Tim Curry's mom did the same thing and he's a great actor.

Ah yes, the old *Rocky Horror Picture Show* punishment!

This hadn't been Gacy's first pair of panties, either. Like four-time serial killer and cross-dresser Jerry Brudos, Gacy developed a fetish for women's undergarments at an early age. To clarify, having a fetish for ladies' underwear by no means makes a person a serial killer or even abnormal. To make that claim would be like saying because some serial killers like orange juice, anyone who likes to start their day with a nice, cold glass might have a makeshift torture dungeon full of corpses in their garage.

But we also don't know that for sure, Marcus.

THINGS BOTH SERIAL KILLERS AND NORMAL PEOPLE CAN LIKE:

Women's underwear
Orange juice
Suffocation fetishes
Red Lobster cheese biscuits
Scat/urine play
Going to a park
It's Always Sunny in Philadelphia
Seeing a picture of a basement filled with corpses
Dave Matthews Band's *Under the Table and Dreaming*

I will say if someone *really* loves kombucha, they might be a serial killer.

However, a love of ladies' underwear is an interesting trait shared by some of these men, specifically because the theft was often as exciting as the possession. And just like Brudos, who eventually hoarded an attic's worth of stolen women's clothing above his garage-cum–torture dungeon, young Gacy had a special hiding place for his ill-gotten gains: a small crawl space under the family's front porch.

Is there any actual purpose for a crawl space other than hiding a body? I've never heard anyone say, "I gotta go grab a beer from the crawl space."

This is a trait that some serial killers show that I find fascinating. A serial killer exteriorizing the compartmentalization of their personality, literally creating another space outside of / adjacent to their home where they can be the "real them." This will be a running theme in JWG's life, with this space under his home later becoming his "unlicensed cemetery," but we also see it with Ed Gein and his mother's room, Jeffrey Dahmer and Infinity Land, Jerry Brudos and the torture garage Marcus mentioned earlier, and many more. They have permission to be the demons that they are in these little ritualistic spaces. It starts in childhood, and as the years go on, the deeper and more serious the compartmentalization becomes.

Unfortunately, Stanley was not the only source of abuse in Gacy's childhood. When Gacy was seven, a friend of his father's, a contractor, began taking him on rides to various jobs around Chicago. Young Gacy was fascinated with construction and Stanley thought a manly influence would be good for his son. Instead, he had turned his son over to a child molester. The contractor started challenging John to "wrestling matches" that usually ended with the boy's face nuzzled between the contractor's legs. But Gacy kept it a secret because he didn't want to be seen in his father's eyes as a "fruit picker"—one of Stanley's favorite homophobic insults.

And that contractor's name was Andy Kaufman! I joke, though Andy did like to wrestle until he was aroused. And then he did it on national television!

"Fruit picker" is a terrible slur unless you actually work in the farming industry; then it's a title of great honor.

The aspersions didn't end there. "Fairy" and "queer" were two of the elder Gacy's favorite words to call his son, especially when John dared to stand between his mother and his father's violent temper. To Stanley, homosexuals were subhuman, an opinion that John would take to heart.

But internalized homophobia alone wasn't enough to make John the monster he eventually became, nor was the anger he inherited from his father. There were other factors contributing to his evolution, episodes that are seen again and again in serial killers the world over. When John was eleven, he suffered a serious head injury when he was knocked unconscious by a playground swing. As a result, throughout his childhood he suffered from periodic blackouts that were frequent and serious enough for hospitalization. And each time, his father would take it as another opportunity to call his son weak.

Not much is known about Gacy's high school years, but he was said to be an excellent student with a fascination for men in uniform. He joined the local civil defense organization and relished the authority that the position provided. When an accident occurred or fire broke out in town, Gacy was authorized to race to the scene to render assistance, with a flashing blue light affixed to the roof of his car. Eventually his father, seemingly unable to let his son enjoy anything, removed the distributor cap from the engine of Gacy's car. The incident was apparently one step over the line for John Wayne Gacy: he moved out in March 1962 at the age of twenty, leaving Illinois for Las Vegas.

There, Gacy was hired as a mortuary assistant, but after spooking himself by crawling into a coffin with the body of a dead boy, he quit soon thereafter. He then moved to Springfield, Illinois, got a job at the Nunn Bush shoe company, and met his first wife, Marlynn Myers. Her father owned several Kentucky Fried Chicken restaurants in her hometown of Waterloo, Iowa, and despite insisting until the day of the wedding that his daughter should not marry John Wayne Gacy, he eventually gave in and invited his new son-in-law to Waterloo to help with the family business.

Do ya think he told her his casket story?

"When he told me he climbed into a coffin with a dead boy because he was curious to see what the body smelled like, I was like, 'Who is this man, and can I get some more of him?!'"

The newlywed received a diploma from the assuredly real Kentucky Fried Chicken University and immediately started overstating his influence to anyone who would listen. According to John, the diploma bestowed upon him all the rights and privileges of the Colonel. He even began telling his employees and others in the community that he was the real owner of four Waterloo locations, despite the fact that he was only a manager.

Honestly, that's the type of vocational education I advocate for. I also wish KFC University had a football team so we could watch them play McDonald's University in the Obesity Bowl.

They have a Chick-fil-A on the campus of KFC University. If you go to it and they catch you, it's immediate expulsion. It's a trick restaurant; really thins the herd.

During this era Gacy also positioned himself as a community leader, joining a fraternal leadership organization called the Jaycees. Gacy was a proud Jaycee until the day he was captured, enjoying both the camaraderie as well as the false sense of power given to him for lording over such an ultimately inconsequential club. He would later describe his years in Waterloo as the best of his life.

We see this need to belong to a group with Bundy and Berkowitz, too. These are men with no real identities. They want to belong to an established body that will give them a societal hierarchy to climb, be it via politics or religion. It might be a way to feel normal, fit in, or have purpose in life. But, with these assholes, it also serves as another sociopathic way to wheedle authority over other people and eventually helps cover up their crimes.

JWG is literally Captain Spaulding from the Rob Zombie films.

With his position of community respectability came other fringe benefits. Much like the rest of the country, Waterloo, Iowa, in the midsixties was a hotbed of promiscuity, and the Jaycees were at the seedy center. Gleefully participating in prostitution, sketchy pornography, and wife swapping, Gacy did his part in keeping the illicit activities under wraps by providing the local cops with all the free fried chicken they could eat.

Ha ha! Bribery through chicken—it really was a better time.

Gacy also played host to what used to be known as stag parties. In these off-putting get-togethers, grown men would set up projectors in garages and watch scratchy pornographic films together, hooting and hollering while drinking cheap beer. But Gacy's actual favorite form of socialization, separate from the stags, had a more sinister bent: he formed a boys' club in the basement of his home, comprised mostly of his teenage KFC employees. Charging monthly dues for free-flowing alcohol and a pool table, Gacy used these lures in the development of his predatory nature.

At first Gacy half-jokingly competed in games of pool with the boys, using fellatio as the ultimate prize. When that ploy fizzled, he claimed that he'd been commissioned by the governor of Illinois to conduct scientific experiments in the field of homosexuality, going so far as to forge a certificate for himself that proved his membership in the program. The boys would be paid for their time, he claimed. Failing in that ruse as well, Gacy would claim that there was a separate branch of the study wherein the participant would have the privilege of sleeping with his wife, the only catch being that Gacy would receive oral sex first. If a club member was stubborn and passed on every sexual deal floated his way, Gacy would not-so-subtly

imply that he knew "some guys" in Chicago, and all he had to do was pick up a phone and his connections would take care of any uncooperative or ungrateful young boys.

Good grief! He was gonna call the blow-job mafia? Those poor kids.

Man, all of this sounds so enticing! Gee whillikers, I wish I could go to a stag party! Gosh darn it, all this really makes me think we need to MAKE AMERICA GREAT AGAIN.

Gacy's victims during this time period are largely unknown, but eventually fifteen-year-old Donald Voorhees did come forward to authorities. According to him, he and Gacy would meet at Gacy's house or a motel, where the older man would flood the boy with drinks and molest him. Gacy would then make Voorhees recount the entire experience, like a player going through a game tape with a coach. Then, as promised, Gacy would pay Voorhees for the service rendered and take him home.

That's better than how most contractors deal with day labor.

Comparatively in Waterloo, Voorhees was one of the lucky ones. Sixteen-year-old Edward Lynch, who worked as a cook and dishwasher at one of the KFCs under Gacy's managerial watch, experienced a special kind of rumpus room hell.

One night in 1968, Gacy privately invited Lynch to his house to watch a movie and play some pool. After a few rounds, Gacy casually floated the blow-job gambit and then threw the game. Upon Gacy's demand to immediately render payment, Lynch tried laughing it off, saying he hadn't thought his boss had been serious, but Gacy pushed it. When Lynch tried moving on to a different subject, Gacy lost control, grabbing Lynch by the arm and dragging him upstairs to the kitchen, where he grabbed a knife and ordered the teenager into his bedroom. Trying to wrestle Lynch onto the bed, he accidentally sliced open Lynch's arm in the ruckus. The sight of blood apparently snapped Gacy out of his aggressive haze, and he became calm and apologetic, going as far as to bandage up the wound.

When Lynch tried to leave, however, his host was adamant that they watch a movie instead. This, predictably, turned out to be from Gacy's pornography collection. After a few uncomfortable scenes, Gacy asked the teenager if he could try a trick.

Check, please!

I think this calls for an "Exit stage right," even!

Lynch agreed so Gacy brought out a chain and padlock to secure the boy's hands behind his back before pushing him down onto a cot, where he secured Lynch's feet as well. Overcome with desire, rage, or both, Gacy wrapped his hands around the boy's throat and began to squeeze, but Lynch was clever. He pretended to black out almost immediately, which possibly saved his life. Suddenly fearful of what he'd done, Gacy stopped short of going all the way, instead unchaining Lynch and taking him home. Even more despicably, all of this happened while Gacy's wife was in the hospital recuperating from the birth of their second child.

You can see JWG blaming her for his crimes: "You left *me* to go 'have a baby!' What was I supposed to do? *Not* try to kill a boy?"

This entire scenario is only made worse by the fact that JWG smelled like fry oil.

Shortly after this incident, Lynch and Voorhees began comparing notes on their experiences. For months, neither boy told anyone else what had transpired, but the secret weighed a little heavier on Voorhees. One night while having dinner with his family, the conversation turned to Gacy. John was planning to run for the local Jaycees presidency and had offered the campaign manager job to Donald's father. At the mere mention of Gacy's name, Donald began sobbing, then spilled Gacy's violent proclivities for teenage boys to his family.

Following Gacy's arrest and indictment for sodomy, the town split into two camps: those who believed the Voorhees family and those who backed their favorite chicken-slinging Jaycee. The division continued even after Gacy demonstrably failed a lie detector test.

If you guys ever wonder why victims are hesitant to go public with abuse suffered at the hands of people in power, this is an example. It was hard to pin down a guy who was some kind of fake lieutenant of the *Jaycees*—just imagine trying to come forward against someone with a real position of influence.

The incident was just beginning to fade into the small-town rumor mill of yesteryear when Gacy's temper got the better of him. Humiliated and vengeful, he contacted one of his more aggressive KFC employees and offered him three hundred dollars to beat Voorhees senseless. That kid, Russell Schroeder, accepted the offer and invited Donald to share some liquor in Black Hawk Park. When the two arrived at the supposed hiding place, Schroeder incapacitated Voorhees with mace and beat him with a thick tree branch. But Voorhees, being tougher than he appeared, scurried away into a cornfield. The would-be enforcer then reported the largely failed hit back to Gacy.

I'm still shocked this is all happening at a KFC! Evidently the recipe isn't the only secret there.

Think this is bad? You do *not* want to fuck with Dave Thomas. On a more serious note, this possibly points to the idea that JWG had accomplices help him with his later crimes. It fits his MO of acting as if he were a low-rent Chicagoland crime kingpin.

After Voorhees quickly identified Schroeder, the boy rolled over on his portly employer with very little hesitation. Gacy's conviction for sodomy was now all but guaranteed. He pleaded for leniency during sentencing but considering the obvious pattern of abuse, Gacy received a sentence of ten years.

I'm no Judge Joe Brown, but I'm just gonna say the crime here isn't "sodomy," it's the whole "forced assault" part, alongside the threats of physical violence.

It's also telling of the true weakness of John Wayne Gacy. These weren't full-grown men he was targeting; these were kids who were easily dominated. He manipulated these kids using his "power" in the neighborhood. They didn't understand that they could say no to an adult, never mind one who was their boss.

To make matters worse, Gacy's wife filed for divorce that same day, taking their two kids. They wouldn't see John Wayne Gacy's face again until his bored, vaguely annoyed mug shot appeared on the front page of every major newspaper in America a decade later. He later told a fellow prisoner that as far as he was concerned, his family was dead.

Astonishingly, Gacy's parents were present at the sentencing. When the judge announced the ten-year sentence, Stanley openly wept in the only display of emotion

besides pure anger that his family ever witnessed. He would die of cirrhosis of the liver one year later on Christmas Day, 1969.

Perhaps dying was the best gift he could give to his family.

And on his tombstone read his final words: NOT GAY!

Gacy hid his sodomy conviction in prison, claiming instead that he'd been sentenced to ten years for hosting good-natured porno parties for teens and had been framed by political enemies. His Jaycees presidential campaign had been going too well, he claimed.

If your excuse is that you're simply in trouble for having "good-natured porno parties for teens," I think it's safe to say you're going to stuff a crawl space with victims in the near future.

Nothing more presidential than making a bunch of minors watch pornography while you watch them watch it. Literally, nothing more presidential.

This might have come off as a completely ridiculous notion had the Jaycees not been a major presence at Anamosa State Penitentiary. Gacy continued his Jaycees work while behind bars, eventually attaining the Jaycee Sound Citizen award, the SPOKE award, and the Spark Plug award while still in prison. In other words, he knew how to both manipulate the system and fool his fellow inmates. Having established himself as trustworthy, Gacy became the prison's head cook and, in a telling display of homophobia, refused to hire openly gay inmates, claiming they would contaminate the food. He even played Santa Claus at Christmas. For his good behavior, Gacy was granted parole only eighteen months into his ten-year term. The Black Hawk County DA issued a strong reproach, but the parole board disagreed. John Wayne Gacy was a free man. Within days, he left Iowa and his criminal record behind, paving the way for even ghastlier crimes to come.

Ugh! Gacy's prison gig as Santa Claus really makes the song "Santa Claus Is Coming to Town" extremely creepy!

Gacy moved in with his mother in Chicago, well out of the purview of his parole board, and got a job at a restaurant as a short-order cook. He soon turned to his childhood hobby of construction and started his own contracting business. His skills and ability to ingratiate himself resulted in success rather quickly, and as a result, Gacy convinced his mother to buy a home at 8213 Summerdale Avenue in Des Plaines to give his business room to grow. This house would play as both stage and storage for Gacy's six-year killing career.

I guess the crawl space technically makes it a tax write-off, like having a home office? I don't know, I'm just gonna go now!

Within months of settling in, Gacy's behavior began to show a murderous edge. One of the first employees at his fledgling construction business said he was searching for a fuse in the garage one day when he felt the thwack of a blunt object on the back of his head. When he turned around, dumbfounded, he saw Gacy standing in front of him with a hammer, looking just as confused. Gacy told him he didn't know what had come over him. All he knew was that he had felt an uncontrollable rage that seemed to guide his hand. The employee left and never spoke to Gacy again.

"So do you want a recommendation on LinkedIn? If it makes you feel better, I can lie and say you know Excel."

Yeah dude, this is the real world, not *Animaniacs*!

This had not been Gacy's first violent incident since his release from prison. In early 1971, he attempted to rape a teenage boy he picked up from the Chicago bus station. Gacy was caught, but since this crime occurred long before the criminal justice system was plugged into a cross-referencing network, his parole board back in Iowa was never notified of the crime. Gacy could have potentially been sent to prison regardless, but the victim didn't show up for the court date and the case was dismissed.

So many of these serial killers get away with this cross-state confusion. He slipped out of the police's hands like a fat, hairy bar of soap!

Later that year, Gacy reconnected with a high school friend named Cathy Hull, and after twelve months of tepid courtship, the two were married in a wedding that was mostly planned by John. Cathy added two young stepdaughters to his life, and with a conventionally normal family at his side, Gacy expanded his business. He named it PDM Construction: Painting, Decorating, and Maintenance, or Polish Daily Maintenance, if he was feeling cute. But unbeknownst to his new family, John Wayne Gacy's journey toward being one of America's greatest monsters had already begun before he said "I do."

On January 2, 1972, Gacy attended a family get-together with his mother in honor of his recently deceased Aunt Pearl. After consuming an excessive amount of scotch, Gacy, his inhibitions lowered, went cruising downtown. He found sixteen-year-old Timothy McCoy as the boy was waiting for a transfer at the Greyhound station. The teenager was looking to kill some time, so Gacy invited him back to his house and began pouring drinks. Oral sex came soon afterward, and once the act was done, Gacy passed out alone in his bed, leaving McCoy on the couch.

POLISH DAILY MAINTENANCE

CALL FOR A FREE ESTIMATE

1-800-KISSMYASS

What happened next is from Gacy's own account. At around 4:00 a.m., he awoke to see McCoy silently creeping toward him, butcher knife in hand. Sensing danger, Gacy claimed to have sprung from his bed to wrestle the teenager to the ground, suffering a deep knife wound to his arm in the process. After a brief struggle, Gacy pried the knife out of McCoy's clenched fist before plunging it four times into the teen's chest and stomach. McCoy was still alive as Gacy composed himself enough to walk to the kitchen to clean the knife. But when arrived at the kitchen counter, he discovered a freshly sliced slab of bacon. McCoy had presumably been in the middle of a nice gesture of an early morning breakfast for his host and had come to tell John the meal would soon be ready. As Gacy realized this, he heard what he called a "gurgulation" from the bedroom as the boy bled out on his carpet—the first of at least thirty-three young men to die in that house.

"Gurgulation" is also the sound Henry makes when eating octopus brains.

THUMBS-UP EMOJI.

The next day Gacy attended his aunt's wake as if nothing had gone awry the night before. He hadn't even bothered to cover the cut on his arm. When his sister asked about it, he nonchalantly told her he'd had an accident while cutting carpet on the job. Tim Cahill points out in *Buried Dreams: Inside the Mind of John Wayne Gacy* that this may have been when Gacy realized he could kill without guilt or fear of being caught. He lied with ease and skill; even with evidence of criminality in plain sight, Gacy found he could just gloss over whatever might come up. This ability to steamroll and manipulate reality would be John Wayne Gacy's greatest weapon against the world for the next six years, and all while he played the part of a respectable member of society.

Well, he was as respectable as a man who works in construction and is involved in politics and also moonlights as a clown can be. Actually, that's exactly how I'd describe Trump! Hot take!

He could have gotten a great deal of pleasure out of the lie as well. I wonder if he actually *did* do a good job of lying, or is Midwestern politeness so strong and powerful that no one pushed too hard as to why John was openly bleeding at his aunt's wake?

During this time, Gacy's love of fraternal organizations led him to join the local Moose Lodge. He was subsequently introduced to the Jolly Joker Club, a group of amateur clowns who participated in everything from Moose Lodge–sponsored events to parades to hospital visits with sick children. And thus, Pogo the Clown was born.

Something tells me the Kenosha Kickers from *Home Alone* provided regular entertainment at the old Moose Lodge!

Sick children were Gacy's favorite and, by all accounts, Gacy was a fantastic clown. He used professionally made puppets—his go-to being an adorable skunk—and his bits were impeccable, the most popular being the invisible dog. In this routine, Gacy would run a tube from his pant leg to a bulb filled with water held in his hand. If the kids were skeptical about Gacy's invisible dog claims, he'd squeeze the bulb and tell the kids they'd upset the dog so much he'd urinated on the floor.

He also had a pastry bag filled with melted Snickers bars just in case the kids *really* upset the invisible dog.

Gacy claimed that his clown alter ego worked as a self-applied tranquilizer. Clowns made him feel *good.* He covered the walls of his home with sad-clown paintings, saying they gave him a warm feeling inside. But even clowning wasn't enough to tamp down the urges Gacy was beginning to feel inside.

What I love about true crime is that there is some stuff that is truly beyond the pale. Gacy's development of this character is like the birth of an archetypal monster out of folklore. John Wayne Gacy, like Ed Gein and Richard Ramirez, would become such a perfect embodiment of evil and mayhem that Pogo's likeness is now burned into the collective unconscious. He is technically an icon.

Following Timothy McCoy's murder, Gacy began cruising the streets of Chicago in search of gay sex more and more often. Naturally, this put a strain on his marriage. After dozens of fights over the lack of sex in their relationship, Gacy came out as bisexual and his wife left him for good. With no one in the house to hold him back, a different kind of fantasy world began to emerge for John Wayne Gacy. In contrast to serial killers like Ted Bundy, who conjured up nebulous demonic beings to explain away their actions, Gacy wrote a story for himself to help justify his crimes, the hero being a hard-bitten detective named Jack Hanley.

Jack Hanley sounds like a character Darrell Hammond would play on *SNL*.

According to what Gacy told psychiatrists years after his capture, Jack Hanley was the persona he inhabited when he went cruising for victims. Based on a cop he'd known back when he was a line cook, Hanley was a tough-guy undercover detective who kept the streets safe from hustlers, liars, and thieves. Gacy would use this persona to intimidate the male sex workers of Chicago's North Side, treating them roughly and sometimes refusing to pay. Hanley also served as a means for Gacy to socially separate from his true identity. In Gacy's own words, he believed that the Hanley persona shielded Gacy from rumor, because he couldn't very well have someone telling the mayor that "Pogo the Clown's queer!"

As Gacy started going out more frequently and his self-hatred metastasized, another persona began to develop, which he named the Other Guy. The personas represented different stages of Gacy's desire. When Gacy would drink to excess, his fear would melt away and Jack Hanley would emerge. Then, when the rage and desire got to be too much, Gacy would claim to black out and it was the Other Guy who took the next step to killing. Whether or not he was telling the truth regarding these switches in identity, we'll never know, but as a result of this supposed blackout state, many of Gacy's murders remain a total mystery. For instance, two years after murdering Timothy McCoy, Gacy strangled a still-unidentified teenage boy and buried him near the barbecue pit in his backyard. The only thing we know about this crime is that postmortem fluid seeped from the boy's nose and mouth and left a stain on Gacy's carpet. The Other Guy couldn't recall any of the specifics, even when Gacy confessed to other murders.

Outside of the home, Gacy appeared to his neighbors to be a man who had everything. His wife's departure was kept a secret, and PDM was making real money, pulling in almost two hundred thousand dollars a year. To show off his wealth, Gacy threw lavish backyard parties every summer, with themes ranging from Hawaiian to cowboy. Sometimes his wife would even attend in order to keep up appearances.

Hmmm, interesting party themes for the obviously not gay John Wayne Gacy.

Gacy was doing fantastic in the political arena as well. A Democrat since the age of nineteen, he served as the assistant precinct captain in the election of a Chicago alderman in 1960. More than ten years later, he decided to try his hand at Chicago politics again. He started by volunteering for campaigns, tirelessly working to establish himself as a player on the city's North Side while growing his construction business. Within a few years, Gacy had amassed enough power and respect to earn the privilege of running the annual Polish Constitution Day Parade, a surprisingly prestigious job for a local politician. For three years, he carried out this task with military precision. In 1978 he even had the pleasure of hosting First Lady Rosalynn Carter as the special guest of honor (just a year after Mrs. Carter had met with cult leader and mass murderer Jim Jones in San Francisco because of Jones' social work). Gacy would tell people that he and the first lady were close personal friends until the day he was caught.

Eureka! Rosalynn Carter is one person away from Jimmy Carter, and what does Jimmy have? Peanuts! Who loves peanuts? Carnival folks. Who works at a carnival? Clowns! It all makes sense, people!

Rosalynn Carter is *still* my hall pass celebrity in my relationship.

The fact that Gacy was a braggart and a blowhard was no secret, but he was still popular in the neighborhood. He was praised as a local business leader who gave opportunities to young boys wanting to earn a fair day's pay for a fair day's work. Nobody questioned his seemingly good intentions, even when his employees started going missing.

I guarantee JWG politically spun this whole thing as not about killing employees, but about creating jobs!

Gacy's third victim, John Butkovich, was one of these employees. Recruited from a local hardware store, Butkovich worked so well with his boss that they earned paired nicknames: Big John and Little John. But when Little John quit in 1975 and the two became embroiled in a protracted argument over a paycheck, Big John's murderous impulses took control.

On the night of July 31, Gacy invited Butkovich over to his house on Summerdale to see if the dispute could be settled peacefully. Both were drunk before Butkovich even showed up. After negotiations turned belligerent, Gacy slapped a pair of handcuffs on his former employee, and then the world went black. When he woke up the next day, Butkovich was dead on the floor with a rope tied tightly around his neck. He quickly buried the body under the concrete floor in his garage, treating its disposal as just another construction project. Though he was questioned by the police and even briefly followed, there was never enough evidence to link him to the disappearance. Butkovich's body would be the first identified when authorities finally discovered what Gacy drolly called his "unlicensed graveyard."

THAT'S A CITY ORDINANCE VIOLATION, JOHN!

Almost a year would pass before Gacy would kill again, but the spring of 1976 initiated a thirty-victim murder spree that wouldn't begin to slow down until he ran out of room to hide the bodies two years later. When four hundred people showed up to his Spirit of '76 party to see John dressed as fat George Washington, nine bodies were already moldering beneath guests' feet.

Just like at the real George Washington's fortieth birthday on his plantation!

While Gacy varied in his methods of murder, he usually began the process with a trick. After bringing his victims home and lowering their guards with either booze or pot, he would ask if they wanted to learn a foolproof method for getting out of handcuffs. If the boys politely refused, Gacy would first demonstrate on himself to put them at ease. He'd pop the cuffs on his wrists and then easily slip out without showing the potential victim how he'd done it. But as soon as the tables were turned and the victim's wrists were cuffed, Gacy would just stare and smile. When they inevitably asked what the next step of the trick was, he would hold their gaze and say, "You need the key."

Excuse me while my skin crawls off my body. Ack!

By October 1976, Gacy took a pause from picking boys from the streets and murdered two more of his employees. Nineteen-year-old William Bundy stopped off at Gacy's home on the way to a party and found his way to the crawl space under the master bedroom. Seventeen-year-old Gregory Godzik actually helped dig trenches for bodies under the ruse that Gacy was replacing the plumbing in his home before eventually occupying one of those ditches himself.

Good leadership means good delegation!

But there were two employees who managed to survive everything Gacy threw their way. Some theorize that these boys, David Cram and Michael Rossi, stayed alive by helping Gacy with his crimes. They may have lured victims to Gacy, just as Dean Corll's accomplices had done in Houston a few years earlier, but it's also possible they just participated in disposal. Or they may not have been involved at all and were merely kept around because Gacy liked them. But it's through Cram's close call with death that we know about the killer's occasional habit of incorporating Pogo the Clown into his murderous plots.

Well, that's not very funny, Mr. Pogo the Clown.

It's showtime, baby! He knew when he bought the clown suit he was going to kill a bunch of boys while wearing it. Which is why most clown suits are purchased.

Cram lived with Gacy for a time, well after the murders began, and on one of his last nights there he'd been out celebrating his birthday with a couple of friends. When he got back to Gacy's, he opened the door to find his host standing on the threshold dressed head to toe in his Pogo outfit, complete with full clown makeup. Gacy's excuse for the strange sight was that he'd been preparing for a clowning gig the next day, but since it was David's birthday, he thought it would be fun to keep Pogo going for the duration of the night. After a few drinks of grain alcohol, a couple of Valiums, and a few tokes from a joint, Gacy gave Cram a private Pogo show, complete with the skunk puppet.

Pretty sure this is still what most clowns consume before they're "ready to perform."

Note to the reader: this is a cocktail meant to be taken BY YOURSELF. Never alone with your boss.

After the show Gacy performed the handcuff trick on Cram. Once Cram was restrained, Gacy grabbed the chain linking the cuffs and swung Cram around the room, laughing his best Pogo cackle, all while the teen screamed to be let go. Eventually, Cram used the training he'd learned during his year in the army and managed to kick his captor in the head, knocking him down. Then he grabbed the keys, unlocked himself, and waited expectantly for Gacy to explain himself. When Gacy got up from the floor, the two stared at each other and shared an uncomfortable silence. Cram then went to his room, locked the door, and tried to forget the incident. He did eventually move out, but he continued working for Gacy until the very last day of Gacy's freedom, never asking questions, even when he was ordered to take over Godzik's job of digging trenches in the crawl space, which no doubt held the unmistakable stench of death.

Just ask why you're digging! It's so easy! If you're not making a moat, you're making a grave!

All you have to say is that you're putting in a pool, *National Lampoon's Christmas Vacation*-style, and everyone will be happy with you.

As Gacy continued his killing spree, his methods became more refined. When he reached the point in the evening at which he was no longer having fun with his victims, he would kill them in one of two ways. The first was the infamous rope trick. Using a rope and a length of wood, Gacy would wrap the rope around his prey's neck and tie three knots: crossover, hammer handle, crossover. The length of wood would then be slipped through the hole provided by the hammer handle, giving Gacy the leverage he needed to slowly twist until the life was choked out of his handcuffed quarry. Although this was Gacy's favored method, at least thirteen of his victims met their ends through suffocation. Instead of wrapping a rope around their necks, he stuffed the victims' own underwear down their throats. Once the underwear was in their mouths, he induced vomiting, causing the boys to choke to death on their own regurgitation.

Amazingly, some of Gacy's victims managed to break free. Arthur Winzell, a sex worker picked up from the streets of Chicago's North Side, survived a night at the Gacy home in the fall of 1977. Gacy eventually got him into the handcuffs and began his rope trick, but as he was twisting the instrument of death, Winzell wrenched his body sideways, grabbed one of Gacy's testicles, and squeezed. Defeated, Gacy let go, complained about the groin pain for a while, and let his young guest loose, even giving him a ride back to his hotel.

Yes, hit him in the balls like you're the kid in *Problem Child*!

What Winzell soon found out was that Gacy was well known in the gay sex worker community. Some knew him as Jack, others by his real name. Three had filed reports for assault, but it wasn't until a straight boy who'd been raped came forward that Gacy was arrested. Despite the fact that Gacy had impersonated a police officer and used a gun to force this victim into his car, the charge was quickly dismissed.

By spring 1978, Gacy's body count had reached thirty-two. Only once had an investigation come even close to touching him. His known victims were mostly younger boys of a lower socioeconomic class, loved by their families but not "important" enough to inspire an intensive investigation following their disappearance. The others were transients and sex workers, faceless young men forgotten by society even before they went in Gacy's crawl space. Six remain unidentified to this day. But his last victim was neither poor nor a transient. He was a popular high school sophomore named Robert Piest.

Gacy had noticed Piest one night while giving an estimate on some new shelves at the pharmacy where the boy worked. Struck with an immediate need to have him, Gacy started a conversation about how much Piest made working there before inviting him to his home, ostensibly to talk about a higher-paying job with PDM Construction. Piest did not survive the conversation.

This murder was the most reckless of Gacy's career, lacking any sort of forethought or regard for consequences. It was obvious that Gacy was the last person to see the boy alive: multiple witnesses had seen him at the pharmacy inviting Piest back to his house, and Piest had even told his mother where he was going that night. Gacy came under suspicion the very next day, and when cops looked up his record, they found the old Iowa sodomy conviction along with multiple reports for sexual assault. A warrant led to the discovery of a receipt for photo development from Piest's pharmacy in a trash can. But what really piqued the police's interest was the sickly sweet smell emanating from the vents in Gacy's home.

"Hey, John, not to pry, but, um, you got a couple bags of Shake Shack in a garbage pail filled with maggots in your house, or is it boy corpses? None of us are sure."

I wonder if some of the cops were hoping he was creating a new secret recipe for the colonel at KFC?

What had finally put the cops on Gacy's case was the discovery that in the previous two years, a whole slew of his employees had gone missing under mysterious and sudden circumstances. With that information in hand, they put a tail on John Wayne Gacy, following him for eight days straight. Gacy tried playing it cool for as long as he could, inviting his tails to dinner and sending over drinks when they followed him into a bar. He even lawyered up, hiring attorney Sam Amirante for a possible police harassment suit. But every time the cops spoke with Gacy, his casual demeanor began to crack a little more. The pressure was mounting and he knew the time would soon be coming when he wouldn't be able to talk his way out of things.

But could he mime or clown his way out of this one? I'll keep reading!

On the night before his capture, Gacy tearfully and in a drunken haze admitted to his lawyers that he had killed over thirty people. The lawyers were understandably shocked, as they thought the extent of their roles in the case was representing their client in a civil suit for police harassment. The next day they contacted the Des Plaines Police Department and informed them that while they could not legally divulge what they'd been told the night before, it might be a good idea to arrest Gacy by any means necessary as soon as they could. According to one of the cops assigned to follow Gacy, the lawyers sounded terrified.

Getting a terrified phone call from a defense attorney has to be near the same level of fear as when the doctor is reading you your lab results and they're on multiple pieces of paper that are stapled together.

As preparations were being made to execute a search warrant on Gacy's home, he was waking up on his last day of freedom feeling hungover and skittish. He drove, with the cops on his tail, to his regular gas station, dangerously speeding through a school zone along the way. When he was stopped, the cop, in chewing him out, used the one insult that for some reason stabbed at Gacy's soul: jag-off. This word usually sent him into a blind rage; his second ex-wife said that the only time she'd seen him lose his temper was when she had pulled that word out of her vocabulary. But on that last day, it seemed to sap Gacy's will to live.

So *jag-off* was to Gacy what being called *chicken* was to Marty McFly, only instead of being a hero, Gacy was also Biff.

Once Gacy was back on his way and had parked at the Park Ridge Shell station, he got out of his car and conspicuously crammed a plastic baggie containing three joints into the attendant's pocket, daring his tail to arrest him. However, the cops were waiting for the main search warrant on Gacy's house, which was due later that day, so they let it go for the moment. After the car was gassed up, the cops followed him to the house of Ron Rhode. Rhode was a fairly good friend of Gacy's, but on that day, Ron was suddenly his best friend in the entire world. He knocked on Ron's door, asked for a morning scotch, and vaguely babbled about how his life was coming to an end. Then he downed drink after drink before finally standing up and announcing that he needed to go to the cemetery to see his dad. Ron stood in his doorway, baffled, as Gacy hugged him one last time and confessed through a veil of tears, "Ron, I've been a bad boy." When Ron asked what he'd done, Gacy replied, "I killed thirty people. Give or take a few."

Yeah, when you gotta start rounding the number of people you've killed, I'd say it's time to get off the streets and into the prison sheets.

When I get scotch-drunk, I mostly sit in hotel rooms and cry about how no one understands the song "Baker Street" like I do. I also haven't committed DOZENS OF MURDERS.

With that, John left and returned to the gas station, where he parked, walked inside, and awkwardly hugged the owner, thanking him for many years of good service. The next stop was to employee David Cram's apartment, where supposed accomplice Michael Rossi was also hanging out. Still weeping, Gacy told them he'd confessed to thirty murders but tweaked the story to impress his teenage friends, saying he'd done them all on behalf of the Chicago mafia. Since Gacy was drunk and full of Valium by this point, Cram volunteered to drive him to meet with his lawyers. Gacy agreed but said they had to make one more stop: his father's grave.

It's almost certain that Gacy intended to kill himself on the grass in front of Stanley's headstone, possibly in some sort of impotent gesture of revenge on the man who helped make him into the monster he became. But the police wouldn't give him the satisfaction. Sensing that he was building up to a dramatic display of some sort, the two detectives on his tail arrested him on drug charges stemming from his earlier stunt at the Shell station.

Later that day police discovered Gacy's makeshift graveyard. It didn't take long for him to begin confessing. He soon became a pariah both in his community and the world at large as the press seized upon the headline "Killer Clown." At trial, Gacy attempted an insanity defense, claiming that his Jack Hanley and Other Guy personas were unfortunate products of the now-discredited syndrome of multiple personalities—he believed he wasn't at fault for his crimes. Thankfully, the shocking amount of premeditation that went into committing and covering up the murders was more than enough to sentence Gacy to death, and he was executed by lethal injection on May 9, 1994, following a last meal of Kentucky Fried Chicken.

Interestingly enough, Gacy didn't inflate his victim count like many other serial killers do during confession. He lowballed his by almost ten. Unlike murderers like Dennis Rader, John Wayne Gacy wasn't proud of his crimes, but he did show a certain curiosity toward his own motivations. He spent years with psychiatrists, alternating between manipulation and genuine self-reflection. But even with these years of therapy, the one thing he could never admit to was his own sexual nature. Whether or not Gacy would have killed regardless of his acceptance of his sexuality is a matter of conjecture. But it is a fact that society's unwillingness at that time to take seriously the disappearances of his victims and his survivors' reports ensured that John Wayne Gacy would earn a place as one of the most prolific serial killers in American history.

HELP WANTED:

PDM Construction is looking for strong, muscular teenagers with a healthy work ethic and good sense of humor to work at laying pipe, drilling holes, and sawing wood. The job pays $2.00 hourly, with bonus pay for those young men who go above and beyond.

The dress code is tight white T-shirts and cutoff shorts. Vagrants welcome.

Please apply on-site at:
8213 W Summerdale, Chicago, IL 60656.

For more information call **1-800-JWG-BOYS.**

MY MEETING WITH ROSALYNN CARTER

By John Wayne Gacy

Cook County News Herald:

May 6, 1978, was a beautiful spring day in Chicago. It was hotter than usual, and the whole neighborhood was alive with the buzz of a summer so close you could taste it. That Saturday began like most. I woke up full of excitement—a bit earlier than usual—shaved, and scarfed down my usual all-American breakfast of bacon, eggs, and a Bellini. I love a good Bellini.

I remember every detail because it was the day that I met former First Lady Rosalynn Carter. I was given the opportunity to meet Mrs. Carter because of my extensive activism, including my work as the director of the Polish Constitution Day Parade, a privilege that came from being a respected cornerstone of my community.

That afternoon, as the kids ran through the sprinklers across the street, a strapping fourteen-year-old mowed our front lawn. As a community leader, I believe in empowering our youth through entrepreneurship, and therefore I always give the young men in our neighborhood an opportunity to work, both at my company and in my own home. Children are our future.

Sitting on my porch, I thought about how Mrs. Carter and our former president, Jimmy Carter, had created over nine million jobs during his term. As I watched Robbie toil, dripping in the heat of that unusually hot May day, I was filled with a deep sense of satisfaction. I was also doing my part.

I chose my outfit carefully that night. I have many nice suits—tan suits, blue suits, and even a purple jacket—but for my meeting with the First Lady, I knew I had to wear my classiest maroon number. My father would have said it made me look like a fruit picker, but that didn't affect me. No, my dad has had zero negative impact on my life choices whatsoever.

As I slipped on my jacket and tied my shoes, I felt more confident than ever, like Sonny Bono without my Cher. I don't understand what people see in her. I always say fishnets are for catching fish, not for wearing.

I combed my hair, poured some salt under the floorboards, and hopped in my brand-new Dodge. Finally, after what seemed like an endless drive, I arrived at the Ponderosa for our big Democratic Party dinner.

I'll never forget walking through those faux saloon double doors and looking up to see Mrs. Carter staring right at me, as if to say, "John, that jacket does not make you look like a fruit picker." I looked back at her and my palms filled with sweat as a bead began dripping down my forehead, like a drunk Canadian driving from Vancouver to Seattle.

Words cannot express how radiant she looked as I approached the table where she was sitting. She was like a peach, but instead of fuzz she was encased in what can only be described as hairs from a baby angel. When I was close I extended my hand, and she nearly lost it when she saw what was in my palm—that's right, even Rosalynn Carter had heard about my famous "rope trick"!

I wanted nothing more than to entertain this woman with the world at her fingertips, and entertain her I did. Anticipating the trick, she extended her wrists, and I did not disappoint. I twisted the rope until her hands were tightly bound, and we laughed as the Secret Service confronted me and forced me to untie her.

Mrs. Carter has an amazing, almost French sense of humor, and I could tell she didn't think I was a fruit picker at all, because I am not. She picked right up on my hypermasculinity. We spoke for what seemed like hours, until security forced us apart. Rosalynn didn't want me to go—her eyes beseeching that we continue our conversation about gas prices, the problems with homosexuality, and, of course, the Bears.

After security sat me at a healthy distance from the First Lady, I made her laugh from afar, rolling my tie up like deli meat and pretending to eat it. She laughed and laughed with her eyes as I channeled my inner Hanley and twinkled my fingers in her direction before holding my breath until my face was purple. Her expression was priceless; I bet I could please her more than Jimmy can.

Indeed, it was a perfect evening!

SEE YOU AT
DIZNEYLAND
HOLLY
AC/DC
HIGHWAY
TO
HELL

CHAPTER 5

RICHARD RAMIREZ

A FAVORITE ARGUMENT AMONG TRUE CRIME BUFFS IS THE debate over which serial killer is the most "evil." The conversation usually begins with killing techniques, moves to victim typology, then gets lost in the details of each killer's most brutal murders. Often, however, the argument ends with one name: Richard Ramirez, aka the Night Stalker.

He is also known as the Stinkbreath Murderer, the Snaggletooth Maniac, and the Gingivitis Killer.

Richard Ramirez is not the most fun subject we've ever covered on *Last Podcast on the Left*. He is downright frightening, driven to murder by the power of the devil, and, to top it off, dude was ugly and smelly. He is everything that is bad about the human animal. The only truly funny thing about him is that he had the same exact taste in music as your stepdad, Wayne.

Over the course of a year and a half in the mideighties, Ramirez maimed, raped, and killed his way through Los Angeles and San Francisco, breaking into randomly chosen homes under the cover of night, dressed in black from head to toe. He ransacked the residences for valuables and left behind mutilated bodies, shattered psyches, Satanic symbols, and memories of bad teeth and the smell of wet leather.

Wet Leather sounds like an Old Spice deodorant marketed solely to people who hunt bigfoot.

While most serial killers tend to have a victim type, Ramirez murdered the young and old, women and men, and, in one case, a child. His victims were white, Asian, and Latino. Even the FBI Behavioral Science Unit was at a loss when asked to profile his crimes prior to capture—it called them "unique." The only requirement Richard Ramirez had for his victims was that they happened to be home that night.

Like our single days! Right, guys? I'm sorry. I'm trying to be as funny as possible for this chapter while I can.

This is why it's important to have a vibrant social life, even if that just means hanging out at Buffalo Wild Wings until 4:00 a.m.

His methods for murder fluctuated as well. He stabbed, strangled, shot, and beat his victims to death, depending only on whatever felt right to him at that moment and whatever would freak out the squares the most. Before Ramirez began his spree in 1984, there had never been a killer like him in the history of American serial killers, and as far as we know, none has existed since. Truly, Richard Ramirez is nothing less than an enemy of humanity.

The deviancy of his methodology and lack of pattern to his choice of victims made Ramirez extremely difficult to catch, ramping up the terror that Los Angeles felt during the period of his crimes. Ramirez was no joke, and even though he's dead, I'm afraid to make fun of him.

To be fair, he *did* buy a lot of AC/DC albums, which helped Angus Young afford those cool hats!

When Ramirez finally admitted to his crimes after months of denying responsibility, he detailed his murders with an attitude that went beyond a lack of remorse. He recounted his deeds the way Christian missionaries might speak of the heathens they converted during their last trip to foreign lands. In other words, Ramirez spoke with pride, joy, and the smugness that comes with believing you have accomplished something in the name of a supernatural being.

This is how I acted after I beat Henry in a White Castle burger-eating competition.

Morgues
THE MAGAZINE FOR FUCKFACE MURDERERS
December, 1984
THE NIGHT STALKER:
"I murder simply because
I love it."
40 UNDER 40

But Richard Ramirez was not a follower of Christ—he believed himself to be a true disciple of Satan. He was raised Catholic in a family that believed the devil to be as real of a presence in their lives as the president, and far more consequential. Although Richard had been an altar boy, when his pubescent thoughts began uncontrollably turning toward violence, sex, and bondage, he figured God and heaven were lost causes and found a darker supernatural being to justify his thoughts and, eventually, his behaviors.

The only two supernatural entities anyone should believe in are Jack from *The Shining* and Brett Favre!

What this really means is that Richard Ramirez had the attitude and emotions of a pot-addled fifteen-year-old metalhead who takes himself way too seriously. He was undoubtedly evil, but his reasoning, motivations, and observations are a far cry from Machiavellian. When asked, his explanation for his behavior sounds more like the lazy philosophizing of a high school student than the grand statements of a diabolical knight in Satan's service. "We are all evil in some form or another, are we not?" he asked reporter Mike Watkins in a jailhouse interview.

The irony is my parents always told me KISS stands for Knights in Satan's Service, which was literally the only thing that made KISS cool.

Unfortunately for Richie, we know that being truly evil takes a lot of money! True evil is creating a fun phone app that slowly ensconces the world in a net of SELF-MADE surveillance. Too bad poor Richie didn't like school; he could've been a Silicon Valley titan with that level of self-importance.

Ramirez wanted to be known as a supernatural force and he was certainly described that way by the media, especially prior to his capture. But as we'll see, the reason he seemed supernaturally good at what he did was because it was what he was trained to do, mostly through the horribly misguided "life lessons" taught by some of his family members.

RICHARD RAMIREZ WAS THE YOUNGEST CHILD OF FIVE born to El Paso, Texas, natives Mercedes and Julian Ramirez. Although Ramirez was a healthy baby, his oldest brother, Ruben, was born in terrible health, covered in golf ball–size lumps all over his head and neck. The second Ramirez son, Joseph, had birth defects, too, suffering from a condition that prevented his bones from properly growing.

Sorta like the universe was saying, "Hey, please stop having babies!"

Joseph would've been a great character actor for a Rob Zombie movie.

Julian and Mercedes blamed these horrific defects on government testing of nuclear bombs in Nevada, almost nine hundred miles northwest of El Paso. While there are myriad examples of nuclear fallout causing birth defects, the Operation Ranger nuclear tests, as they were known, didn't begin until 1951, years after the Ramirez brothers were born. Although no cases of birth defects as far south as El Paso were officially reported, if any of the Ramirez children would have been affected by windswept fallout, based on time line alone, it would have been Richard and his sister, Ruth.

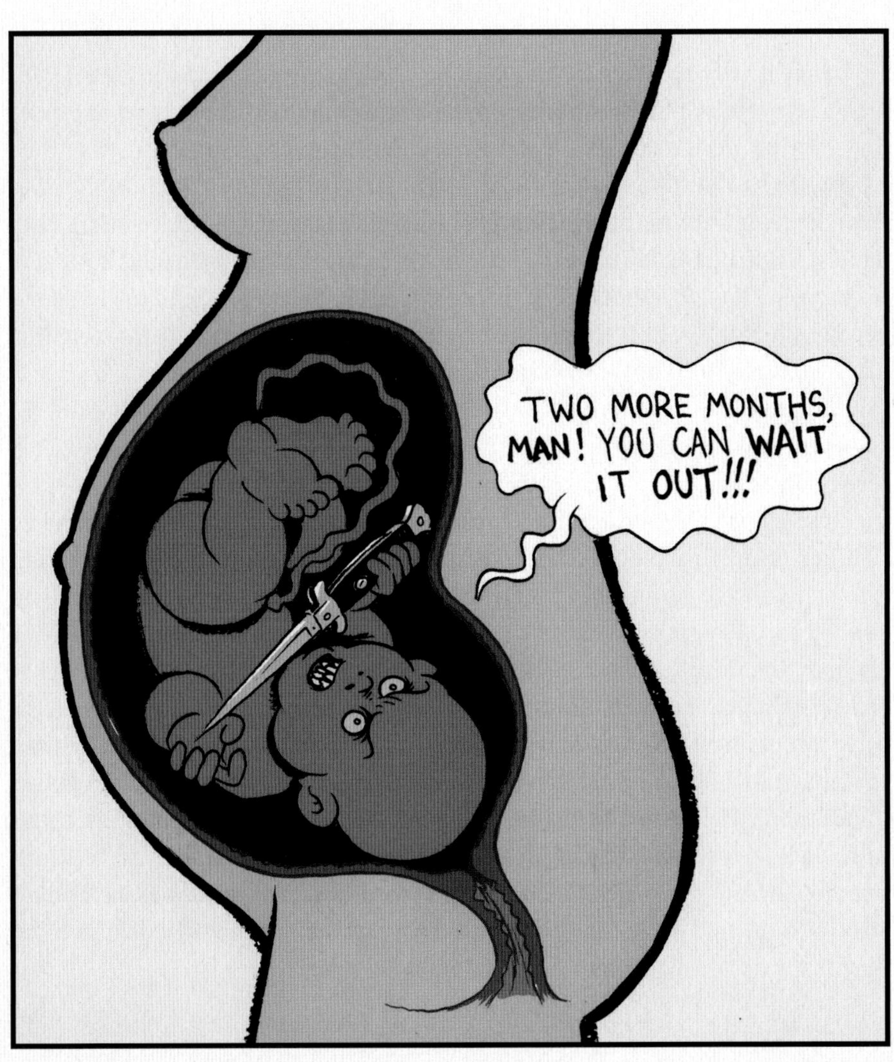

It's never good when your hometown's residents resemble the desert people in *The Hills Have Eyes*.

That's not to say Richard Ramirez was lacking in the chemical exposure department. His mother worked at the Tony Lama boot factory for the first five months of her pregnancy with him. During that time she was exposed to noxious chemicals on a daily basis without the aid of ventilation or a protective mask. It was so bad that halfway through the pregnancy, Mercedes came close to losing the fetus as her body repeatedly attempted to reject it.

He was dangerous even as a zygote.

It sounds like Ramirez had the same experience in utero as the baby in *Eraserhead*.

Despite this, when Richard was born he was healthy, happy, quiet, and blessed with a love of music that made him move his tiny limbs to whatever song happened to be playing on the radio. But that initial happiness quickly soured. In 1962, when he was just a toddler, he was home with a babysitter named Socorro while his father was out laying track for the railroad and his mother resumed her career at the boot factory. Little Richie, as he was called, wanted to listen to the radio, but it sat atop his parents' dresser, a spot he couldn't easily reach. Socorro refused to get off the couch so Richie decided to scale the dresser, which couldn't handle the weight of a two-year-old. It fell forward on top of him, knocking him unconscious for fifteen minutes, and it took thirty stitches to sew his scalp back together. He also suffered a concussion, providing the first ingredient in the recipe for Ramirez's personal serial killer soup.

A 2014 study published in the journal *Aggression and Violent Behavior* found that just over 20 percent of 239 serial and mass murderers studied suffered definite or suspected serious head injuries in childhood, and sometimes more than one. Richard Ramirez was one of the unlucky who suffered two documented head traumas, the second one occurring during a playground mishap when he was five years old. In that incident, his sister, Ruth, was on the swing set, and not realizing what sort of force a forward-moving swing has, Richard ran toward her. She tried to stop but Richie was hit right in the frontal lobe, which once again knocked him unconscious. He seemed to be fine in the immediate aftermath, but when he hit fifth grade, the seizures began. Ramirez suffered from both grand and petit mal seizures throughout his childhood, which manifested as episodes in which he'd stare into the middle distance, unable to move, as well as full-on convulsive fits. Eventually he was diagnosed with temporal lobe epilepsy.

Serial Killer's
CONDENSED
KILL
RAMIREZ
SOUP
NUTRITION FACTS
SERVING SIZE 1/2 CUP
SERVINGS PER CONTAINER 3.5
CALORIES 210
9 MONTHS OF NUCLEAR
FALLOUT EXPOSURE
3 SQUIRTS OF TOXIC
BOOT CHEMICALS
1 SEVERE HEAD TRAUMA
1 FUCKED UP VETERAN UNCLE
6 TEASPOONS OF SATAN

I am certain this made him very popular at school. Children are notoriously kind to kids with weird conditions that cause them to collapse and flagellate themselves in front of everyone.

This condition only added to an issue Richard Ramirez had been born with: the explosive Ramirez temper. Except for Joseph, nearly everyone in the Ramirez family line had extreme problems with anger, bursts of rage triggered by the smallest inconveniences, flaring up at random. Richard's grandfather beat Julian and his siblings almost daily, something Julian swore he'd never inflict on his own children. Instead, Julian took his anger out on objects. During one incident, he became so enraged at an ill-fitting car part that he screamed the worst words he could think of while slamming his head against the side of the house, leaving behind a dark-red splatter of blood. A few years later, he took a hammer to his skull after having trouble repairing a sink.

Is it better or worse to watch your father beat himself in the head with a hammer instead of you? At some point I might've said, "Hey, Dad, want to try beating me for a change? You're not getting it all out!"

Julian kinda sounds like the dad from *A Christmas Story*.

Richard's childhood was rife with demonstrations of abusive and abnormal behavior from the adults in his life. In addition to the violence of family members, he witnessed a neighborhood pedophile sodomize a young boy with a candle, and received regular home visits from a teacher who sexually abused both of his brothers. When asked if he had been molested, Ramirez said he couldn't remember.

What goes in does eventually come out. This is the fishbowl Ramirez found himself in, and as a kid, he absorbed all of it. He would eventually spit this violence and rage back into the face of the world.

But the most influential person in Richard's life was, without a doubt, his cousin Miguel. Miguel was a bad influence on all the Ramirez children: he was impulsive, seriously into drugs, and extremely violent. That behavior was only reinforced when Miguel went to fight in Vietnam in 1965. There he found that his uninhibited violent tendencies were not only accepted but rewarded. During patrol, he took every opportunity he could to rape the women of the villages his squad came across. In one instance, Miguel shot a series of pictures of a woman fellating him against her will while he held a .45 to her head. The last photo showed Miguel smiling, holding the decapitated head of the villager with pride and satisfaction.

CHECK! PLEASE!

After two tours, Miguel returned to America with four medals pinned to his chest, having faced no repercussions for his brutality. Vietnam had turned an already unstable individual into a base creature, someone who believed that if you played the game correctly—i.e., violently and without mercy—you could become God. The lessons Miguel learned and the crimes he committed would be taught in detail to a twelve-year-old Richard Ramirez, who took it as gospel.

This is a very bad heavy metal cousin. My heavy metal cousin taught me about Metallica, Anthrax, and Dungeons & Dragons.

Until Miguel, Richard had been a relatively normal child despite his occasional bursts of anger. He was a bit of a loner, but his grades were average and those who knew him described him as a generally sweet kid. But everything changed after his cousin became a consistent presence in his life. The photographs of rape and murder Miguel brought back from Vietnam were shown to Richard again and again as proof of his supposed godhood. This came as Richard was just hitting puberty, and these images soon became a regular part of the teen's masturbation fantasies. Something had clicked in his psyche and he soon privately denounced his disappointed God for the always-game Satan of his imagination, which made him comfortable with his burgeoning sexual deviancy.

God must've been more disappointed with him than He was when His son went through his long hippie hair and Birkenstocks phase.

In taking his cousin under his wing, Miguel gave Richard a master class in murder, bringing the brutality of Vietnam back home as a horrid gift and presenting it to an angry and impressionable teenage boy. And until Miguel's anger tangentially touched fourteen unlucky souls a decade later, the last person to be a direct recipient of it was his wife, and young Richard was there to see it.

This episode is unique in the world of serial killers; many had traumatic childhoods, but none had their hand held through a moment of mayhem and murder like Richard did. Miguel planted this seed in Richard that would grow to terrify all of Los Angeles.

The day seemed like any other. Richard, who had been spending most of his free time with his cousin, was over at Miguel's place for a casual hang. The two were in the middle of a game of miniature pool when Richard walked to the fridge for a Coke. When he opened the door, he found a .38 automatic pistol sitting on the top shelf. He asked why a gun would be in the fridge, and Miguel casually said he might have to use it later and he wanted to keep it cool.

Soon after, Miguel's wife, Jessie, walked in with her two kids and berated him for playing pool with his cousin all day instead of looking for a job. Miguel walked to the fridge, opened the door, and removed the gun, telling her to shut her mouth.

Jessie dared him to shoot her as Richard and the children watched. Calling her bluff, Miguel pointed the gun at his wife and shot her point-blank in the face. She dropped to the ground and died within seconds. Miguel then turned to his nephew and told him to leave, and Richard complied, dazed and shaken.

Ramirez never told his family he was there when Jessie was killed, but a few days later, he returned to the house with his father to pick up some valuables. After walking past the dark bloodstain on the kitchen floor on his way to the bedroom, he began rifling through Jessie's possessions and, at that moment, another switch flipped in Richard's psyche. He discovered that looking through the belongings of others, particularly someone who had been violently killed, gave him a special feeling like none he'd had before. Just being in the house post-murder gave him a charge. He later said, "That day I went back to that apartment, it was like some kind of mystical experience. It was all quiet and still and hot in there. You could smell the blood." But it was a long time before Richard himself would spill the blood of others—until then he made do by breaking into houses and prowling through them while bondage fantasies danced in his mind.

Citing PTSD, Miguel was sentenced to a mental institution for the murder. Without his cousin, Richard became rudderless and spent less time at school and more time smoking pot and breaking into people's homes. At the end of the school year, he briefly left El Paso to visit his brother in Los Angeles. Ruben was yet another criminal in the family, and spending the summer with him did little more than reinforce Richard's skills as a break-in artist. He also discovered the truth that either repels or attracts people to the City of Angels: it's all about sin and sex. The brazen downtown sex workers who walked the streets and the hard-core sex shops openly advertising the sorts of bondage fantasies he'd already been entertaining helped Richard fall in love with LA. He was still only twelve years old.

Richard returned to LA the following year and moved in with his sister temporarily. He now had one more family member to teach him the ways of the world: Ruth's husband, Roberto. Roberto was an inveterate pervert, particularly fond of peeping into the windows of neighborhood women. He must have seen something in Richard because he began bringing his teenage brother-in-law with him, showing him all the best peeping spots and teaching him how to evade capture. Richard would use his newfound skills to break into houses while the occupants were there, just to see if he could. And with this, he had learned everything he needed to become the Night Stalker.

How did Richard get so many mentors in being a serial killer? It's like he went to Professor Xavier's School for Horrible Youngsters.

Richard had started smoking pot when he was ten, but when he reached adolescence he began experimenting with LSD and peyote as well. When he tripped, he believed he could speak to Satan, whom he turned into an imaginary friend of sorts—this childish delusion would become a permission slip for every evil act he would commit. His belief in a higher being never abated; he merely switched from Jesus to Satan because there was no absolving necessary with the latter.

I am really upset that he has the same origin story as Dio.

Richard's other source of justifying evil was "heavy metal" music. Ramirez famously loved AC/DC, Judas Priest, Billy Idol, and all the other bands that passed as dangerous in the seventies and eighties. These fun-time party boys who had found a niche and ran with it wrote songs that Ramirez said inspired him as his crimes grew in ferocity.

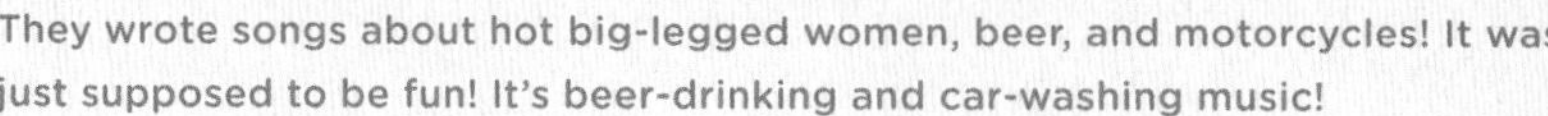

They wrote songs about hot big-legged women, beer, and motorcycles! It was just supposed to be fun! It's beer-drinking and car-washing music!

His first foray into violent crime came in 1975 at the age of fifteen. Richard had gotten a job back in El Paso at a Holiday Inn as a gofer, and he used that setting to kick off a crime spree.

Wait, a gopher like in *Caddyshack*? Now *that* guy was a real nuisance!

No, Kissel, a gofer like the umbrella guy who used to hang out with P. Diddy.

The work was menial, but Richard had managed to obtain a master key from a friend who'd been fired. He used it to sneak into rooms while the guests were asleep, stealing whatever valuables he could find. Other times he'd hide in women's closets to watch them undress.

One day Richard decided to take it to the next level. He hid in the room of a woman who was alone and waited for her to get close. When she walked by the closet where he was waiting, he tackled her to the ground, gagged her with her underwear, and told her not to scream or look at him. Then he tied her up and attempted to rape her, but at that very moment her husband returned, beat Richard unconscious, and called the police. However, the couple was from out of state and just wanted to forget the whole thing had ever happened, and so the charges were dropped, allowing Ramirez to get away with his first major crime with nothing more serious than a concussion and a few stitches.

These are Richard's training days, where he slowly builds the allowances he needs to become the brutal predator he wants to become.

And this is why you need to immediately place the "do not disturb" sign on your hotel door and hook the chain-link lock.

After a year of honing his craft in El Paso, Richard finally answered the siren song of Los Angeles, hopping on a Greyhound bus with a sack of dirt weed that he hoped to sell upon his arrival. When the Greyhound pulled into the downtown station, Richard disembarked with a smile, excited that he'd finally arrived in what he considered to be Satan's hometown. He then walked to the nearest dirty bookstore and bought the most extreme bondage magazine he could find before renting a room at one of the many ratholes a newly arrived Skid Row transient could count on for a night's sleep. In Ramirez's mind, he'd made it.

Honestly, entering Satan's hometown does require arriving by Greyhound.

That seems a heckuva lot happier than I was when I moved to New York City with my dashiki, a copy of *Dune*, and a sketch comedy group with an impossible dream.

Within a year, Ramirez was mainlining cocaine. Although the effect is similar to snorting the drug, injecting it supercharges the high, giving the user an almost impossible boost of focus and confidence. But that high comes with a price: high aggression and increased psychosis. In Richard's case, he felt cocaine brought Satan closer, and the closer his imaginary Satan got, the more vivid his violent fantasies became. However, an intravenous high isn't cheap; the effects wear off after five to ten minutes, making this highly addictive drug even more habit-forming. So, before he knew it, Richard was in the depths of addiction, trying to support a fifteen-hundred-dollar-a-week habit.

To do this he turned to the only source of steady income he'd ever known: burglary. Occasionally, if he had enough extra cash after getting his night's fix, he'd rent a room at the Frontier or the Cecil, but for the most part during this time, Richard lived in stolen cars, either hot-wiring them from the streets or swiping them from gas stations when the owners were paying for their fill-up. During the day, Richard learned the highways and byways of Los Angeles, studying maps and amassing an encyclopedic knowledge that he would soon use to horrific purpose.

And remember, this is long before Google Maps, when it wasn't so easy to remember all those highway exits!

If only he'd put all of this work toward creating a business, he would have been very successful. I'm just spitballing here, but a late-night breakfast drive-in pancake restaurant called the Night Stacker could've really worked, especially with the "niche eats" craze that has popped up in this country. Honestly, Richie could've done a lot of things if he wasn't mainlining pure cocaine with the Master of Deviance as his only friend.

Richard then expanded his drug repertoire, adding another anger-inducing powder into the mix: PCP. And with the PCP came Richard's first violent act in Los Angeles. His victim was an unnamed woman, a transient who was searching for PCP when the two met. Richard obliged and the two went to her apartment to smoke what he had on his person. After a fair amount was consumed, he came on to his new friend but was quickly rejected. When the dust ran out at 3 a.m. Richard left the apartment, making sure to surreptitiously unlock the window on the way out. He then made his way to the roof and dropped to the ledge once he was certain she'd gone to bed. Finally, he slipped inside, gagged the woman and tied her up, and raped her repeatedly, fully realizing his fantasies for the first time. The act filled him with a vile joy that was without compare.

A few days after committing his first assault on a woman, he came across a copy of Anton LaVey's *Satanic Bible*. Predictably, just as Richard had approached the obviously over-the-top lyrics of AC/DC with deadly seriousness, he completely misinterpreted the lessons of LaVey's book. Since we've got our very own avowed Satanist at our disposal, let's let Henry explain just what it was that Ramirez misunderstood.

Soapbox has been prepared—aaaand *go*. My interpretation of Satanism: Satanists do not believe in "The Devil." Anton LaVey's *Satanic Bible* is a tongue-in-cheek essay collection meant to inspire people to imagine life from the perspective of someone portrayed as a villain for his entire existence. In my opinion, the intended purpose was also to inspire people to defy the Christian standard of total obedience to a deity we cannot see or understand, and the concept of "blind obedience" in general. Lucifer, the devil, Satan, the serpent, whatever you want to call it began its role as the Christian villain after he tempted Eve with the apple of knowledge, which revealed to her and Adam the true nature of their universe: they were in a utopia but they were essentially pets for God. When God saw that they'd become enlightened, they got kicked out of the party and the serpent's been blamed for it ever since, even though he was doing them a solid by educating them. All the devil ever wanted was to create an even playing field between the creator and his creations! LaVey's book is intended to parody the smug Roman Catholic worldview that pleasure is supposed to be felt when you're dead in heaven and not here on earth (except for priests, of course, who are chosen by God and are his mouthpiece, so they can molest whoever they like). There are rituals in the *Satanic Bible* that outline the "practice" of Satanism, but mostly they stand as a response to the many rules of worship in the Christian Bible. The *Satanic Bible* teaches the tenets of Satanism, which are to have respect for yourself and others; advocate for free speech; live a life of happiness and pleasure while you can; and understand that the villain or adversary in your life has a story, too. NONE OF IT SAYS TO MURDER PEOPLE.

Richard felt LaVey had cultivated a personal relationship with Satan not unlike his own, so he stole a car and took a trip to San Francisco, where LaVey was welcoming the public to attend Church of Satan services. Years later, after Richard Ramirez's capture, LaVey would claim to remember meeting him, commenting on Richard's good manners. But knowing LaVey it's likely he said this just to provoke a reaction. Richard's own memories of the service, however, were clear as day. He recalled that as LaVey performed a ritual over a woman's naked body, he'd felt the icy hand of Satan touching him. Afterward, Richard returned to LA, read more of LaVey's work, and, like a sullen teenage boy who thinks he's got it all figured out, stopped smiling, grew serious, and proclaimed himself a true Satanist.

Holy shit, what I would have given to have been there! A lot of Satanists lean heavy on the "destroy those that bother you" commandment, but I'm way more into the "naked lady acting like a table, wearing a cape, and doing magic rituals to get TV work" side of Satanism.

Everyone knows a true Satanist just wants to hang out at Ren faires and play D&D.

After finding Satanism, Richard's life took a nosedive in every way, including personal hygiene. He refused to brush his teeth and only ate candy, which led to a gnarly case of halitosis. Showering became sporadic at best, and the smell of wet leather followed him wherever he went.

As his life deteriorated more and more, Richard's sister took a bus from Texas in a futile attempt to bring him back home. He responded to her pleas by shooting cocaine, blaring *Highway to Hell*, and proclaiming Satan to be the only thing he needed. The sociopathic influences of three different relatives, combined with a scrambled brain and hard-core drug use, had turned this relatively sweet-natured boy from El Paso into a dead-eyed, hard-faced, inhuman Angeleno. The time was nigh for murder.

He's finally ready for Hollywood!

Richard's transient nature meant that downtown LA was not the only place he called home during the eighties. After visiting San Francisco, he found that the town agreed with him, so he spent his time in the early part of the decade bouncing between the two cities. His home up north was San Francisco's infamous Tenderloin District, known for its high crime rates and shady characters. It would also serve as the location for Richard's first murder, although this fact wasn't uncovered until 2009, almost twenty-five years after his capture.

It has been assumed that the Night Stalker was born in Los Angeles in June 1984. That all changed in 2009, when a San Francisco cold case detective named Holly Pera ran a twenty-five-year-old DNA sample that had been found in April 1984 at the murder scene of nine-year-old Mei Leung. The child's body had been discovered in the basement of an apartment building only six blocks from where Richard was known to have lived. She had been stabbed, raped, and strangled, her limp body hanging by her shirt from a water spigot. Inspector Ronald Schneider remembered the arrangement of the body vividly, saying, "If you can picture Christ on the cross, that's the way she looked. Her head was dropped and her chin down."

At the time, this statement was used by the more sensational news outlets like the *New York Post* to argue that Leung's murder was ritualistic in nature. While that may be the case, it seems like Schneider's comparison to Jesus was merely a description rather than a judgment of intent, though it does eerily fit into the narrative Ramirez was looking to build.

After the murder of Mei Leung, Richard returned to Los Angeles and continued in the sleazy rut he'd dug for himself. Days were spent sleeping while nights were for burglary and stuffing as much cocaine into his veins as his body could handle. The night of June 27, 1984, was one such night.

That evening, Ramirez bought two grams of cocaine from his brother Robert, who had set up shop in front of the Greyhound station on Skid Row. Having spent his last dime on the coke, Richie drove his latest stolen car to an alley behind an abandoned building. There he found a discarded Pepsi can, cut off the rounded bottom, and used it to melt down the coke before injecting it directly into his system. He returned to that spot three times that night, filling the time in between with aimless joyrides, blasting his Black Sabbath and AC/DC tapes. When the drugs ran out, he was twitchy, irritable, and aggressive. If he wanted more cocaine, he'd have to go to work.

And that's when he got a job at a local grocery store and worked his way up the ladder to eventually purchase his very own Publix . . . Oh, that's not what happened.

Weed makes me want to watch movies, eat a burrito, and stare at the sky to see if any stars move. So what I'm saying is I'm also an addict.

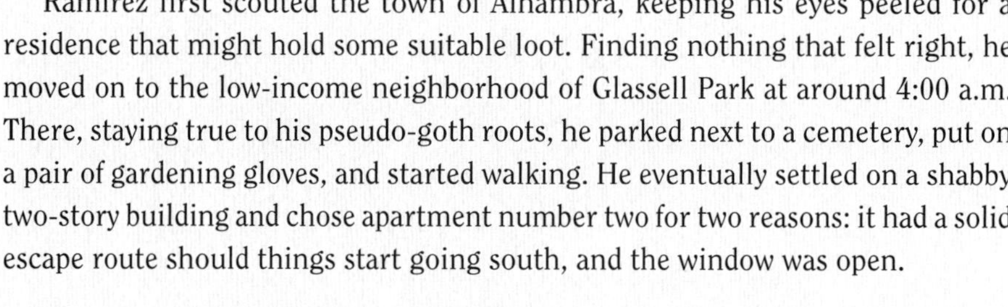

Ramirez first scouted the town of Alhambra, keeping his eyes peeled for a residence that might hold some suitable loot. Finding nothing that felt right, he moved on to the low-income neighborhood of Glassell Park at around 4:00 a.m. There, staying true to his pseudo-goth roots, he parked next to a cemetery, put on a pair of gardening gloves, and started walking. He eventually settled on a shabby two-story building and chose apartment number two for two reasons: it had a solid escape route should things start going south, and the window was open.

This is a very good time to remind our readers to always make sure your doors and windows are locked before going to sleep at night.

Richard removed the screen and climbed in, but when he looked around, he realized he'd chosen the wrong apartment for any kind of score. He quietly searched the usual hiding places people used for valuables, such as drawers and suitcases, but found nothing. The more he searched, the angrier he became.

Seventy-nine-year-old Jennie Vincow had been asleep the entire time Richard had been rummaging through her things. She was awakened by a six-inch hunting knife to the chest. Her hands flailed wildly as her survival instincts kicked in, but he sank his knife into her throat and cut across so deeply that he came close to decapitating her. Ultimately, he stabbed her three more times before finishing his gruesome game. Then he spent the next hour in Vincow's apartment, drinking glass after glass of water while savoring the sights and smells of a fresh murder of his own making.

Returning to his stolen car with only a small portable radio, Ramirez drove off into the night, his clothes still wet with his victim's blood. In his reverie, he almost ran a stop sign, but some sort of criminal instinct kicked in. As he pulled away from the intersection, he looked to his right and saw an LAPD cruiser watching him, only half a block away from Jennie Vincow's body. This close call could have been why he waited almost a year before murdering again.

Ramirez spent the remainder of 1984 committing up to three burglaries a day to support his addiction. After doing time for stealing a car and crashing it into a bus station in a cocaine-fueled frenzy, he decided he didn't want to be just another junkie holed up at the Frontier. He wanted to be a murderer, plain and simple, and he understood that he could never get away with it if he was permanently gakked out on coke. Richard realized killing gave him a high that cocaine couldn't hope to top, so when 1985 rolled around, he jettisoned the junkie lifestyle and emerged as a cunning, deliberate murderer capable of any cruelty he could imagine.

Good Lord, it took me fifteen years to stop smoking. I guess it just shows that you only quit when you're ready. How is he so disciplined when I have to give myself a forty-five-minute pep talk every time I go to the gym?

Hold on, so he only got clean because it was negatively impacting his murdering? This is the worst drug rehabilitation story ever!

Ramirez's reign of terror began in earnest in March 1985 with the purchase of a gun. He picked a .22 revolver as his weapon of choice, as he'd been told that it was the preferred caliber of professional assassins around the world. That night, using one of his tried-and-true theft tactics, he hopped into a Toyota at a gas station while the owner was inside paying. He then sped off, put on his headphones, and listened to *Highway to Hell* while wearing his AC/DC hat, staying completely on-brand. It was time for Richard to choose a victim.

AC/DC must have been so mad about all this free advertising.

Rather than searching for a house, he decided to pluck the unlucky soul from the pavement of the San Bernardino Freeway. Maria Hernandez was driving her gold Camaro back home after dinner with her boyfriend when Ramirez spotted her, and he watched as she pulled into the complex where she shared a condo with her roommate, Dayle Okazaki. When Maria opened the garage to pull in her car, Richard parked and silently ducked inside just as the door was coming down, knocking his hat off in the process. Maria walked toward the door with her keys in hand only to find Richard Ramirez in a combat pose, drawing on the skills that had come from Cousin Miguel's Vietnam experience. She gave a panicked plea for mercy and brought her hands to her face, but Richard fired, unmoved. Though she fell to the ground, by some piece of extraordinary luck the bullet had hit her keys. She ingeniously played dead, mystified at her fortune, but her roommate would not be so lucky.

Dayle Okazaki was upstairs in the kitchen when she heard the gunshot. When she saw the black-clad maniac enter, she ducked behind the counter. Ramirez waited silently and, when Dayle poked her head up to see if the coast was clear, he fired a single shot to her forehead, killing her instantly.

Having accomplished his mission of murder, Richard walked out the front door to find that his first victim had seemingly risen from the dead and had walked around the building to the front door. He pointed the gun at her again but this time her pleas for mercy were heard. Ramirez lowered the weapon, got in his car, and sped away to the freeway from whence he came. But the single murder hadn't been enough.

He quickly spotted a thirty-year-old law student named Veronica Yu and followed her when she exited at Monterey Park, just a few miles from the scene of the first murder. But Yu was an observant woman so she stopped to let Ramirez pass, and when he did, *she* started following *him,* yelling angrily. He got out at a red light and walked back to her car, trying to explain away his behavior by saying she looked like someone he knew, but Yu was having none of it. Tiring of the situation, Richard grabbed her and tried pulling her out through the window, but when he couldn't do it, he opened the passenger door and shot her in the side. The second shot came as she tried to run from the car, and she fell to the ground screaming as Ramirez returned to his stolen vehicle and drove away. Yu was still alive when first responders arrived, but she didn't survive her trip to the hospital.

Within a day, veteran detective Gil Carrillo of the Los Angeles Sheriff's Homicide Division followed a hunch and made the connection between the two murders. When the ballistics were returned the bullets didn't match perfectly, but it was determined that they had more than likely come from the same gun. That being said, the murders had been senseless to the point where no motive could be discerned. Fortunately, Detective Carrillo had recently taken a course with the FBI Behavioral Science Unit. Knowing that sex and violence can be interchangeable when it comes to serial murder, he called on fellow sheriff's department detective Frank Salerno, aka the Bulldog, who had been the point man on the Hillside Strangler murders. He suggested that Carrillo search for similar unsolved crimes in the area. So with only a couple of bullets, an AC/DC hat, and Maria Hernandez's description of a bug-eyed, curly-haired gaunt monster who looked more like Lou Reed than anyone else, Gil Carrillo began hunting Richard Ramirez.

Cut to Lou Reed being dragged out in cuffs screaming he didn't do it, and that murder was *not* what he meant by taking a walk on the wild side.

Meanwhile, the press was covering Richard's first murder spree extensively. Multiple names for LA's new killer were bandied about in editors' offices around the city: the Walk-In Killer, the Valley Intruder, and the Screen-Door Intruder were all tried, but none seemed to stick. Although Richard himself preferred the Night Prowler owing to the AC/DC song of the same name, the media eventually dubbed him the next best thing: the Night Stalker. Thus dubbed, Richard Ramirez would soon escalate his reign of terror at the home of Vincent and Maxine Zazzara.

The night Richard slaughtered the Zazzaras was not the first visit he had made to their home; the year before he had burglarized the couple while they were sleeping. This time, although he apparently hadn't left his hotel with the express purpose of ending their lives, as he drove down the San Gabriel River Freeway waiting for inspiration, the home made its way to the forefront of his mind.

Ramirez began as he always did, probing the house for weakness. He found his point of entry at a high-up open window that let sunshine into the laundry room. Although the Zazzaras surely thought the window was too high for anyone to use as an entrance, Richard picked up a garbage can from the backyard and used it to hoist himself up. Once he was through the window, he removed his shoes and began prowling.

He first found Vincent Zazzara asleep in the den. Carefully aiming his .22, Richard fired a shot above Zazzara's left ear, causing a geyser of blood to erupt from the wound. Mrs. Zazzara was awoken by the shot, but before she had a chance to get her bearings, Richard was upon her. He slapped her and began berating her verbally, singing the same song he'd sing time and again in the murders to come: Where's the money? Don't look at me. Bitch.

He then tied her up and began ransacking the bedroom, but Maxine wasn't giving up. She managed to wriggle herself free from the ligatures and then quickly reached under the bed to grab a shotgun put there for just this purpose. Richard froze when he turned around to see the forty-four-year-old woman pointing the scattergun at his chest, but when she pulled the trigger, nothing happened. Her husband had taken out the shells the week before during a visit from their grandchildren.

Richard had been briefly shocked and terrified by the close call, but those feelings were quickly supplanted by rage. He raised his gun, shot Zazzara three times, and beat her mercilessly as she lay bleeding out. But he didn't stop there. Finding a ten-inch carving knife in the kitchen, he brought it back and tried cutting out her heart. But as his anatomical knowledge was nonexistent, he failed to breach the rib cage. Instead, he decided that her eyes would make an equally gruesome trophy. He cut the lids away, forced her eyeballs from the sockets, and placed them in a jewelry box. Then the stabs continued: one to the neck, one to the stomach, and multiple wounds in the pubic area. Finally, he attempted one last degradation—necrophilia—but the shock of his near death made it impossible, or so he said, so he put his shoes back on, gathered up what valuables he could find, and fled the scene to fence his ill-gotten gains.

Afterward, Ramirez returned to a residence where he felt comfortable, all too fitting considering its history of hauntings and mysterious deaths: the Cecil Hotel. There was only one thing from the Zazzara house that he hadn't sold, and he finally had the privacy to enjoy it. He later said that when he opened the jewelry box containing Maxine Zazzara's eyes, he looked at them and laughed.

Most people who are staying at the Cecil are coming home from a night like this.

I have a feeling the Cecil Hotel leaves this off their website. The Cecil Hotel is more haunted than Demi Moore in *Ghost* or Mickey Rourke in *The Wrestler*.

The officers on the scene of the Zazzara murders were shocked by what they found. Such horror hadn't been seen in Los Angeles since the decades-past bisection of Elizabeth Short, more famously known as the Black Dahlia. Police searched for fingerprints but they came up short because Ramirez had been meticulous in his savagery. There was only one thing he hadn't thought of: his shoes. Even though he had taken them off upon entering the house, he'd left footprints in three different locations outside. The discovery was only significant because of the relative rarity of his footwear: Richard wore Avia Aerobic sneakers, of which only 1,354 pairs had been made. Out of that total, police would discover that only six pairs had been sold in Los Angeles. That distinctive footprint would be the only forensic evidence that linked all the Night Stalker's crimes together when no one was left alive to tell the tale. (Victims did sometimes survive their encounters with Ramirez. In those cases, his only seeming objective was to spread misery and terror.)

Avia's horrible branding and marketing team deserve some credit for barely selling any shoes in the LA area, which helped the police in this case.

The next time Ramirez left behind an Avia footprint was on May 14, 1985, when he sliced open a flimsy screen window and slipped inside the home of Bill and Lillian Doi, where he found the couple sleeping in separate bedrooms. Bill's end began when Richard fired a .22 bullet into his mouth as he slept. The victim struggled to stay alive as he listened to the Night Stalker beat and rape his invalid wife in the next room. As he choked back the blood pouring down his throat, Bill's last earthly act was to call 911 for his wife. Richard fled without killing her, and although it was difficult because of the stroke Lillian had suffered years earlier, she managed to communicate that her assailant was tall and had jagged, rotting teeth with a putrid smell to match.

You can hear the sound of the five Avia stores in existence shuttering forever.

After that night Ramirez's subsequent attacks came in quick succession. Although he failed to immediately kill his next victims, two octogenarians named Mabel Bell and Nettie Lang, he found a way to increase the level of fear the public was starting to feel. Taking a tube of Mabel's lipstick, Richard drew a pentagram on the back of her left thigh and another above her bed, and then finished by tagging Nettie's bedroom wall. The two were found the next day by Mabel's gardener, comatose. Nettie would survive the attack, but Mabel succumbed to her injuries seventeen days later.

Ironically, the pentagram that Richard had used as a sort of signature led the police to believe that an entirely different killer had descended upon Los Angeles. Since there was no Avia footprint at this scene and he'd never left pentagrams before, they didn't immediately make the connection. In fact, Gil Carrillo, who was now completely in charge of the case, was having great trouble convincing the rest of the sheriff's department that all the crimes were likely committed by one man—just the mere suggestion had all but gotten him laughed out of the room. The attacks on Nettie Lang and Mabel Bell had momentarily thrown him for a loop, as no other known serial killer varied in their choice of victims the way the one he was tracking had. The implication was chilling: two or even three men with specific MOs would be easier to catch than one who held to no pattern whatsoever. Carrillo wanted to be wrong, but his instincts wouldn't let him let go of the idea that a single perpetrator was responsible.

I'm completely romanticizing the life of a detective, but I picture Carrillo drinking whiskey every night in a white undershirt, pacing his living room while tying the murders together like in *True Detective*.

Richard's next victims were forty-two-year-old Carol Kyle and her eleven-year-old son, Mark. They were wrenched from their rest by a litany of terrifying catchphrases: Wake up, bitch. Don't look at me. Scream and you're dead.

Both survived but still endured a terrible ordeal. Carol was bound and raped while her son was forced to sit in the closet with his hands cuffed behind his back. After the vile act, Richard decided on a whim to let the woman and child live, for reasons unknown even to him. Carol later told the police, "The look in his eyes was absolutely demonic."

After Carol Kyle, Richard started slipping. One attempt at breaking into a house was aborted after the residents called out to each other when they heard him coming inside. He bolted but left the telltale Avia shoe print in his escape. Unable to find another house that felt right, he drove around all night and then tried abducting a six-year-old girl in Eagle Rock the next morning. She managed to escape Richard's grasp, and a witness called the police. He sped away toward the freeway, ran a red light in the process, and was pulled over by a motorcycle cop. As the officer wrote out the ticket, a call came over his radio about a Mexican man with black hair driving a blue Toyota who had just attempted to abduct a little girl.

This was a great scene in my old VHS copy of *Serial Killer Goof 'Em Ups.*

Completely oblivious to the fact that he was in the presence of one of the great monsters of the twentieth century, the cop, Officer John Stavros, made small talk about the series of murders plaguing their fair city. Stavros jokingly asked Richard, who exactly matched the description of both the killer and the attempted kidnapper, if he was "that guy killing people in their homes." Reportedly, Richard responded, "No way, man. When are you guys going to catch that motherfucker?"

"Richie, we love curious citizens just like yourself. Want to go on a ride along? You ever shoot a gun? Power is fun, Richie. You can do anything . . . with a gun."

Stavros assured Ramirez that the suspect would soon be in custody, and then, with the friendly, casual tone one would use in the good-natured ribbing of a friend, asked one more time, "You sure you're not him?" When Officer Stavros's back was turned, Richard drew a pentagram in the dust on the hood of his car and easily escaped on foot, leaving his car behind.

No! Officer, you had one job! Seriously, even the cop in *Dumb and Dumber* would recognize Ramirez is the killer!

However, it's unfair to place the blame for police incompetence completely on Officer Stavros. When Detective Carrillo arrived at the LAPD Northeast station where Ramirez's car was being held, he was told that as a member of the sheriff's department, he wouldn't be allowed to even look at it, much less dust for prints. It was a matter of jurisdiction: until the LAPD was forced to by an edict from above, they wouldn't let Carrillo anywhere near what was, at that point, his most valuable piece of evidence thus far. The Northeast station assured Carrillo that they were more than capable of dusting the car themselves, but they never proved their claim. By the time Carrillo was given access to the vehicle, the oil from Richard's fingers that was required to lift a print had been scorched away by the sun.

LA is a great place to commit crimes, because THE SUN IS YOUR ACCOMPLICE.

If ya ask me, we gotta charge the sun.

Admittedly, there are times when we can forgive the limited resources of the police officers of America's past. The first system to link interstate reports of sexual assault and murder—ViCAP—didn't debut until the year of Richard Ramirez's arrest. Before then, police had no feasible way of connecting the dots between crimes committed in the faraway corners of America. But Ramirez's spree was not one of those cases; while his crimes occurred in different neighborhoods, they were all within relatively close proximity.

In the case of the Night Stalker, oversize egos and a desire to be the department that landed the big fish prevented many jurisdictions from working together in any meaningful way. It seemed as if the only two men truly who cared about bringing this case to an end were Gil Carrillo and Frank "the Bulldog" Salerno. These two sheriff's department supercops had partnered up in light of the enormity of the crimes they were facing. Infighting and jealousy had infected the task force investigating the Hillside Strangler from the beginning, which allowed the killers, Kenneth Bianchi and Angelo Buono, to take even more lives. Salerno's current case was in very real danger of succumbing to those same mistakes, so partnering was the best choice. Meanwhile, the suspect was demonstrating that there was no end to his bloodthirst.

Richard's next victim was Patty Elaine Higgins, who was found nearly decapitated and badly beaten. Next was seventy-five-year-old Mary Louise Cannon, who met almost the exact same fate by way of a ten-inch butcher knife to the neck. It was these two murders that finally brought the rest of the department around to Carrillo and Salerno's way of thinking: Los Angeles had a serial killer in its midst. Everything, from the Avia shoes to the revolting smell of wet leather and bad teeth, was pointing toward one man. As a profile of the killer took shape, detectives guessed at a fact that turned out to be somewhat true in its own bizarre way: when they considered that many of the victims were Asian, combined with the efficiency and brutality of the crimes, it was suspected that the killer was most likely a Vietnam veteran. Cousin Miguel's training was showing through.

But, as with all good soldiers, the most important skill is adaptation. Richard bought a police scanner to track their movements, avoiding areas where patrols were thick. However, the promise of an increased adrenaline rush was too good to pass up, so he slipped through the Arcadia dragnet on July 4, 1985, and arrived at the home of Steve Bennett, his wife, Anna, and their teenage children, Whitney and James.

You'd be amazed at the Venn diagram of people who primarily listen to police scanners and Alex Jones.

That night, Richard decided to try a different method of murder and planned to bludgeon the entire family to death with a tire iron. Sixteen-year-old Whitney Bennett had forgotten to lock her bedroom window that night and Ramirez used that as his point of entry. He brought the tire iron down on her head twenty times, but still she screamed. Fearing her cries might alert the rest of the household, he yanked a telephone cord from the wall and began strangling her with it. But as he pulled the cord tighter around Whitney's neck, sparks shot from the exposed end and the escaping electricity produced a blue haze over her body. To this disciple of Satan, it seemed as if Jesus Christ himself was intervening to save the girl's life. Richard fled in fear and astonishment, leaving Whitney behind to miraculously survive.

Once again Richard had left behind a witness talking of wet leather and bad breath, and he'd also left behind another footprint just like at most of his crime scenes. Just three days after this attack, his footprint was revealed in the gruesome death of Joyce Lucille Nelson. He had beaten the woman to death, stomping her head so hard that the shoe's imprint was left on her face. Then it was found at a crime committed later that night at the home of Sophie Dickman, whom he let live only after making her swear to Satan that there was nothing of value hidden in the house. During this period, Ramirez seemed to be enjoying himself, experimenting with different methods of murder and intimidation as the press continued its frenzied reporting on "the Night Stalker."

He loved the attention! He'd finally become a somebody. This is a very compelling motive for most serial killers. They spend their childhood being "invisible" or abused, and now they can feel powerful. When they're in the newspaper, they can see that someone finally gives a shit! Which is also why they tend to want to be caught. Their deeds won't go down in the history books with their names attached unless they're caught.

The press glorifying killers has encouraged more murder than tax season.

On July 20, 1985, Richard Ramirez stole another Toyota and went stalking. He stopped at the Glendale home of Maxon and Lela Kneiding, slicing open their screen door. As he walked into their home, he held an industrial machete, newly purchased from a knife store downtown. Richard was planning theatrics—he had a vision that when the sun came up the next morning, people would look out their windows to see the bloody, decapitated heads of their neighbors staring back at them from their front lawn.

Luckily for the people of Glendale, however, Richard's plan did not come to fruition. Upon encountering Max Kneiding, Richard sunk the machete deep into his victim's neck but found it wasn't sharp enough to slice through the spinal cord. Instead, he shot Max in the head and fired three more shots into his wife's face. Then the machete was put to use in the couple's mutilation before Richard fled with a pillowcase full of their belongings. As usual, Richard had chosen a house close to the freeway and, within thirty seconds, was out of Glendale and on his way downtown to unload his score on his regular fence, who was beginning to get suspicious due to the fact that most of the items Richard sold him seemed to be covered in blood.

"Richie, I don't mean to pry, but all this jewelry, is it covered in blood?"
"No, certainly not, it's . . . raspberry preserves."
"Hell yeah—I just gotta ask one time."

I can see Chumlee from *Pawn Stars* paying Richard a bunch of money solely *because* all of the items are covered in blood.

After the transaction, Richard headed north, arriving at the home of Chainarong and Somkid Khovananth at 4:15 a.m. The Khovananths lived in Sun Valley, far outside of what was thought to be the Night Stalker's killing zone, so Richard was able to enter the house easily through a pair of unlocked sliding glass doors. Mr. Khovananth was killed instantly by a shot to the head as he lay sleeping next to his wife, but Somkid endured a horrifying ordeal at the hands of Richard Ramirez, who once again invoked his imaginary friend Satan during the torment. The next day, after showing off what he'd stolen to the scumbags downtown, Richard took in a porno, thinking that if the cops *did* catch and kill him, he'd be welcomed in hell as a hero.

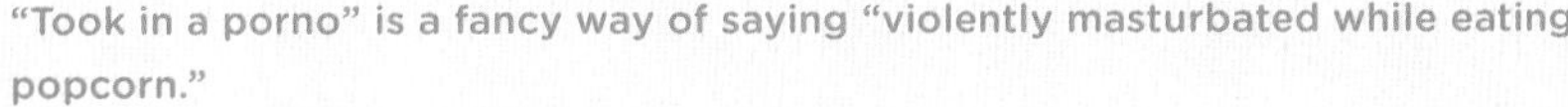

"Took in a porno" is a fancy way of saying "violently masturbated while eating popcorn."

Like *you* haven't stroked it covered in popcorn!

As Richard fantasized about what awaited him down below, his actions on earth were causing panic in Los Angeles. Just like the rumor in New York that the Son of Sam only killed blondes, coincidence also caused irrational action in the Night Stalker case. Somehow, Richard had managed to only invade yellow or beige houses, so hundreds of homes got a new paint job. People were made even more miserable by the oppressive heat of that summer, the hottest in a hundred years, because most didn't dare to sleep with their windows open. And yet, even with all the anxiety coursing through the city, things were actually much worse than people believed. The Sun Valley murders weren't immediately attached to Ramirez, so no one knew that he'd expanded his killing grounds when his sinister urge returned.

Ramirez found his next unlocked door, twenty miles from his last known point of attack. This time, he'd brought an Uzi, but Elyas Abowath, the patriarch of the Abowath family, still got his from Richard's .25 caliber.

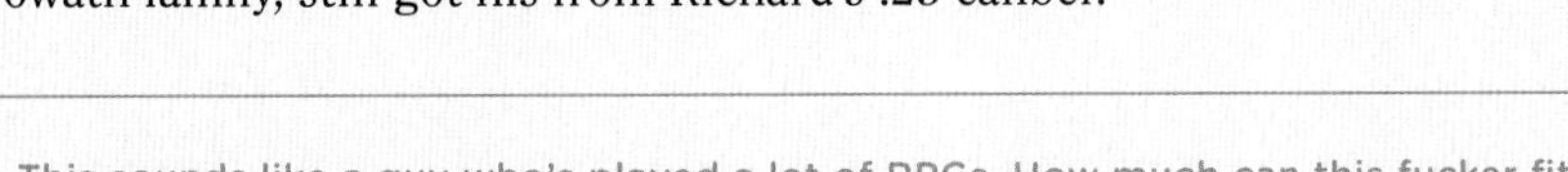

This sounds like a guy who's played a lot of RPGs. How much can this fucker fit in his pack?

Killing the husband first had become habit for Richard. Much like Richard Chase, Ramirez liked to take charge of a situation immediately, using shock and awe to rattle victims so badly that rational thought was nearly impossible. Elyas's wife, Sakina, felt that shock as she was awoken by the gunshot that killed her husband. She survived, and kept her children alive as well, only by repeatedly swearing to Satan that she would not scream.

The senseless killing of Elyas Abowath, Richard's fourteenth murder, brought the reward money for the Night Stalker's capture to eighty thousand dollars, making him the most sought-after serial killer in history at the time. That reward certainly caught the attention of Richard's friends at the Greyhound station who were starting to put two and two together concerning the burglar named Rick who wore all black, jabbered on and on about Satan, and sold loot covered in blood. The fence had long suspected him but couldn't claim the reward money without incriminating himself. Another bus station denizen, a gypsy-cab driver named Jesse Perez, had no such baggage. He recognized the foul odor and bad teeth the survivors had reported, but by the time he asked his daughter to contact the sheriff's department on his behalf, it was too late. Richard, sensing the heat but refusing to stop his killing spree, had left Los Angeles for the streets of San Francisco.

No honor among thieves! It's actually very nice. There has to be a movie about the scene of Richie and his "friends" all hanging out at the Cecil Hotel. A three-card monte lady, two sex workers, a taxi driver, and then Richie, the Andy Kaufman of the group, yammering on about Satan.

Life in San Francisco continued much the same as it had in LA. His first victim was an unknown Asian woman whom he spotted on the sidewalk and followed into her building. When she entered the vestibule, Richard beat the old woman so badly he didn't know whether he'd left her living or dead. He then tested his waters in the San Francisco burglary game, breaking into an empty home in the Marina District. Within days, Richard felt comfortable enough in his new surroundings for a full invasion.

On August 18, he removed the screen from an open window and slunk into the home of Peter and Barbara Pan, both in their sixties. First Peter was killed by a shot to the temple as he lay sleeping, then the same was done to Barbara. Before leaving, Richard took a tube of lipstick and wrote "Jack the Knife" on their wall. For good measure, he finished off the tag with a pentagram, and then left to find a streetwalker on the Tenderloin.

Fortunately, the San Francisco Police Department immediately recognized the killings at the Pan home as the work of the Night Stalker. Dianne Feinstein, future senator and then mayor of San Francisco, held a press conference and added ten thousand dollars to the reward money. This press conference wouldn't have merited even a mention had Feinstein not kept talking afterward. In the course of her time behind the podium, she blabbed about every bit of confidential evidence the police had on Richard Ramirez, including the footprints and ballistic matches. Up until that point, he'd had no idea how the police were linking all of his murders, but he sure as hell knew afterward. And so the Avia Aerobics, which were central to the investigation in the Night Stalker case, were tossed off the Golden Gate Bridge.

And we are still loving the immortal Dianne Feinstein here in Los Angeles as she recently tried to recriminalize marijuana. Love her, love her work.

Dianne Feinstein was the Nancy Grace of mayors. The only difference is Nancy Grace actually helps perpetrators get caught.

Richard soon returned to Los Angeles but discovered the city had become more vigilant in his absence. He needed to travel farther to feed the beast, so for his next crime he drove seventy-six miles south to Orange County, where he found a couple named Bill Carns and Carole Smith. Bill was shot three times but survived. When Carole awoke, Richard reveled in the opportunity to reveal himself as the bogeyman, proudly telling her he was the infamous Night Stalker. When she invoked the name of God in fear, he demanded, "Don't say 'God,' say 'Satan.' Say you love Satan!" After she complied repeatedly, he raped her. Later, he said that the only reason he didn't kill her was because she happened to have four hundred dollars in cash hidden in her home.

However, as he drove away in an orange Toyota, he didn't notice a teenager fixing his scooter on the front lawn. The astute thirteen-year-old had taken note of the orange Toyota earlier, when Richard had been driving slowly through the neighborhood with his lights turned off. Then, when he left the scene of the crime, the kid had the forethought to write down what he could see of the license plate number. This action would provide the key to uncovering the Night Stalker's identity.

And this child grew up to be Robert Mueller!

This whole thing actually ends with Richie pulling off his mask and screaming, "If it wasn't for those meddling kids, I would have gotten away with it!"

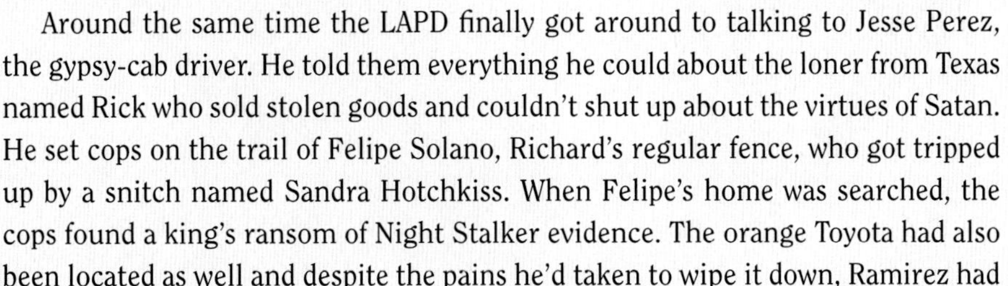

Around the same time the LAPD finally got around to talking to Jesse Perez, the gypsy-cab driver. He told them everything he could about the loner from Texas named Rick who sold stolen goods and couldn't shut up about the virtues of Satan. He set cops on the trail of Felipe Solano, Richard's regular fence, who got tripped up by a snitch named Sandra Hotchkiss. When Felipe's home was searched, the cops found a king's ransom of Night Stalker evidence. The orange Toyota had also been located as well and despite the pains he'd taken to wipe it down, Ramirez had left a single print on the rearview mirror.

Of course Richard wasn't good at cleaning; he hadn't brushed his teeth or washed his clothes in ten years.

The San Francisco Police Department was busy as well. Richard's criminal friends there were starting to turn on him. They had seen pictures in the newspaper of jewelry taken from the Pan household and had noted that they were identical to items Richard had given them before leaving town. After calling the cops, they said all they knew was that Rick Ramirez was a guy who broke into houses, listened to a lot of AC/DC, and continuously talked about Satan. And with that, the police had a last name to go with the prints and traced him back to the Bristol Hotel in the Tenderloin through another fence. When investigators entered room 315, they found more fingerprints, along with a pentagram drawn on the bathroom door. When the prints from the Bristol and the orange Toyota were sent to Sacramento and cross-referenced, the system turned up a petty thief from El Paso named Richard Ramirez.

The next day, newspapers and television stations across the country revealed the Night Stalker's real name and face for everyone to see, but Richard had no idea—he was on a bus to Tucson, on his way to visit his brother. Upon his arrival, Richard

tried calling Robert from the bus station, but his sister-in-law wanted nothing to do with her husband's psychopathic Satanist little brother. He was milling around the bus station, trying to kill time until his brother got home, when he noticed plainclothes police entering the station. Spooked but still unaware that he was a wanted man, he bought a ticket back to California and returned to the Greyhound station in downtown Los Angeles for the last time.

When Ramirez arrived at 7:25 the next morning, he looked out the bus window and noticed the police keeping an eye on outgoing buses, as the smart money was that the Night Stalker would try to leave town. No one suspected that he might have been returning from somewhere else. Richard avoided the police and ducked into Mike's Liquor Store on South Towne Avenue for coffee and a pastry. As he was paying, two elderly Latina women pointed at him from the back of the store, terrified, and said only two words: *El Matador*. Confused, Richard looked down at the newspaper rack. There, on the front page of every newspaper, was his mug shot staring right back at him.

GET THE MURDERER!

That's gotta be worse than when you get a glimpse of your face in the reflection on your laptop screen after crying while watching the one and only season of *Firefly*.

Richard ran but the store owner had alerted police to his presence long before. Darting across the freeway, Richard managed to catch a bus but was immediately recognized by everyone on board. He fled and attempted a carjacking, but the owner, who also recognized Richard, not only beat him back but chased him down the street. Continuing to run, he jumped over fences and raced through yards, trying to find some sort of escape. Invading one yard earned him a couple of spatula whacks from a man having an early morning cookout. Each attempt at escape or car theft failed, and every person who saw Richard only added to the chorus filling the streets: "El Matador!"

Finally, a man named Manuel De La Torre chased Richard down and brained him with a steel rod, sending him to the ground and ending the Night Stalker's reign of terror forever. The cops arrived and threw Richard into an interrogation room, where the deadliest killer in the history of Los Angeles banged his head against the table and hummed "Night Prowler," his favorite tune, all while wondering what he'd done to displease Satan.

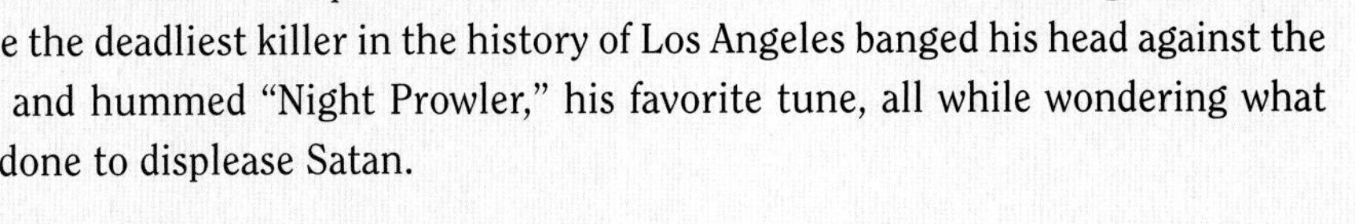

You did nothing from the *Satanic Bible* that he would have been happy with, you fucking idiot! You get everything back three times!

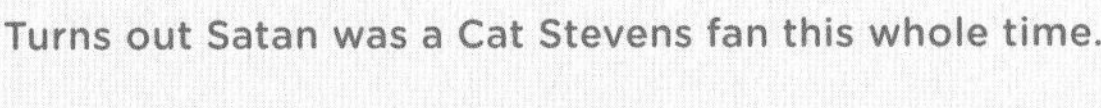

Turns out Satan was a Cat Stevens fan this whole time.

Richard Ramirez's trial was a farce worthy of his level of maturity. He hired and fired a Supreme Court's worth of lawyers on whims, all while calling the judge a motherfucker whenever he could, snarling at the press, and wearing sunglasses in open court so he could sleep through his own trial.

Technically, that is super metal. He never stopped being Richie, that stupid fuck!

He's like a demented Zack Morris in Miss Bliss's homeroom.

Surprisingly to most people, fan mail flooded Richard's jail cell from admirers around the world who all wanted a piece of Satan's bad boy. Women literally lined up to visit him, some of them going so far as to smuggle phallic vegetables into the visitation booth so he could watch as they pleasured themselves. One of his jurors even baked him cupcakes for Valentine's Day.

He's an influencer on Insta!

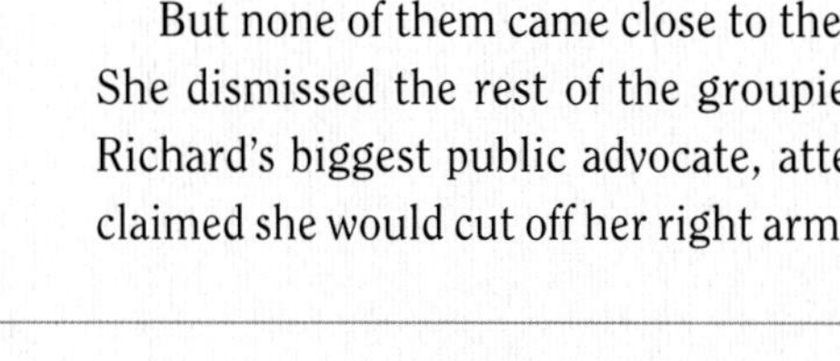

But none of them came close to the devotion of true crime author Doreen Lioy. She dismissed the rest of the groupies as a "bunch of street sluts" and became Richard's biggest public advocate, attending every day of the trial. She famously claimed she would cut off her right arm for Richard, and eventually the two married.

Every pot has a lid that is covered in blood!

It's like a royal wedding with halitosis.

Richard pleaded not guilty, possibly just to hear the anguished testimonies of his victims as they faced their attacker for the first time since the crimes occurred. Sometimes he looked bored, sometimes aroused, but mostly, he just laughed.

From arrest to conviction, Richard Ramirez spent four and a half years of the court's time and $1.8 million in taxpayer money, making his the most expensive trial in California's history until O. J. Simpson came along. When the ruling finally came down, Richard was found unanimously guilty on every single count brought against him and was sentenced to death by lethal injection. Cindy Haden, the juror who had baked him cupcakes, mouthed the words "I'm sorry" to Richard as the sentence was read. Afterward, Richard famously said, "Big deal. Death always went with the territory." Then, echoing a sentiment that was once a Ramirez family inside joke, he added, "See you in Disneyland."

He wouldn't be able to afford Disneyland if he went now. You have to go multiple days if you want to see everything because of the way they designed the FASTPASS system. Sorry, I became my father for a second.

The first rule of comedy is no inside jokes! Ramirez and Bill Engvall need to both learn that lesson!

The Night Stalker never made it to the lethal injection chamber. On June 7, 2013, Richard Ramirez was dragged down to hell by the twin maladies of lymphoma and liver failure, brought on by almost thirty years of prison hooch in addition to a hepatitis C infection. It was the death of true Skid Row scum, a bad death for a bad man who would have been nothing more than an inconsequential drag on society if not for the training he'd received. Unfortunately for all of us, though, Richard Ramirez left behind a legacy that reverberated far beyond the lives of his victims and their families.

For some, Richard Ramirez was proof that the supernatural force of Satan had made its way to earth, possessing its children and forcing them to perform unimaginable cruelties in his name. It might not be a coincidence that the "Satanic panic" began roughly around the same time as Richard's many public devotions to the devil. Hundreds of lives were destroyed in modern witch hunts across the country, from the twenty years John Stoll served in prison under the bogus claim of Satanic ritual abuse, to the near-execution of Damien Echols in the case of the West Memphis Three. While Richard Ramirez was not the only factor driving the panic in America during that era, when it came to spreading misery and making people believe that Satan was real, the Night Stalker certainly held up his end of the devil's bargain.

RICHARD RAMIREZ'S REJECTED LETTER TO *HIT PARADER*

To Whoever Edits This Piece of Shit,

I'm AC/DC's number-one fan. None of these so-called fans love AC/DC as much as I do because they aren't willing to go the distance. I'll go the distance. I started the first AC/DC fan club in LA. Well, right now it's just me and my pal Lloyd Stevens, who turned out to be a total pussy because he won't even come to the meetings anymore. I met Lloyd in a mosh pit at a concert in Sacramento. He seemed like a real hard-dicked motherfucker. He punched an old lady in the face, and I thought, "This guy can rock." Well anyway, Lloyd and I started this club and I made us like thirty patches. I hand-stitched every one of these fuckers. I put blood, sweat, and tears into every stitch. Only we've had some trouble recruiting and now Alma is mad because I threw a tire iron at his mom when she told us we couldn't hang out in her garage anymore. But that's not the point. The point is I want more articles about AC/DC.

I'm so sick of looking at David Lee Roth's dick through his tight pants I could stab someone. RATT sucks. Ozzy looks like a bloated Avon lady, and if I see one more article about Journey, I'm gonna puke. I want more Angus and less Winger. Mötley Crüe looks like weak cum covered in leather. Your rag mag isn't even good enough to be used as toilet paper, and trust me, I've tried. I'm gonna go absolutely insane unless you give more credit to AC/DC for being the most badass guys other than myself. And trust me, I shoot to thrill and fucking shake people all night long. You pussies wouldn't know how to do either of those things, though, 'cuz you're too busy putting KISS on the cover so ten-year-old girls will buy your shit.

KISS pretend to be metal even as they market their bullshit band on kids' lunch boxes. KISS doesn't stand for Knights in Satan's Service 'cuz Satan doesn't want dudes like Peter Criss, who looks like a gay cat trying to paw a mouse to death when he drums, and Gene Simmons, who uses that long tongue of his to lick his own ass. Ha, I guess they really are both like gay cats.

How the hell can you call yourself a metal mag when you put Warrant on the cover? Jani Lane looks like he blow-dries his hair as much as he blows Rob Halford's dong. His breath is worse than mine, and mine smells like a cemetery fucked a landfill and aborted the baby. You guys should be ashamed to call yourself men.

Guns N' Roses need to change their name to Guns N' Posers because that's what they are. Slash looks like a stoned tumbleweed, and Axl Rose is such a skinny bitch I'm surprised Dio hasn't tried to fuck him on his party bus yet. Paradise City for Guns N' Roses is filled with weak-ass drugs and dudes.

And in case you were wondering, I am AC/DC. The bells that ring in hell ring for me, for I am the night prowler, the one who is about to rock and the heatseeker of destruction. Angus Young is my spirit animal. I practice doing his kick dance on every screen door I see. AC/DC inspires me to be the screen-door intruder my mother never wanted me to be, but fuck it, my cousin would be proud.

So put AC/DC on the cover, assholes.

Richard

CHAPTER 6

DAVID BERKOWITZ

NEW YORK CITY IN THE MID-1970S WAS A TERRIFYING place. The Bronx was burning, junkies openly lined up outside of apartment buildings on the Lower East Side waiting for a fix, and intermittent garbage strikes gave the city an almost tangible smell of decay. In 1975, the *Daily News* printed a headline that summarized in two words President Gerald Ford's refusal to bail NYC out of debt: "Drop Dead." It was a bitingly appropriate statement considering the city's rising crime rates. On average, almost two thousand New Yorkers fell victim to murder every year during that decade. But six murders in particular petrified locals more than the seventies' other twenty thousand combined. During the wild years of 1976 and 1977, New York City was in the thrall of a man who would eventually come to be known by a name so cryptic, so scary, that you almost have to give its creator a nod for its literary merit. That killer's name was the Son of Sam.

The media succeeded in creating a bogeyman to sell papers. And here's a little-known fact: the comic strip *Mallard Fillmore* also saw a rise in fame during the time. Love the *Daily News* comic section!

During this era, lore about Son of Sam took on an almost-mythic feel. He was New York's own modern-day Jack the Ripper who stalked the streets using a .44 caliber instead of a knife. But when the nightmare finally ended, New York City discovered that their monster was not the demonic genius they'd assumed him to be; rather, he was a slightly overweight postal worker with the seemingly innocuous name of David Berkowitz. As people watched news footage of him being led into a Manhattan police station, their reactions matched David's own bewildered and confused expression. Despite the knowledge that Berkowitz was a dangerous and unstable individual, the dark romance surrounding the Son of Sam vanished in a haze of vague disappointment. New York City's famed serial killer was nothing more than another schlub from the Bronx.

Can you imagine the disappointment of the NYPD pulling Berkowitz out of his car? "Oh, I'm sorry, Mr. Berkowitz, we're looking for a serial killer. Do you need an escort to the 'Dumpy Boys of Queens' calendar shoot?"

DAVID BERKOWITZ, BIRTH NAME RICHARD FALCO, WAS THE illegitimate offspring that resulted from an affair between a married real estate agent named Joseph Kleinman and Betty Falco, a former fishmonger. Falco, a single mother who was already struggling to care for a young daughter, expected Kleinman to provide financial support for her new son. Kleinman refused and, with no other realistic options, Falco put little Richard up for adoption, where he was soon taken in by a Bronx couple and renamed David Berkowitz.

His adoptive parents, Nathan and Pearl Berkowitz, had conflicting views of their son. He was said to be unusually close to his mother, but according to David, his father repeatedly told his adopted son that not only had the adoption been a mistake, but the world would have been a better place without little David.

Normally, it is incredibly cruel and wrong to tell a child that their birth was a mistake. But in this case, they were absolutely correct.

Apparently his father read the "How to Make Your Adopted Child a Serial Killer" guide to parenting.

Adoption is actually a somewhat common experience among serial killers. The FBI estimates that 16 percent of known American serial killers were adopted, as opposed to the 2 to 3 percent of the general population. Aileen Wuornos was adopted by her grandparents when her mother abandoned her at the age of four; Kenneth Bianchi of Hillside Strangler fame was the son of an alcoholic teenage sex worker; and Joel Rifkin, New York's number-one serial killer with seventeen murders under his belt, was the unwanted byproduct of a college romance. In fact, Rifkin attempted to use his adoption as a long-shot defense in his murder trial, saying the lack of nurturing in his early life led to the aggressive behavior that fueled his crimes.

To be fair, none of these people had identical upbringings: some remember their birth parents, some knew their birth mother but in a different role, and some didn't find out the truth about their adoption until later in life. Berkowitz was one of the latter. When he was seven, his mother sat him down and told him that he was adopted, but she changed some of the details, saying that his real mother had died during his birth. When he discovered the truth over a decade later, the reality was devastating to his psyche. This isn't to say that there is a causation between adoption and serial killing, or even violence in general, but it can definitely be a spice in the serial killer soup.

Don't let this discourage you from adopting. Ray Liotta was adopted and he only kills people in movies.

Another interesting quirk in Berkowitz's place in the annals of serial killer history is that he was truly Jewish, both in the ancestry of his birth and his adoptive parents. Many point to the aforementioned Joel Rifkin as another example, but he was only raised by a Jewish family and was not a Jew himself. The only other mother-vagina-Jew serial killer besides Berkowitz was Harvey Glatman, aka the Glamour Girl Slayer, who murdered at least three women while posing as a photographer in the late fifties.

Ladies and gentlemen, Marcus Parks is very Texan, and apparently "mother-vagina-Jew" is a common saying in his neck of the woods.

"Mother-Vagina-Jew" is also a very controversial Leonard Cohen B side.

As a child, Berkowitz was hyperactive and an early bloomer, taller and heavier than the other kids his age. He wasn't what you'd call grossly overweight, but the word *pudgy* would dog Berkowitz for his entire life, used at some point in just about every article, book, or documentary that mentions him.

Despite his hyperactivity and slow metabolism, Berkowitz was a relatively normal child until he suffered a series of traumatic head injuries. The first came at the age of four, when one of the neighborhood boys dropped a rock on his head from the top of a building. The second came three years later when Berkowitz was accidentally hit by a car. The first injury reportedly had no lasting effect, but after the car accident Berkowitz's psyche became a low-key war zone, wherein he suffered from long periods of calm punctuated by fits of rage. His teachers described him as an easily upset bully who would lose control and act out. This behavior occurred at home, too, such as the time a preteen Berkowitz tore down all the curtains in his parents' house. Pearl responded by spoiling him with toys.

Some people would call this reinforcing behavior, as in, he's getting rewarded for destroying the house and thus learns to associate negative attention with love. But *those* people are nerds.

From there, Berkowitz's conduct began to edge closer to typical serial killer territory. He began burning insects with a magnifying glass—arguably somewhat common among kids—but eventually graduated to suffocating his six-legged victims with rubber cement. At the age of thirteen he moved on to higher-functioning animals, when he slowly poisoned his mother's parakeet with cleaning products over a series of weeks. The reason behind the bird murder was simple: David's mother would talk to the bird when she gave her son a spanking, telling the animal what a bad boy her son had been. Coincidentally, the bird's name was Pudgy.

David's behavior took a turn for the worse after Pearl died of breast cancer, her diagnosis a secret to David until two months before her death. The teenage Berkowitz blamed himself, later saying in an interview that he felt his mother died because he "wasn't good enough."

That is very sad, but he could've used it as motivation to become a lawyer, doctor, or drive-time radio host!

You see how he made his mom's death all about him? Do you? IT'S NOT ABOUT YOU, DAVEY BOY.

Soon after his mother's death, Berkowitz started to develop an obsession with uniforms, as many serial killers do. For example, Dennis Rader was a compliance officer, aka dogcatcher, while Ed Kemper famously enjoyed hanging out with the cops who investigated his murders. Berkowitz was no exception. He began by sneaking into the nearby fire station to try on the uniforms, then escalated to taking them home so he could casually wear them around the house. He even worked as an auxiliary police officer in the Bronx in his late teens, which in New York City translates to "officially sanctioned neighborhood watch."

Uniforms can give a person who feels inconsequential in life a way to gain social status. It can give you authority over other people—and there's nothing a serial killer wants more than power. That said, anybody who worked for Hollywood Video from 1998 to 2002 knows for a fact that uniforms can be a really great way to get made fun of in a parking lot.

Despite this behavior, David did end up having a social circle, however tenuous, in early adulthood. He had something of a sweetheart in Iris Gerhardt, and he even had a group of pals who threw him a party the night before he left for his army deployment in 1971.

I bet his friends look like a pack of sitcom losers.

Hey, that's more than what Forrest Gump got when he joined the army.

Berkowitz's time in the military would prove influential to his serial killing career, but not from exposure to combat. In fact, he managed to skip Vietnam altogether and was instead sent to Korea. (Interestingly, no other known American serial killer who served in the military during the Vietnam War ever actually saw combat. Leonard Lake, who killed eleven people in tandem with his partner, Charles Ng, rode out his tours as a radar technician. In addition, Gary Ridgway, the Green River Killer, served on a navy supply ship, while Dennis Rader was stationed in Japan. The closest connection to actual action was Richard Ramirez's cousin Miguel.) That said, it was here that David's mental state began to shift toward instability. Taking a cue from his fellow soldiers, Berkowitz dabbled heavily in the paranoiac's trio of pot, cocaine, and acid. The army was also where the .44 Caliber Killer first learned to shoot a gun. By the end of basic training, he was able to bull's-eye thirty-seven shots out of a hundred.

I wonder if the lack of structure later on caused him to go off the rails. The day-to-day structure of the army helps a lot of people, and sometimes the bottom falls out when that ends. I wouldn't know because I haven't had structure in my life since I was fifteen. I am a performer! (*Doffs cap.*)

The aspect of his experience in Korea that was potentially most damaging to his psyche was an encounter that Berkowitz had with a sex worker. He lost his virginity during this incident, but the woman he'd chosen was wet with the clap, which David promptly contracted. David felt that this "betrayal" was indicative of the fact that all women were liars, and beings to be feared and hated.

Once again, ladies and gentlemen, "wet with the clap" is evidently a Texas saying. Also, it might be the worst name for a band of all time.

Personally, I feel dry with the eczema.

Berkowitz underwent one more somewhat confusing change during this period: he found Christ and became an evangelist for others to follow. As a result, he spent his last few months in the army either trying to convert his fellow soldiers or bothering the locals by street preaching in downtown Louisville, Kentucky.

Possibly due to his newfound religion, Berkowitz shifted from a hard-core hawk into a full-blown pacifist. In one of his many letters to his high school sweetheart, Iris, he rambled on about the efficacy of nonviolence, America's undue reverence for "war pigs," and the power of love. He even went so far as to refuse to carry a weapon and was almost discharged as a result. But by the time his army career was almost over, his drug abuse had caused a change in his rhetoric. In one of the last letters to Iris, he wrote, "I might turn out to be a lifetime freak. They taught me about many weapons. I will use these tactics to destroy." In closing, he had scratched out the name Dave and written "Master of Reality."

WEE-oo WEE-oo WEE-oo, we've got a nerd alert!

In other words, much like the Manson Family, too much acid turned David Berkowitz from a peace-and-love pacifist into a paranoiac living in a land of violent delusions. Those feelings would eventually bubble over onto the streets of New York City, where he returned in 1974 as an overbearing, obnoxious fire-and-brimstone evangelist.

Bleeeechh, I hate new Jesus freaks. Totally get ones that are raised in a weird church and become tattoo artists later, but freshly hatched Jesus freaks? Get away from me!

Honestly, having violent delusions is a must for truly great brimstone evangelists. No one's gonna believe the world is ending unless you sell it like the Rock sold the Stone Cold Stunner!

Between his new Jesus freak persona and his constant antiwar ramblings, not a single person who knew David before his army experience—not even his father—could stand to be around him. He began lashing out at everyone, calling his best friend, Ed, who had merely served in the coast guard, a war pig and a rightist militant, ending their friendship.

He's like the dude who's the first out of his group to become straight edge at the hardcore show. "Whoa, Brian, are you drinking beer? Have you thought about your choices?" Get away from me, Jeremy, you have Sharpie all over your hands!

So he's like a combination of Michael Moore and Jack Van Impe, but perhaps slightly more self-aware.

Once Berkowitz successfully alienated himself from what small social circle he had, he went searching for his birth mother with the scant details provided by his adoptive father. He eventually found Betty Falco in a 1965 Brooklyn phone book and decided to send her a bizarre, almost anonymous Mother's Day card that just read "You were my mother in a very special way." He signed the back with the initials RF for Richard Falco and left his phone number.

Betty did indeed follow up, but things didn't work out as David had hoped. After reconnecting with his mother, he discovered that she had kept her first child, Roslyn, and that David had been given up after his birth father had completely rejected his entire existence. According to Berkowitz, the rage he felt upon learning this information was directed not at his birth father, but rather toward his mother, himself, and eventually New York City. The reality of his patrimony was too much for his fragile psyche to take, and his personality continued unwinding. In a letter to his adoptive father he wrote, "It's cold and gloomy here in New York, but that's okay because the weather fits my mood—gloomy. Dad, the world is getting dark now."

Go write a grunge album, David! You and Gavin Rossdale could be having drinks at Spago right now, but instead you're a fake Christian in a jumpsuit upstate!

This makes me a bit sad! He just wanted to be loved, but his birth dad rejected him like Hollywood rejected the Steve Harvey biopic.

Eventually, David Berkowitz turned to pyromania as an outlet for his frustration. From 1974 to 1977, Berkowitz was responsible for more than fourteen hundred fires in New York, each one detailed in a journal. Every entry had precise details of the incident, including the location of the firebox where the alarm was sounded, the address of the fire, the kind of equipment used when the fire department responded to the call, the time of day, and the weather. When David himself sometimes called 911 to report these arsons, which ranged from simple trash-can fires to blazes that overtook vacant buildings, he always referred to himself as the Phantom of the Bronx. The inner fantasy world that had begun with Berkowitz calling himself Master of Reality in Korea had come home, and it was about to get bloody.

By 1975, simple arson wasn't satisfying his growing need to create chaos in the world so he decided it was time to make it personal. However, the revolver that would eventually make him famous wasn't what he took with him the first time he left his apartment to kill. His first weapon of choice was a hunting knife.

His *first* first weapon was a sandwich but he used it against himself. Hell yeah, I'm good, I'm funny. Give this guy a book deal!

Some of you might wonder why a New Yorker needs a hunting knife, and the short answer is rats!

Like many would-be killers, Berkowitz assumed from the media he'd consumed that knifing a person was an easy process: stab, fall, die. But on Christmas Eve 1975, he discovered that stabbing someone to death could be a prolonged, messy, and earsplitting process.

Ed Kemper also said something to that effect, claiming it seemed easy enough to stab someone based on how it was portrayed in the movies. These guys live a life of horrible fantasy, and when they face the reality of how physically difficult murder can be, some of them realize they don't have the constitution for it.

Fortunately, David's first night of prowling was a failure, considering his ultimate goal. That first victim, who has never been identified, was attacked as she left a grocery store. Berkowitz said he stabbed her several times, but she was able to run away within moments of the attack. The second victim, Michelle Forman, would not go as quietly, although thankfully this attempt would be largely unsuccessful as well. Berkowitz stabbed her six times as she was walking into her apartment building, but she screamed and fought him, eventually scaring him away. The squeamish aspiring murderer had learned a lesson: the knife was too difficult of a weapon for him. Up close and personal just wasn't his style. When discussing these attempted murders, Berkowitz said, "I didn't want to hurt them. I only wanted to kill them."

About a month after his failed night out, Berkowitz moved from the Bronx to New Rochelle, just north of New York City. Supposedly his demonic delusions began in earnest out there in the suburbs, with Berkowitz claiming that it was his landlord's dog that first told him to kill young girls. The dog was under the command of the landlord himself, who, in Berkowitz's imagination, went by the alias General Jack Cosmo. Using powers bestowed by Satan himself, General Cosmo commanded an army of devil dogs scattered across the suburbs.

"Army of Devil Dogs" should be a Sam Raimi movie starring Ash from *Evil Dead*. That would be so cool!

All of this nonsense was strung together after Berkowitz had already been caught. He created an entire mythology to explain his actions. There was no real army of devil dogs, and if there was, they would have been delicious.

Berkowitz lasted only three months in the presence of the general before moving to a studio apartment in Yonkers, but even there, he couldn't escape the forces of canine evil. This time he claimed that Satan was speaking through the presence of a black Lab named Harvey, owned by his neighbor, Sam Carr. David said that Sam was possessed by a six-thousand-year-old demon, coincidentally also named Sam, but it was that demon's son who finally convinced Berkowitz to begin his reign of terror—and with that, the Son of Sam was born.

Hmmm, well this is in direct opposition to the theory that all dogs go to heaven!

All of this is a lie, of course. In 1979, David Berkowitz admitted to FBI profiler Robert Ressler that he fashioned his entire demon story in order to prepare for an insanity defense if he ever got caught. It was all smoke and mirrors, although what lay behind them was still a homicidal maniac.

About a month before the murders began, Berkowitz drove from New York City to Houston, Texas, to visit an old army buddy. There, he convinced this man to buy the gun, a Charter Arms Bulldog .44 caliber revolver, that would give him his original nickname. A Bulldog .44 was the perfect choice for Berkowitz: small enough to be easily concealed, but with enough firepower to do serious damage at close range.

Gun in hand, David returned to New York, quit his job as a security guard, and became a cabdriver, learning the streets of the Bronx, Queens, and Brooklyn by heart. After work, he'd go home and listen to records by his favorite artists, Carole King; Peter, Paul and Mary; and James Taylor. And even though it was released about a month after the killings began, Berkowitz cites "Rich Girl" by Hall & Oates as an inspirational tune that kept him going.

The only thing Hall & Oates inspires me to do is dance in boat shoes and tease the four remaining hairs on the top of my head.

The setting where these sweet, private moments occurred, however, was disgusting. David's studio apartment consisted of a bare mattress on the floor, with one naked light bulb swinging above. The windows were covered in filthy quilts to keep out the light, and the walls were full of his twisted graffiti, eerie statements like "In this hole lives the wicked king. I turn children into killers. Kill for my master." The ambience was completed by the smell of sour milk, as the shag carpeting was soaked with the remnants of empty cartons that Berkowitz would toss on the floor after finishing them. The parts of the floor that weren't covered with milk cartons were obscured by empty liquor bottles and used-up pornographic magazines. In other words: this man was ready to be a serial killer.

On July 28, 1976, David Berkowitz would finally begin his journey into serial killing in earnest. That night, two young girls, Donna Lauria and Jody Valenti, were talking in their car after returning from the Peachtree's disco in the Bronx, where they were regulars at the Wednesday night backgammon tournaments. Berkowitz approached the passenger side of the Oldsmobile Cutlass, pulled his .44 out of a brown paper bag, crouched, and fired three shots into the side of the car. While Jody would survive with a bullet wound in her thigh, Donna Lauria died instantly, struck in the head as she opened the door while attempting escape.

Naturally, there were no leads. The best theory the police could come up with for this chaotic crime was that it could have been a case of mistaken identity and the girls had ended up on the wrong end of a mob hit. Donna Lauria's father, a bus driver, was even investigated for being a "made man," but even the police knew they were reaching with that one.

The young girl's death was newsworthy enough to feature in the local cycle for a day or two, but it soon faded from the public eye. After all, this was New York City in 1976. That year, 1,622 murders were committed across the five boroughs. The death was admittedly tragic, but it would take several more victims for police to notice a pattern. That pattern would begin to emerge three months later in Queens.

On October 23, 1976, the opportunity for murder presented itself again. That night, Carl Denaro and Rosemary Keenan were sitting inside a VW when Berkowitz approached and fired five shots inside the vehicle. Luckily, neither was killed, though Denaro was struck in the head and had to have a metal plate implanted in his skull.

Unsatisfied, less than a month later David returned to his hometown of the Bronx for attack number three, taking down two teenage girls on their way home from a movie. He approached them on the sidewalk, asking for directions in a high-pitched voice. But before he finished the question, he yanked his gun from his coat and opened fire. One girl got away with a superficial wound, but the other victim would be permanently paralyzed from her injuries.

To me, nothing is scarier than David Berkowitz doing a Michael Jackson impression before killing people. "What you ladies doing tonight? Want to meet my llama? SHAMONE!"

Berkowitz was already one successful and seven attempted murders deep into his killing career, yet the public still had no idea who or what was stalking their streets. The totally random nature of the attacks had prevented the police from even linking them together, much less reaching the point where they could warn the public. As such, vigilance was virtually nonexistent. The following January, Berkowitz approached Christine Freund and John Diel in Queens as they were enjoying ABBA on the radio while waiting for their car to warm up after a showing of *Rocky*. Berkowitz fired three shots this time, hitting Freund in the neck and shoulder. Diel survived the encounter unscathed, but Christine died the next day from her injuries.

As busy as Berkowitz was with murdering, however, it didn't pay the bills. About six weeks after killing Christine Freund, he landed a job working at the post office as a Zip Mail Translator operator. During its heyday, the ZMT became infamous as an example of capitalism run amok in the government sector. Letters whooshed through the machine at a rate of sixty per minute, giving workers only a literal second to process the zip code and type it onto a keypad. Eventually it was proven to deteriorate the mental state of the people who used it and was partly blamed for the rash of workplace massacres perpetrated by postal workers in the seventies and eighties. True crime wags have pointed to Berkowitz's time at the post office as possible motivation for his crimes, but he was already three attacks deep—five, if you count the stabbings—by the time he started this job, so the connection is tenuous at best.

Two months after killing Freund, Berkowitz would stalk another Queens neighborhood, the relatively posh Forest Hills. There he approached student Virginia

Voskerichian on a darkened sidewalk and pulled his gun. Virginia's instincts took hold and she tried covering her face with her schoolbooks, but the Bulldog made quick work of the paper shield. The bullet ripped straight through and killed Virginia instantly.

It was this murder that led the NYPD to realize that a serial murderer may have been stalking the streets. The lack of motive in Christine Freund's murder had raised suspicions, but now that two more young girls had been shot on the streets with a .44, police started looking into other crimes with similar circumstances, a process that was arduous and analog in its execution. It may seem strange and woefully incompetent in today's terms, but it's again important to mention that New York City averaged almost two thousand murders a year throughout the seventies, and there was no computer system to link similar crimes throughout the five boroughs, population 7.4 million. In addition, the city was on the verge of bankruptcy, which had resulted in seventeen hundred officers losing their jobs to budget cuts.

I will say that my dad was a cop in New York during this time period, which was difficult. But even crazier, in order to be a cop, he actually quit his job as a taxi driver. That's how awful driving was in New York City.

For the city to gain the win that it so badly needed, on April 14, nine months after Berkowitz's first murder, the NYPD formed a task force named Operation

Omega. Soon after, Police Commissioner Michael J. Dodd held a press conference and announced that there was a serial killer loose in the city. Panic immediately followed, and the Summer of Sam began. Unfortunately for the people of New York, however, none of the things they were warned about had anything whatsoever to do with the case. Attendance at discos dropped drastically even though the only disco-related event was backgammon at the Peachtree. Women flocked to beauty salons to have their hair cut short and dyed blonde because it was said that the .44 Caliber Killer, as he was known at that point, only killed girls with long brown hair. This proved to be nothing more than a coincidence. In fact, when it came to choosing his victims, Berkowitz said, "I was out almost every night, driving, looking for game. I'd look for a parking space for my car. If I found one right away I'd know I was being commanded. Then I'd hit 'em." In other words, the most feared serial killer the city of New York had ever seen chose victims based more on alternate-side-parking rules than appearance or behavior.

Three days after the commissioner's announcement, Berkowitz made his public debut as a known serial killer—and he would do it in an audacious way. At 3:00 a.m., he approached Bronx resident Alexander Esau's car, where he and his girlfriend, Valentina Suriani, were chatting after a party. Drawing his gun, Berkowitz fired four shots into the closed passenger-side window, shattering the glass. Suriani was killed almost instantly, and Esau succumbed to his injuries at the hospital hours later. Berkowitz had committed this crime only four blocks away from his first murder.

It was a textbook .44 Caliber case, and now that the city was aware of his presence, Berkowitz decided to formally introduce himself. After murdering the couple, he left a letter on the street next to the car, addressed to Captain Joseph Borelli, head of Operation Omega. Written in neat, all-caps handwriting, the letter read:

> I AM DEEPLY HURT BY YOUR CALLING ME A WEMON HATER. I AM NOT. BUT I AM A MONSTER.
>
> I AM THE "SON OF SAM." I AM A LITTLE "BRAT."
>
> WHEN FATHER SAM GETS DRUNK HE GETS MEAN. HE BEATS HIS FAMILY. SOMETIMES HE TIES ME UP TO THE BACK OF THE HOUSE. OTHER TIMES HE LOCKS ME IN THE GARAGE. SAM LOVES TO DRINK BLOOD.
>
> "GO OUT AND KILL" COMMANDS FATHER SAM.
>
> BEHIND OUR HOUSE SOME REST. MOSTLY YOUNG—RAPED AND SLAUGHTERED—THEIR BLOOD DRAINED—JUST BONES NOW
>
> PAPA SAM KEEPS ME LOCKED IN THE ATTIC, TOO. I CAN'T GET OUT BUT I LOOK OUT THE ATTIC WINDOW AND WATCH THE WORLD GO BY.
>
> I FEEL LIKE AN OUTSIDER. I AM ON A DIFFERENT WAVE LENGTH THEN EVERYBODY ELSE—PROGRAMMED TOO KILL.
>
> HOWEVER, TO STOP ME YOU MUST KILL ME. ATTENTION ALL POLICE: SHOOT ME FIRST—SHOOT TO KILL OR ELSE. KEEP OUT OF MY WAY OR YOU WILL DIE!
>
> PAPA SAM IS OLD NOW. HE NEEDS SOME BLOOD TO PRESERVE HIS YOUTH. HE HAS HAD TOO MANY HEART ATTACKS. TOO MANY HEART ATTACKS. "UGH, ME HOOT IT URTS SONNY BOY."

I MISS MY PRETTY PRINCESS MOST OF ALL. SHE'S RESTING IN OUR LADIES HOUSE BUT I'LL SEE HER SOON.

I AM THE "MONSTER"–"BEELZEBUB"–THE "CHUBBY BEHEMOUTH." I LOVE TO HUNT. PROWLING THE STREETS LOOKING FOR FAIR GAME–TASTY MEAT. THE WEMON OF QUEENS ARE Z PRETTYIST OF ALL. I MUST BE THE WATER THEY DRINK. I LIVE FOR THE HUNT–MY LIFE. BLOOD FOR PAPA.

MR. BORELLI, SIR, I DONT WANT TO KILL ANYMORE NO SIR, NO MORE BUT I MUST, "HONOUR THY FATHER."

I WANT TO MAKE LOVE TO THE WORLD. I LOVE PEOPLE. I DON'T BELONG ON EARTH. RETURN ME TO YAHOOS.

TO THE PEOPLE OF QUEENS, I LOVE YOU. AND I WANT TO WISH ALL OF YOU A HAPPY EASTER. MAY GOD BLESS YOU IN THIS LIFE AND IN THE NEXT AND FOR NOW I SAY GOODBYE AND GOODNIGHT.

POLICE–LET ME HAUNT YOU WITH THESE WORDS:

I'LL BE BACK!

I'LL BE BACK!

TO BE INTERPRETED AS–BANG, BANG, BANG, BANK, BANG–UGH!!

YOURS IN MURDER

MR. MONSTER

The letter was not immediately made public, but the hype began almost immediately. Talking to a reporter for the *Daily News*, one officer said, "He lives in a nightmare world where he sees bloodsucking vampires and Frankenstein monsters." The off-the-record police statement only served to heighten the .44 Caliber Killer's reputation, and the panic worsened. Eventually whole excerpts of the letter were leaked to the press, who passed over Berkowitz's chosen sign-off, Mr. Monster, and latched on to the name given in the opening paragraph: Son of Sam. Although less conventionally menacing than the .44 Caliber Killer, Son of Sam was decidedly more frightening. It was an amorphous nightmare of a name, indefinable and nonsensical. The .44 Caliber Killer sounded like the name of a human; Son of Sam could be whatever people imagined. And with their imagination fueling them, the people of New York lost their minds.

I mean, in their defense, a chubby behemouth was on the loose! Of course they lost their minds. New Yorkers can deal with pretty much anything, but a bad poet with a gun is especially stressful. Berkowitz was like an armed Jim Morrison without the drug problem.

A good name is very powerful. Many serial killers tried to carefully choose what the press would call them. Luckily, most of the time the experts at writing did it for them. Son of Sam sounds like a sweet black metal act. Mr. Monster sounds like a goddamn cereal.

Chaos took hold across the city as New Yorkers frantically looked for a way to end their nightmare. In Westchester, two men who believed they'd solved the case took their suspect and dragged him to his father's grave, where they beat him with baseball bats to elicit a confession. In Sheepshead Bay, Brooklyn, a bar crowd emptied out onto the streets after they heard someone had been apprehended outside with a .44. They surrounded police during the arrest chanting, "Kill him! Kill him! Kill him!" In the Bronx, cops were called after residents saw two men dancing on the grave of a Berkowitz victim.

See, back then you actually had to go to the streets to chant "Kill him!" You couldn't just go to Twitter. It really was a different time for angry mobs of people.

Police were overwhelmed with tips. At its height, the suspect list would edge on seven thousand. And as it is with any serial killer manhunt, some used it as an excuse to get rid of rivals. Others used it to seek revenge, as it was with one woman looking to settle a score with her ex-husband. The official report from her call said:

> She said that just before her divorce he told her that one of the things he will miss is her long brown hair. She also stated that he loved Italian girls. He has sexual hang-ups and wanted her to get into the sado-masochistic scene with ropes.

It sort of sounds like he was just trying to save the romance in the relationship, but it's hard to be sexy with ropes if you're big, goofy, and Italian.

Over time, there had been enough survivors and witnesses to form sketches of the Son of Sam, but none of them remotely resembled David Berkowitz. Some point to this as evidence that he didn't act alone, but with the exception of Dating Game Killer Rodney Alcala, police sketches generally aren't conclusive when it comes to identifying a serial killer. For instance, as we mentioned in chapter five, the sketch of Richard Ramirez looks more like Lou Reed with a perm, and his victims often spent extended periods of time in his presence. In other words, people's memories, especially when they're in shock, are fallible. There is a slight possibility that other people were involved in these killings, sure, but the smart money is on Berkowitz acting alone.

About a month after the first communication, journalistic legend Jimmy Breslin, who had been covering the case extensively in his column for the *New York Daily News*, received a letter from the Son of Sam. Neatly printed on the back of the envelope were the words "Blood and Family—Darkness and Death—Absolute Depravity—.44." This is what Jimmy Breslin read when he opened the letter in his office:

HELLO FROM THE GUTTERS OF N.Y.C. WHICH ARE FILLED WITH DOG MANURE, VOMIT, STALE WINE, URINE, AND BLOOD. HELLO FROM THE SEWERS OF N.Y.C. WHICH SWALLOW UP THESE DELICACIES WHEN THEY ARE WASHED AWAY BY THE SWEEPER TRUCKS.

HELLO FROM THE CRACKS IN THE SIDEWALKS OF N.Y.C. AND FROM THE ANTS THAT DWELL IN THESE CRACKS AND FEED ON THE DRIED BLOOD OF THE DEAD THAT HAS SETTLED INTO THESE CRACKS.

Looks like we got ourselves a little Allen Ginsberg here! Nice!

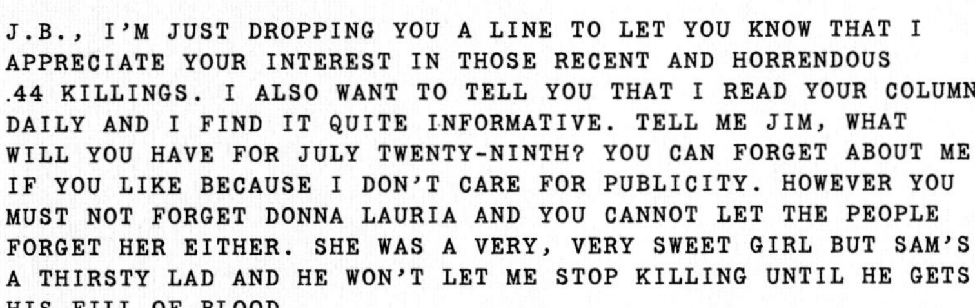

J.B., I'M JUST DROPPING YOU A LINE TO LET YOU KNOW THAT I APPRECIATE YOUR INTEREST IN THOSE RECENT AND HORRENDOUS .44 KILLINGS. I ALSO WANT TO TELL YOU THAT I READ YOUR COLUMN DAILY AND I FIND IT QUITE INFORMATIVE. TELL ME JIM, WHAT WILL YOU HAVE FOR JULY TWENTY-NINTH? YOU CAN FORGET ABOUT ME IF YOU LIKE BECAUSE I DON'T CARE FOR PUBLICITY. HOWEVER YOU MUST NOT FORGET DONNA LAURIA AND YOU CANNOT LET THE PEOPLE FORGET HER EITHER. SHE WAS A VERY, VERY SWEET GIRL BUT SAM'S A THIRSTY LAD AND HE WON'T LET ME STOP KILLING UNTIL HE GETS HIS FILL OF BLOOD.

MR. BRESLIN, SIR, DON'T THINK THAT BECAUSE YOU HAVEN'T HEARD FROM ME FOR A WHILE THAT I WENT TO SLEEP. NO, RATHER, I AM STILL HERE. LIKE A SPIRIT ROAMING THE NIGHT. THIRSTY, HUNGRY, SELDOM STOPPING TO REST; ANXIOUS TO PLEASE SAM. I LOVE MY WORK. NOW, THE VOID HAS BEEN FILLED.

PERHAPS WE SHALL MEET FACE TO FACE SOMEDAY OR PERHAPS I WILL BE BLOWN AWAY BY COPS WITH SMOKING .38'S. WHATEVER, IF I SHALL BE FORTUNATE ENOUGH TO MEET YOU I WILL TELL YOU ALL ABOUT SAM IF YOU LIKE AND I WILL INTRODUCE YOU TO HIM. HIS NAME IS "SAM THE TERRIBLE."

NOT KNOWING WHAT THE FUTURE HOLDS I SHALL SAY FAREWELL AND I WILL SEE YOU AT THE NEXT JOB. OR, SHOULD I SAY YOU WILL SEE MY HANDIWORK AT THE NEXT JOB? REMEMBER MS. LAURIA. THANK YOU. IN THEIR BLOOD AND FROM THE GUTTER—

"SAM'S CREATION" .44

HERE ARE SOME NAMES TO HELP YOU ALONG. FORWARD THEM TO THE INSPECTOR FOR USE BY N.C.I.C:

"THE DUKE OF DEATH"

"THE WICKED KING WICKER"

"THE TWENTY TWO DISCIPLES OF HELL"

"JOHN 'WHEATIES'—RAPIST AND SUFFOCATOR OF YOUNG GIRLS."

PS: PLEASE INFORM ALL THE DETECTIVES WORKING THE SLAYING TO REMAIN.

PS: JB, PLEASE INFORM ALL THE DETECTIVES WORKING THE CASE THAT I WISH THEM THE BEST OF LUCK. "KEEP EM DIGGING, DRIVE ON, THINK POSITIVE, GET OFF YOUR BUTTS, KNOCK ON COFFINS, ETC."

UPON MY CAPTURE I PROMISE TO BUY ALL THE GUYS WORKING ON THE CASE A NEW PAIR OF SHOES IF I CAN GET UP THE MONEY.

This is where Berkowitz and my mom from Queens blend together. "Oh God, I hope they have tight-fitting shoes! When you police officers get tired, I made forty steak-and-pepper sandwiches you can take for the road."

Objectively, it's fantastic writing, but some people claim that the quality of the prose suggests that Berkowitz was not the author of this letter. However, as we know from early-twentieth-century supercriminal Carl Panzram, whose autobiographical prison journals could easily be compared to the best of Hemingway, just because a person is a serial killer does not mean that they can't be talented when it comes to the written word. Even Jimmy Breslin praised Berkowitz's writing, saying Son of Sam's big-city cadence had the stuff necessary to take over his own column.

But the *Daily News* was by no means the only paper on the case in New York City. Although the *News* was getting the exclusives, media magnate Rupert Murdoch of NewsCorp, who had just purchased the *New York Post*, ordered a reporter to get a scoop at any cost.

I met Rupert once and I felt like when Chris Farley meets Dan Aykroyd in *Tommy Boy*—he seemed like a nice guy! And then I thought of David Spade yelling at me about some of the horrible things he's done.

Since the *Post* didn't have their own line to the killer, the reporter tried the next best thing: a victim. After hearing about a suspected Son of Sam murder on a police scanner, the *Post* reporter raced to the hospital where the victim had been taken. Once there, he snuck into the ER, found some scrubs, located the victim's family, told them he was a grief counselor, and pumped them for information.

This *Post* reporter is like Fletch! And no, I will never let nostalgic comedies die.

The police continued their unsuccessful bids for information throughout the summer. They were so desperate to latch on to any part of the letter that they even hosted a screening of *The Wicker Man*, in which a Scottish police inspector is burned alive as a sacrifice to ancient pagan gods, to see if the public made any connections between that and Berkowitz's "Wicked King of Wicker."

Berkowitz's next attack came on June 26. Sal Lupo and Judy Placido had met that night in the Elephas nightclub in the Bayside neighborhood of Queens. As they sat in the car at 3:00 a.m. waiting for a friend, Placido turned to her date and started talking about Son of Sam. No sooner had she said, "You can't stay home forever" did David Berkowitz fire five shots into the passenger-side window. Luckily, both June and Sal survived. Just over a month later, David Berkowitz would claim his last victim: Stacy Moskowitz. She and her new beau, Robert Violante, had met only a few nights before at Beefsteak Charlie's in Sheepshead Bay during Gong Show Night. Stacy and Bobby were well aware of the dangers of the killer on the loose, but they weren't worried: after all, Stacy was blonde, and furthermore, none of the attacks had occurred in

Brooklyn. But that evening, since it was so close to the one-year anniversary of Son of Sam's first murder, the cops had invested most of their manpower into Queens and the Bronx, blanketing those areas with three hundred officers. Knowing this, Berkowitz traveled south for one last magic parking spot. He found it near Coney Island, right next to Gravesend Bay.

This reads like an almanac of "Things to Do by the R Train 1977" written by a guy named Tommy Spaghetti.

As Stacy and Bobby kissed in a parked car following a showing of the Liza Minnelli movie *New York, New York,* Berkowitz squeezed four rounds into the open passenger-side window before retreating into the darkness. Bobby would survive, blinded by the bullets, but thirty-six hours later Stacy died in the hospital.

It seemed to Berkowitz that he had once again gotten away with murder, but that night, the thing that had led him down this dark path would be his undoing. Usually, serial killers get caught because they get sloppy, and Berkowitz was no exception. While he was normally careful to park his Ford Galaxie in an inconspicuous spot, he'd gotten impatient on the night of July 31. At 2:05 a.m., about twenty-five minutes prior to the shooting, David Berkowitz had received a parking ticket for parking too close to a fire hydrant. Then, just a few minutes before the shooting, a woman named Cacilia Davis had been out walking her dog Snowball when she saw a shifty-looking pudgy man in his twenties angrily grab a parking ticket from under his windshield wiper. According to her, the man was holding something and had stared at her before walking away. Not too long after, she'd heard the shots.

No parking spots is the number-one reason why people move out of NYC.

We can all agree finding parking in New York City is more difficult than putting together IKEA furniture while tripping on shrooms.

Although the police initially ignored Cacilia's report, filing it in the "crackpot" bin of Son of Sam tips, her local precinct finally followed up after she badgered them for three weeks straight. Berkowitz's ticket was only one of four issued in Coney Island that night, and the sole citation for parking in front of a hydrant. The car listed on the ticket was a cream-colored Ford Galaxie registered to one David Berkowitz, who lived at 35 Pine Street in Yonkers. Initially, police only wanted to talk to David as a potential witness, but after making a couple of calls, they discovered that this might be the man they'd been looking for all along.

After searching through the thousands of files related to the Son of Sam case, Operation Omega discovered that throughout the summer, Berkowitz had been reported for sending multiple threatening letters to neighbors. Local police had forwarded the reports to the task force, but again, they'd been lost in the flood of tips. One letter, addressed to Craig Glassman, his downstairs neighbor, had a familiar, haunting tone:

> **How dare you force me into the night to do your bidding. True, I am the killer, but Craig the killer kills on your command. The streets have been filled with blood at the request of Craig. Because Craig is Craig so must the streets be filled with Craig.**

Wow, nothing would be scarier to me than a whole street filled with Craigs. Hundreds of craft beer fans, LA comedy writers, and the dude you met at Christmas who dated your cousin for a while.

When detectives called the Yonkers Police Department to get more information, they found that dispatcher Wheat Carr suspected that Berkowitz may have killed her black Lab. Amazingly, Wheat's father was Sam Carr, Berkowitz's former neighbor, whose dog was supposedly possessed by a demon. In a strange cosmic flip-flop, Wheat Carr was quite literally the Daughter of Sam.

After learning of the dog and the letters, two detectives from Operation Omega, Ed Zigo and John Falotico, headed up to David's apartment in Yonkers. Looking in the back seat of his Galaxie, they saw the butt of a rifle sticking out of a large duffel bag. Stupidly, Detective Zigo opened the car door without a warrant and searched the glove compartment. Inside he found a letter detailing an upcoming mass murder in a disco. Berkowitz later claimed that he had driven to a nightclub in the Hamptons on August 6 with the intent to go down in "a blaze of glory"—suicide by cop—but bad weather had stayed his hand.

You know Berkowitz and rain: "Oh God, I can't get murdered by the cops tonight! I can't catch a cold before getting shot in the face!"

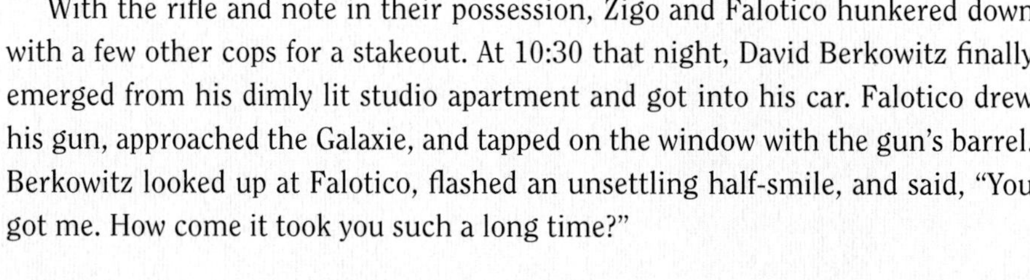

With the rifle and note in their possession, Zigo and Falotico hunkered down with a few other cops for a stakeout. At 10:30 that night, David Berkowitz finally emerged from his dimly lit studio apartment and got into his car. Falotico drew his gun, approached the Galaxie, and tapped on the window with the gun's barrel. Berkowitz looked up at Falotico, flashed an unsettling half-smile, and said, "You got me. How come it took you such a long time?"

Investigations take time, man! Jeez!

A backup officer on the scene said Berkowitz's demeanor made it seem as though he thought the whole thing was "a kid's game," and the first detective to have an actual conversation with the Son of Sam said talking to him was like "talking to a head of cabbage." But even though the conversation was slow going, after only thirty minutes Berkowitz confessed to all the murders and was placed under arrest.

Adamant that he be punished for what he'd done, Berkowitz steamrollered his defense team and skipped the insanity plea. He pleaded guilty to every charge brought forth and was sentenced to twenty-five years to life for each murder. Two years after the conviction, he would openly admit to FBI profiler Robert Ressler that he killed not because a six-thousand-year-old demon commanded it, but because he was devastated by the revelation of the circumstances surrounding his birth in addition to his general feelings of inadequacy around women. Jimmy Breslin would also tone down his estimation of the Son of Sam after Berkowitz was caught, describing him in an interview with NBC News as "goopy."

I, too, suffer from Goopy Body. But all it takes is a good attitude, well-fitting jeans, and little bit of LUCK and things can turn around for ya, just like they did for me.

Oh, nice! I think that's why Gwyneth Paltrow named her brand Goop: because they sell disgusting products that only a sociopath would buy.

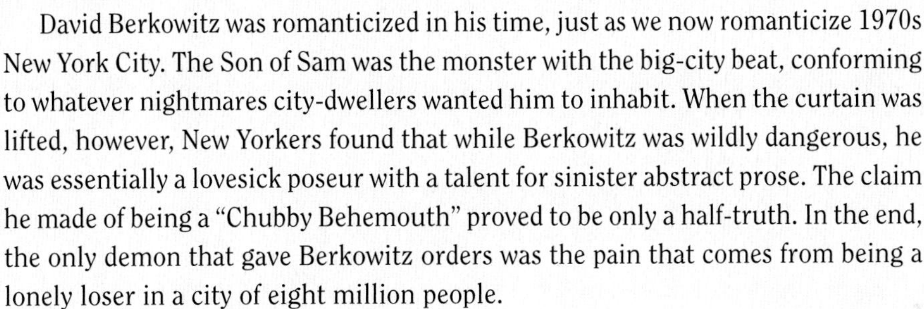

David Berkowitz was romanticized in his time, just as we now romanticize 1970s New York City. The Son of Sam was the monster with the big-city beat, conforming to whatever nightmares city-dwellers wanted him to inhabit. When the curtain was lifted, however, New Yorkers found that while Berkowitz was wildly dangerous, he was essentially a lovesick poseur with a talent for sinister abstract prose. The claim he made of being a "Chubby Behemouth" proved to be only a half-truth. In the end, the only demon that gave Berkowitz orders was the pain that comes from being a lonely loser in a city of eight million people.

HARVEY THE DOG SPEAKS OUT

My name's Harvey, but you might know me better as the talking dog who told David Berkowitz to murder six people from July 29, 1976, to July 31, 1977. There are only a few talking dogs in the whole world, like Duke, the Bush's Baked Beans dog, the Chihuahua from Taco Bell, and of course that cop dog from TV's short-lived *Poochinski*. But none of them, except maybe the bean dog, were possessed by the devil.

I'm not one of those sweet, stupidly curious dogs you see in movies like *Up*. Life made me a stone-cold bitch. I got my start like most: a kid saw my cute puppy eyes in a shop window, begged her parents for me, and, like suckers, they took me home. But it wasn't long until my cuteness wore off and little Cindy's mom had enough of me humping her bridge club. What's up with that doggy in the window? He's got a urinary tract problem.

Just like that, I was on the streets—that's where David found me. It was fate, I suppose. He was a lonely psycho looking for a pal to putz around with. I was a sad, abandoned black Lab with an ear infection. I had hit rock bottom. If I could've had a quaalude addiction, I would've, you know what I'm saying? It was around that time that I made a deal with the devil for eternal life. In exchange he possessed my body and made me a demon creature. See, it's simple!

It all started the hot-as-balls summer of 1976. New York City in the summer is hog heaven for a dog. The streets smell like trash, people feed ya scraps from their brunch tables, and the human brain is ripe for manipulation on account of the madness caused by the oppressive heat.

People always tell me dogs are man's best friend, but think about it—would *you* make your best friend pick your shit up off the sidewalk? No. We're not man's best friend, we're manipulative bastards with one goal in my mind: murder. It was prime time to convince a young dude to commit heinous acts of meanness.

I'll never forget the day I met David Berkowitz. Being a black Lab, it usually takes people a few days to get comfortable around my hard exterior, but it didn't take long before Mr. Berkowitz was giving me belly rubs and as much spoiled 2 percent milk as I could lap up. Dave was an interesting guy. He kinda looked like if a meatball rolled on the floor of a barbershop and was then shaped into the form of a human. He mostly spent time listening to romantic melodies and lying on his mattress (which was on the floor, by the way—and they call *me* an animal!). This guy lived like a sewer rat, only he ate more cheese.

David was always a little depressed and I wanted to cheer him up. I promise, this all began because I thought he'd enjoy starting a couple of fires around the city. I mean, I'd also had a couple of feuds with some neighborhood joints for kicking me out. What's the big deal, I peed on some cereal boxes, who cares? Humans are so sensitive. Anyway, it worked. David loved starting fires. He would come home happier than a priest in a preschool.

I saw true potential in this loafy dump of a dude, but I knew in order to get to the next level, he'd need a cool nickname—something to give him the confidence he needed to kill. It was then that I thought of it: Son of Sam.

Now, despite the fact that I came up with a kick-ass handle for him, he still signed a bunch of letters to the police as "Mr. Monster." That's a horrible name! As if "Mr. Monster" wasn't corny enough, he also called himself "Beelzebub" and "Chubby Behemouth." (Note: that's the way he spelled it.) "Chubby Behemouth" sounds like a great name for a Tulsa jiggle joint but it's a horrible name for a serial killer.

Despite the fact David's voice sounded like a stressed-out mattress, it was only a matter of time before he raised his crime ante from arson to straight-up murder. In fact, I'm the one who told him to purchase the .44 Caliber Bulldog revolver, which he used in shootings from the Bronx to Queens and then to Brooklyn.

So I know what you're thinking: Why? Why would a friendly dog like me convince a fragile man like David Berkowitz to kill? The answer is simple: I WAS POSSESSED BY THE DEVIL! For crying out loud, I'm so sick of people blaming me for the murders. Have you ever been a demon spawn? It's not easy. In fact, it's downright difficult. Pissing fire, crapping fire, breathing fire . . . I was basically living like someone who competitively eats jalapeño poppers.

Once the media coverage began to intensify, I realized we were in deep. I figured I was safe on account that I'm a dog, but I was a little worried David would snitch, which he did. Thankfully, no one believed him. It still ruffles my fur just thinking about it: I was the one who gave him the confidence to be his best self, the puppy who pushed him to become an icon. Yet he still ratted me out like a canary in a courthouse. At least he didn't go into great detail about the activities of our Satanic death cult—let's just say that no one was wearing clothes under their robes.

So there you have it: Harvey the dog is very real. I am him, and although I did not actually commit any crimes, I definitely got that meatball rolling. David Berkowitz will go down in history as the man who terrorized New York City in 1977, but I'm the brains behind the operation, the top dog. It's about time I got a little credit for it.

CHAPTER 7

BTK

NOBODY LIKES DENNIS RADER. DON'T GET US WRONG, we're not saying that any reasonable person has an affection for men like Andrei Chikatilo or David Berkowitz. Everyone covered in this book is a monster, committing heinous acts that collectively destroyed hundreds of lives. But when it comes down to it, the killers outside of Rader covered herein all have something that can elicit even a *hint* of sympathy, whether it be the extreme mental illness suffered by Richard Chase and Ed Gein or the childhood abuse heaped upon John Wayne Gacy and Richard Ramirez.

Dennis Rader had none of that. Infuriatingly self-aware and driven by nothing more than psychopathic desire, Rader murdered ten people in Wichita, Kansas, between 1974 and 1991. His first foray into serial killing wiped out nearly an entire family, while a subsequent murder occurred as the victim's children were listening behind a locked bathroom door. Normally this would be the part of the introduction where we might provide some sort of trauma or psychological defect to explain this type of behavior, something that sets the general public apart from people like Dennis. Such evidence does not exist.

He's like if Tom Selleck had a three-way with a literal puddle of tapioca pudding and the hair of every bassist in a cock-rock band.

He was also head of IT for a church. He did computers for God, which to me is like being head caterer for Thor.

Rader was an ordinary creature of spite and sexual malice, a copy-and-paste serial killer fanboy whose imagination was fueled by inflicting misery and pain. But even though his crimes were the very definition of sadistic, his drug was not necessarily murder. Control was his game. The concept was such a turn-on for Dennis Rader that he could reach ejaculation simply by applying to himself the same bondage techniques he used on his victims, sometimes even taking self-portraits with a camera set on a timer.

Maybe if he had some sort of hobby all of this could have been avoided. Tom Hanks collects vintage typewriters!

To the public, Rader appeared to be a doting, loving parent who was among the most respected Boy Scout leaders in Wichita. But in reality, many a Boy Scout trip saw Rader sneaking off from camp for a private bondage photo session in the woods. Eventually those trips were used as a cover for murder, all of it carefully planned and controlled with maddening patience.

Seriously, it's embarrassing enough when your dad is the local weatherman, but this is like "sweater tucked into his jeans dad"—level embarrassing.

Rader is a classic example of a killer who used and manipulated his family as a front. His deception went so deep that his kids don't understand that even their births were a gigantic con. What a horrible asshole!

Rader's obsession with control even extended to the narrative of how his crimes were depicted in the press. He'd send horribly misspelled letters and poems to the Wichita media, demanding recognition for his many crimes, choosing his own moniker in the process: BTK. Bind, Torture, Kill. And perhaps that's part of why we hate Dennis Rader so much in comparison to the others we've covered in this book. We don't just hate Dennis because he's a monster; we hate him because he is a monster of his own creation.

DENNIS LYNN RADER WAS BORN IN PITTSBURGH, KANSAS, on March 9, 1945, to loving and supportive parents. The worst that could be said of his World War II veteran father, William, was that he could be a bit strict, while the most detrimental act committed by his mother, Dorothea, was that she once humiliated Dennis by making him return a toy he claimed not to have stolen but only borrowed from another child.

His mom was so confused. "I'm punishing him. Why is he erect?"

The most traumatic thing he had to contend with was having "Lynn" as a middle name, and that's not nearly as bad as being named "Adolf."

His mother does admit to dropping little Dennis on his head when he was a baby and heavily smoking throughout her pregnancy. These are two possible explanations that Dennis has put forward to explain his aberrant behavior, but if every child whose mother smoked while pregnant turned out to be a serial killer, America in the seventies would have been an even more hellish nightmare than it already was.

Even Rader's so-called "origin story," dating back to when he was only three years old, isn't all that bad or even special. Rader's version of the story has varied over the years, but the theme is essentially the same. In the initial version written in his old journals, he claims that he waddled into his mother's room to find her in bed, inexplicably sobbing and wrapped up in the sheets, unable to move. Dennis had no idea why she was in such a state, but he said that this moment made bondage a permanent part of his sexuality. It's possible there was more going on in the Rader household than we know—he'd alluded to his father's collection of ropes and cords in the family basement—but a different version of the story told more recently to author Katherine Ramsland is much more plausible. In this tale, Dorothea simply got her wedding ring caught in a couch spring and Rader witnessed his mother weeping in panic, her anxiety increasing with every second it was trapped. He said that as he watched her, he "had a strange feeling in the pit of [his] stomach and groin area."

He would have had a hell of a time if his family had competed on *Double Dare*.

Concerning his bloodlust, Rader had a story to justify that as well, but it's still a scenario that millions throughout history have experienced and come out of the other end murder-free. He said that he would sit and watch his grandmother on the back porch of her farmhouse as she twisted the heads off chickens meant for dinner, the sight of which gave Rader a thrill that brought blood, pain, and death into his sexual equation.

That same feeling would be brought forth when his mother would spank him. Rader said that when he was ten or eleven years old, his mother found a semen stain in his underwear. While she certainly was unwittingly raising a deviant, Dorothea went over the top in her admonishment of young Dennis, telling him that God would come and kill him if he masturbated. She then held his hands behind his back and whipped him with a belt. Rader was surprised to find himself aroused, later saying, "Sparky liked it." When his mother noticed that her young son had an erection, she stopped and said, "Oh my God, what have I done?"

This is another thing that makes me hate BTK with all my heart. He had a nickname for his penis by the time he was ten years old. You earn a nickname for your penis only in your twenties, as a means to help entertain you while you're in a dorm room all alone.

It's official, I'm never having children.

Rader's interest in bondage only grew over the years, particularly when he discovered the pleasures of binding. Dennis's fascination with strings and cords sent him on adventures down alleyways and through garbage cans on the hunt for scraps to add to his collection. The fantasies soon extended to voyeurism. As Rader approached adolescence, he began peeping on neighbors and cousins. The fantasy went even further with his fifth-grade teacher, who had humiliated young Dennis in class. As revenge, Rader began going to her house to watch her from her backyard, holding ropes he'd brought from home while fantasizing about tying her up. Soon, the peeping wasn't enough. His urge became so strong that he began tying himself up to approximate what it would be like to tie up others, and doing so gave him his "first male release."

My "first male release" was pretty terrifying, but I can't imagine STARTING with bondage. All I had to do was see Jenny McCarthy on the cover of *TV Guide*—this rope play seems like a lot of work.

Once Rader discovered his sexual buttons, he learned how to push them himself, sneaking out to empty fields to satisfy his curiosity. He would spend hours alone in the dirt, binding himself by tying knots around his wrists and ankles with his teeth. He would then lie there until the sheer pleasure of being tightly bound made him ejaculate. These solo ventures were coupled with masturbation trips to the barn with garments from his mother's underwear drawer.

At least he kept himself busy. That's how millionaires are born. Tommy Hilfiger. The ShamWow Guy. Oprah. Bruce Wayne. I'm saying words because I'm horrified.

This behavior suggests that Dennis Rader would have been a social pariah, a demented masturbation addict devoid of relationships. It is true that he was a solitary child for the most part, but this was by choice. Author Peter Vronsky, in a conversation with Katherine Ramsland in her BTK book, *Confession of a Serial Killer,* opined that childhood loneliness is a key factor in serial killer development. This is certainly backed up by everyone from John Wayne Gacy to David Berkowitz, but Rader's loneliness seems to have been self-imposed. He had no shortage of childhood chums by his own admission, but he also chose to engage in acts that he knew would horrify others, so solitude was a necessity. Those around Dennis Rader didn't see him as anything other than a normal boy. Every so often, though, Rader would give them a peek into his innermost desires.

I spent a lot of my time alone, but it helped me create characters until a child therapist had to tell me they were not real. But now I'm cool!

By the time Rader was in sixth grade, he'd already learned about the grotesque wonders of the nineteenth-century murder hotel owned and operated by the infamous H. H. Holmes. Holmes's nightmare world of suffocation rooms, trapdoors, and corpse chutes all designed to murder and neatly dispose of young women seemed like heaven to young Rader. Thinking that perhaps a friend would share in his fascination, he decided to sketch his version for another boy during a free period in school. He called it his "girl trap." In Rader's version, he took the murderous ingenuity of Holmes's original design and added Kansas flair, incorporating threshers and combines into the setup.

The only thing that could've made it more Kansas is if he added the largest ball of twine. That's located in Cawker City!

The boy who was unfortunate enough to share a desk with Dennis later told FBI profiler and author John Douglas that Rader sketched like a boy possessed. Yet when Rader recalled this memory, it was with fondness. He claimed that he and his friend Bobby would let their imaginations run wild, drawing their "castles of doom." Rader never let go of this fantasy-making, either. He would continue doodling vast complexes that he called BTK Lairs well into adulthood, including hot boxes to drown women in their own sweat and urine, and train tracks that Rader imagined tying his victims to as they screamed for help.

Always a creature of fantasy, Rader's adolescent imagination extended beyond Kansas. He would watch *The Mickey Mouse Club*

obsessively, paying particular attention to famed Mouseketeer Annette Funicello. As he watched her bright, expressive face entertain America, Rader could only think of kidnapping her and bringing her back to Kansas. He dreamed that she would become his slave girl, kept in a cage attached to his family's chicken coop. That fantasy became real in a sense when Rader began getting inside that cage on hot summer days, tying himself up, and pretending to be Funicello. He later said, "In many ways, AF started me on the female stalker road. I became the werewolf to chase her down on a full moon, the Dracula to bite her, my teeth sinking into the wonderful flesh of upcoming womanhood, or the Mummy wrapping her up tight defenseless at the mercy of me."

He never once got caught in these compromising positions. In fact, Dennis Rader never got caught doing anything because he always made sure to give the appearance of normalcy. Rader knew that the less attention he attracted, the more he could get away with.

This is why I only hung out with the troublemakers in school!

With fair regularity, Rader would catch stray cats using traps of his own design and take them, still alive, to one of the abandoned barns near his home. Once there, he'd bind them to a pole with rope, then wrap baling wire around the animal's throat. He'd twist the wire ever so slowly, bringing the animal to the brink of death before loosening the wire to let it catch its breath. Then he'd twist again, repeating the process over and over while whispering his darkest thoughts. Finally, as the creature was taking its last gasp, Rader would masturbate and ejaculate on the dying animal, then dispose of the body near a pond belonging to his grandparents.

Worst strip of *Garfield* I ever read. Jim Davis needs to retire.

Nobody taught any of this behavior to Dennis Rader. These actions were entirely of his own creation, experiments in cruelty that would one day be put into practice on actual human beings. However, that is not to say he didn't take inspiration from others. Nothing excited Dennis Rader quite as much as a juicy true crime story, and few inspired him more than the murder of the Clutter family in 1959. Rader was fourteen when the Clutters were tied up and killed in the middle of the night 225 miles away in Holcomb, Kansas. He was on a date when he heard the news of the murders over the radio. He said that hearing about the terror the family must have experienced made him so excited that he sat there and imagined binding and killing his date right there in the car.

The Clutter murders were only the beginning of Rader's obsession with serial killers, or, as he pathetically called them, Minotaurs. Over the years, he would study everyone from Albert DeSalvo to Ted Bundy, whom he affectionately called "Ted of the West Coast." But he wasn't like you or me, reading about these men out of a fascination with human nature; he wanted to be listed alongside them, believing that they all shared a trait that Rader referred to as Factor X. He's given a long, convoluted explanation of what exactly Factor X is, but just like all the other explanations these people give, it's just an excuse for bad behavior.

My hatred scale goes 1) BTK, 2) Donald Trump, 3) whoever shit on the seat at the rest stop in OKC when *LPOTL* was on tour there.

Rader's obsession with serial killers was only amplified by his discovery of detective magazines at the age of fourteen. Long since replaced by the internet and shows like ours, detective magazines were once one of the few places where a true crime junkie could get his or her fix. Rader's introduction into this world came when he discovered one in his father's car. A vicious kismet seemed to be at work that day, as the featured story fell right in line with Rader's violent bondage fantasies. Harvey Glatman, aka the Glamour Girl Slayer, spent the late fifties hiring young models under the presumption that they would be doing photo shoots for pulp fiction magazines. Instead, Glatman would tie them up and photograph the terrified girls before strangling them and dumping them in the desert. Rader took this magazine to the family's chicken house, where he read the article again while masturbating into a stolen pair of his mother's underwear. This publication would lie side by side with issues of *Sports Afield* and *Stag* along with other stolen items of clothing in what Rader called his hidey holes. He would have dozens of these holes over the decades, in locations ranging from his own home to his workplace to his own children's tree house. Eventually, Rader would also fill these with jewelry and driver's licenses, trophies from his murders.

Rich people call those safe-deposit boxes.

Glatman notwithstanding, the Clutter murders stayed with Rader more than any other he read about during his teenage years. The thought of breaking into a home, tying up an entire family, and killing them one by one was exhilarating, and he slowly started to envision how he himself could enact such a scenario. His first foray into B&E was decidedly less dramatic than the one immortalized by Truman Capote—he broke into his old high school through a skylight, walked around, and wrote some dirty words on a chalkboard—but it was the beginning of what he thought of as his cat-and-mouse game, risky behavior that taunted authority figures.

I'm just really happy Bart Simpson will never grow up.

That's a very scary thought, Kissel.

Dennis's first B&E may seem silly, but it demonstrates a patience that would prove invaluable in his later killing career. As we've discussed, serial killers evolve through a series of allowances. These tastes of the dark life may seem innocuous, even goofy at first, and oftentimes the killers aren't even conscious that they're making that slow march toward serial murder. Rader did, though. His allowances were training, pure and simple, and he came to call these escapades projects, or PJs for short.

I fucking hate him.

In 1966, almost a decade before he killed for the first time, Rader enacted what he called PJ Mountain #1.

Project Mountain #1 was also the name Stephen King would give to his first pile of cocaine for the day.

When he was not yet twenty years old, Rader traveled an hour and a half north to Salina, Kansas. Much like Richard Ramirez's first home invasion, Rader's was done while the house was empty. All Rader wanted was to inch himself into the world of concrete violation while picking up a fresh pair of panties along the way. On his way out the door, though, he decided to take it a step further. He grabbed a loose set of car keys, stole the car that was parked in the driveway, and drove it to the outskirts of town, where he masturbated into the seat before abandoning the vehicle.

Surprise! You got carjacked by the horny Pillsbury Dough Boy!

While Rader was entering the world of the serial killer, he was learning another skill that was essential to his overall plan: how to be human. He decided that

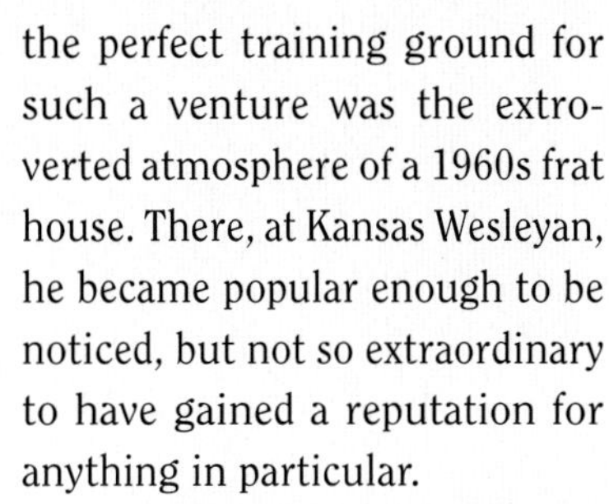

the perfect training ground for such a venture was the extroverted atmosphere of a 1960s frat house. There, at Kansas Wesleyan, he became popular enough to be noticed, but not so extraordinary to have gained a reputation for anything in particular.

Learning how to be human by attending a frat is like learning how to ride a horse by going to a Tijuana donkey show.

He also discovered an important social tool and cover: the church. Dennis Rader became a Lutheran while in college and, under a mask of piety and faith, quickly rose to the rank of deacon. The religion itself meant nothing to him; all it did was give him another avenue to fall deeper into the tapestry of "normal" American life. He was settling into the persona of a man who would be the last person you would suspect of a sadistic violent crime.

Rader added to that facade by volunteering for the air force at the height of the Vietnam War. This decision was also calculated. He figured that if there was a war going on, his best move would be to volunteer instead of waiting for a draft notice. As a result, Rader was stationed north of Tokyo as a mechanic, joining David Berkowitz, Leonard Lake, and Gary Ridgway among the ranks of serial killers who served during the Vietnam War but never saw combat.

My dad also volunteered for the Vietnam War but saw no combat. It was like McHale's Navy, a bunch of wet men in an undersea tube pulling pranks and getting drunk. My dad would have given the Vietnam War four stars on Yelp.

While in Japan, Rader's fantasies continued to poke their way into reality. Most of his alone time was filled by constructing what he called his "slick ads." Rader trawled magazines looking for photos of scantily clad women and then, when he found a model who was suitable, he'd cut out the image and sketch bindings around her body and a noose around her neck. He considered these artistic endeavors collectibles, his own brand of homemade pornography that was better than the real thing.

He reminds me of guys who refuse to let a mechanic change their oil. "I do it better and I can cum faster."

They sound more like sticky ads to me. #ClassicKissel #OnFire

#NewCokeKissel

Japan was also where Dennis Rader first began stalking women. On multiple occasions, he would escape over the fence from the air force base and take a bus into a populated area. Along for the ride was the prototype for what Rader called his "hit kit": a knife, a gun, rope, and gags.

Some purple drink, a bland cola, and SUNNY D!

Each time Rader took one of these trips, he would choose a young woman to follow home, knowing that he could kill her at any moment should he choose to do so. He wrote in his journals that he thought of this as a hobby, nothing more than a passing fancy that would end as soon as he got back to the States. Instead, it eventually led him to commit a quadruple murder.

But before it came to that, Dennis Rader got married. Soon after he returned from Japan in 1970, Dennis met Paula Dietz at church, and the two wed less than a year later. Like so many other serial killer wives, Paula fell prey to the actions of her psychopath husband and swore that she had no idea that her spouse of thirty-five years was the bogeyman of Wichita. There certainly were signs that Rader had a kink or two, but as far as their sex life went, Rader said it was normal. Paula did walk in on him during self-bondage sessions twice and threatened to leave him, but suburbia is lousy with such secrets. The closest she ever got to uncovering his true identity was when Dennis was reading the paper one morning after the publication of a BTK letter. Paula leaned over his shoulder, looked at the letter, and remarked that the killer misspelled a word in just the same way that Dennis usually did.

After which followed five minutes of pure silence.

Shortly after the two were married, Rader was hired at the Cessna Aircraft Company as an assembly line worker. All seemed to be going well: work was steady, the marriage was happy, his standing at Christ Lutheran Church brought him great respect in the community, and there had been no more "projects" since his return from Japan. That changed in 1973, after Dennis was laid off from Cessna. This sort of incident is depressingly common in the lives of serial killers. Stressful events blow the charges on whatever it is that's holding these people back from murder, and the fantasy becomes a focal point for their anger and frustration. For a creature such as Rader, who was already prone to a rich fantasy life, it was only a matter of time before these emotions bore bitter fruit.

It's a good thing BTK wasn't in the entertainment business, 'cuz it's nothing but rejection—though it is a perfect place for a sociopath to shine!

Paula was the breadwinner during those times, spending her days earning a paycheck as a bookkeeper at the local VA hospital. Feeling worthless, Rader found that reviving his PJs gave him purpose. It began with a simple B&E, once again while no one was home. This PJ made Rader feel like his heart was going to burst from his chest, and yet the action both relaxed him and made him feel alive—he now had a new hobby. His days at home were no more wholesome. The moment Paula was out the door, Rader would pull his stash of detective magazines from one of his hidey holes and masturbate while putting himself into the violent bondage scenarios he was reading about.

Accordingly, Rader decided to try his hand at writing one of these himself. Entitled "The Child Killer Who Dressed Like a Women," Rader's first creative foray was at the same time laughably bad and highly disturbing. Over the course of four single-spaced pages, Rader placed himself in the shoes of a killer out and about looking for a victim on Christmas Day while dressed as a woman, as the title suggests. The action begins when the killer picks up a couple of young girls looking for a ride, holds them at gunpoint, and takes them to a deserted farm on the edge of town. There, the protagonist takes them into a barn, chains them to a post, and gags them, then leaves them in the cold while he digs two shallow graves. He soon returns and quickly murders the first girl by hanging her, but the second is forced to perform fellatio on the titular child killer after the character gives instruction to "Suck badly on it real hard."

We passed it on to our publishers here at HMH and the response was "Fuck no, leave us alone."

At least he didn't have a bunch of kids having sex with each other, like in *It*.

The killer then garrotes his victim and follows it up by mailing the panties to her parents with a note saying, "MERRY CHRISTMAS TO YOU ALL . . . I hope this small present of goodwill will brighten your day up, for now you know that the girl in not in her pants, so where is she? Have a good day." The letter is signed DTPG: Death to Pretty Girls.

Is he in some sort of SCREAMO band?

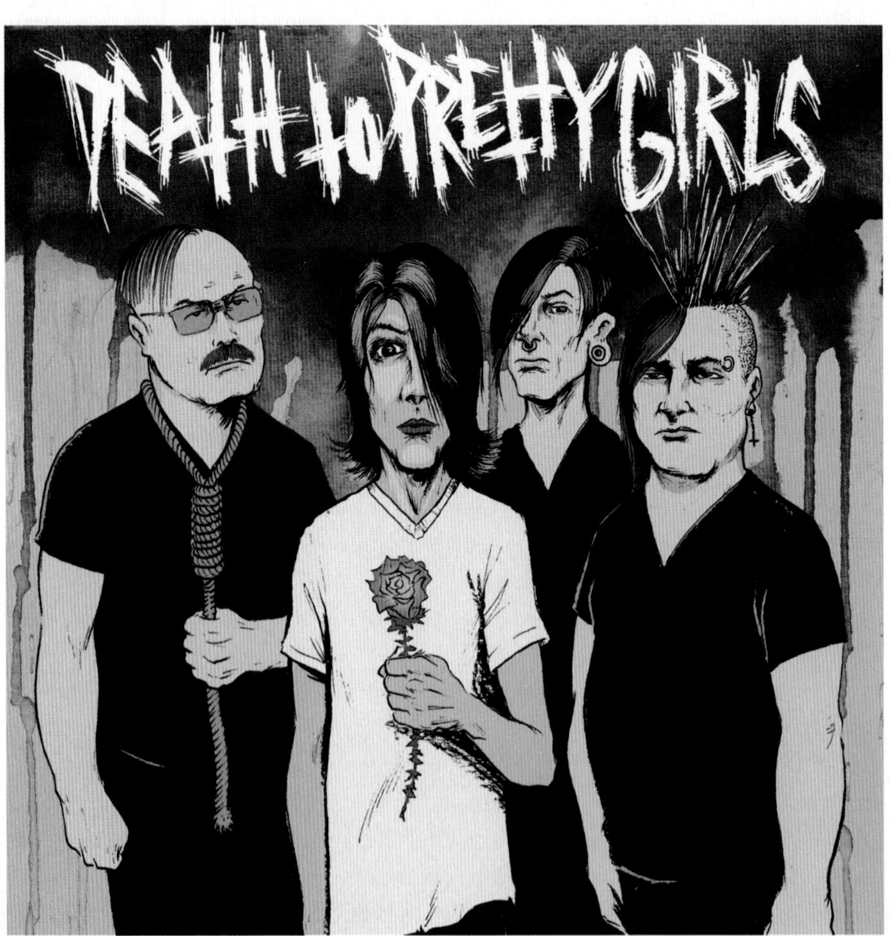

Now that Rader's fantasy life had begun gaining steam, it was only a matter of time before his stories became reality. After dropping off his wife at work each day, Rader would let his mind wander while sitting in the parking lot of the Twin Lakes Mall, watching girls enter and exit the shopping center. He became focused on a brunette who worked as a teller at the bank contained therein. Soon, a plan began to formulate in Rader's head based upon what he'd been reading in the detective mags. According to the magazines, women were kidnapped from parking lots with alarming regularity and a fair amount of ease. Rader became convinced he could do the same, and set off to do so one winter day in 1973. Unsuccessful attempts were rarely reported in Dennis's favorite crime rags, so he was wholly unprepared when his would-be victim fought back ferociously from the moment he tried laying hands on her. She screamed and let loose a fury Rader never thought possible. He ended the debacle by shoving her to the pavement before running away, utterly defeated.

Always fight hard, guys! Most of these pussies can't handle any sort of resilience. One of the best things my dad taught me is there is no cheating in a street fight, baby! . . . I have the soft hands of a professor.

I would pay a crapload of cash to watch BTK versus WWE superstar Ronda Rousey in a Hell in a Cell match! Make it happen, Vince!

Rader, however, had learned a lesson. If reality would not bend to his fantasy, then his fantasy would need to change. Snatch-and-grab wasn't his style—too difficult and risky to enact. If he truly wanted to actualize his homicidal fantasies, it would need to be done in the victims' homes, where Rader could control the situation from beginning to end. When that nightmare was finally realized, the people of Wichita were left with a horrific quadruple murder that haunted the cold cases for over thirty years.

In January 1974, Rader was cruising a Wichita neighborhood when he spotted a mother loading three children into a station wagon. Julie Otero had moved to Wichita with her husband and five children only months before. To this day, Rader has never been able to pinpoint exactly why he targeted the Otero family. The idea of using both a mother and daughter as playthings certainly played a part, but as it is with most serial murder victims, it was most likely that they just happened to catch the murderer's eye during a chaotic moment of decision.

I think the answer is "because he's a fucking monster," Marcus.

They caught his attention the same way that special slice does at your favorite pizza joint. Yep. Just like that. I'm trying to add some humor here!

With his victims officially chosen, Rader returned the next morning to observe the family's routines. He named this Project Little Mex. Day after day, week after week, Rader came to the Oteros' street, gathering intel. The discovery that Julie Otero was not a single mother was a disappointment, as Rader had no interest in tangling with a man. His only desire was for Julie and her eleven-year-old daughter, Josephine, so Rader began taking notes on the schedules of various family members, from nine-year-old Joe Jr. to patriarch Joseph Otero. Rader discovered that Joe Sr. left every morning at 8:00 a.m., the teenagers left soon after, and Julie would take the youngest children to school at 8:45. The fantasy, as Rader later said, was beginning to crystallize sharply.

On the morning of January 15, 1974, Julie and Joe were getting their two youngest children ready for school. At the same time, Rader was walking into the Oteros' backyard. Only one car was parked in the driveway, so Dennis assumed that Joe Sr. had gone to work early. When the appointed time came, Rader stalked his way to the back of the house dressed in a heavy air force parka and cut the phone line. Just as he was slicing the cord, the back door opened, and Rader was faced with nine-year-old Joey Otero. Rader pulled his Colt Woodsman .22 and a large knife from his jacket, pointed the weapons in the young boy's face, and directed him back inside. It had begun, but a hitch in Rader's plan presented itself almost immediately. Joe Sr. had wrecked his car a few days before—hence his car not being in the driveway—and he was standing there in the kitchen when Rader walked inside. Improvising, Rader told Joe that this was a stickup. Otero, seemingly unable to comprehend the situation, asked if this was some sort of prank orchestrated by his brother-in-law. Rader assured him that the situation was all too real.

Ugh, I can't even imagine how I would react if a mustachioed loser broke into my house, looking like the tour manager for the Village People.

Rader gathered the four members of the family who were home that morning and learned their names: Joe, Julie, Joey, and Josephine. Knowing that he was murdering people with names and stories of their own gave the experience the flavor of reality he'd been craving all these years. He even made small talk with Joe, telling stories about his time in the air force and discussing the merits of trade school. As far as the Otero family knew, this mysterious man only needed money and a car to get to California. He was on the run from the law, but if they cooperated, then everything would be just fine. Naturally, this was all part of Rader's plan. He was later quoted as saying, "You win if people think they are going to be okay."

The opposite of politics.

At this point, Rader had not yet decided to put down the whole family—his focus was still on Julie and Josephine. But in his haste to shoo young Joey back through the door, Rader had forgotten to pull the ski mask he'd brought over his face. He realized in that moment that the whole family would have to die, no matter what.

This is one of the reasons I watch the movie *The Ref* as a horror movie.

Rader tied up each family member in the master bedroom and, one by one, began to exact his murderous fantasies. The patriarch was taken first. Rader slipped a plastic bag over Joe Otero's head and held it tight as he gasped for air. Otero attempted to chew through the material in desperation, but he eventually succumbed. Julie was next. She was strangled as her two youngest children begged Rader to stop, but their pleading only made it more enjoyable to him. Believing he'd finished the job, Rader moved on to little Joey, but just as he was about to place a bag over the child's head, Julie woke up screaming. Rader returned to her and resumed strangling her until he was sure she would never wake again, then he carried Joey to his bedroom. There, Rader tied up the boy, laid him on his bed, and wrapped a T-shirt around his face before sliding a plastic bag over his head just as he'd done with Joe Sr. Suffocating, Joey struggled against the bindings and fell to the floor, trying to break free. Rader pulled up a chair and watched. After the young boy stopped moving, Rader returned to the master bedroom where his last victim, Josie, was waiting. She was taken to the basement, undressed, and hung from a pipe next to a half-junked dirt bike. There, Rader strangled the eleven-year-old girl and masturbated on her body.

With his fantasies finally satiated, Rader walked back up the stairs to the kitchen and performed what he called his "secret trademark." He took a glass, filled it with water, drank it, wiped it clean, and replaced it. It is certainly simple and seemingly stupid, but the mundanity of this signature move was just another way for Rader to bring his fantasy life into the real world. It made even the most basic of biological necessities into something sinister.

He should have been aborted.

After quenching his thirst, Rader left in Julie Otero's car, carrying a small radio and a few mementos from his first successful kills. He then drove to the grocery store, but by the time he got to the parking lot, he realized he'd left his knife at the Otero home. He returned to the scene of the crime and fetched the only piece of evidence that might have led police to his doorstep and continued on, still unnoticed. He then drove back to the grocery store parking lot, switched cars, and headed home. Once there, he went out to the woods with the notes and sketches he'd made in preparation for the murder and burned them all. He returned home just in time for his wife to walk through the door, suspecting nothing.

It's like if Ferris Bueller spent his day off massacring innocent people instead of going to a Cubs game, only to pop into bed just before his mom opened the door.

Oh yeah, this all makes me think of Matthew Broderick.

It was around this time that the Oteros' other children discovered their parents and younger siblings. Police were baffled by both the brutality and the brazen nature of the crime. Almost an entire family had been brutally wiped out in broad daylight, but nobody had heard a thing. It was long assumed that, due to the multiple strangle marks on Julie Otero's neck, the killer had taken her to the brink of death then let her return to consciousness as part of a torturous game, but Rader insists this wasn't the case. According to him, he just wasn't very good at strangling people yet. Once again, he learned his lesson and adapted. Following the Otero murders, Rader claims to have strengthened his grip with a rubber stress ball labeled "Life Is Good," often while wearing the watch he'd taken from Joe Otero's dead body.

BTK has more one-liners than Mitch Hedberg, and dare I say he also has a similar body.

For Rader, murder was something that demanded training and forethought, and he aimed to improve his methods. He took this notion even further when he began taking classes in justice administration at Wichita State University. He couldn't have given a damn about helping others; his only interest was in how to better prepare for future murders. To help contextualize his knowledge, he wrote extensively about his first experience in his personal journals, both to relive what he'd done and to analyze where he'd gone wrong.

He had the game tape. He did a lot of homework. Rader is different from other serial killers because of the sheer amount of the Malcolm Gladwell-approved hours he put into it. He would have been a very successful Nazi.

Rader detailed every step of the slaughter of the Otero family in his journals, from the original planning process to the disgusting climax, but he still wasn't done with his debasement of these poor souls. Rader continued to imagine his power over them even after their deaths, writing out elaborate scenarios wherein he imagined the Oteros as slaves to him in his eventual afterlife. Joe would be his bodyguard, Julie would bathe and serve him, Joey would be a servant and sex toy, and Josephine would be his "young maiden," an expert in sex and bondage who existed to please Rader. This was his AFLV: After Life Concept of Victim.

He sounds like he is trying to sell supplement powders on YouTube.

Once Rader completed this chronicle of events to his satisfaction, he began more PJs. Multiple women were followed and considered before Rader settled upon a pretty single blonde named Kathryn Bright, calling this PJ by the cringeworthy title of Project Lights Out. Kathryn had been spotted while Rader was out driving with his wife, and once again, he spent weeks preparing for the kill. The plan was to gain entrance by playing the part of a frustrated student looking for a quiet place to study.

Ah, he's a regular ol' Drew Barrymore in *Never Been Kissed*.

"Anyone here for the 9:00 a.m. How to Wash Your Car to Styx class?"

He even had props, carrying an armload of books to bolster his story. But when he knocked on Kathryn Bright's door on the day he'd planned to kill her, nobody was home. Improvising yet again, Rader walked to the back of the house and smashed the glass on the back door. Once he gained entrance, he cleaned up the shards, lest she see them upon her entrance. His new plan was to hide in the bedroom and then leap out, brandishing his .22, once she got home. But when he pulled out his gun to take off the safety as he lay in wait, he accidentally pulled the trigger and fired a bullet into the floor. The house now smelled of gunpowder but Rader decided to take the risk anyway, hiding for an hour before Kathryn finally walked through the door.

This almost reads like a spaghetti western starring Don Knotts, if you can ignore the fact that it's a tale of pure terror.

Much to Rader's chagrin, however, his carefully laid plot was once again spoiled by the presence of an unexpected male: Kathryn's brother Kevin. Determined to go through with the murder no matter what, Rader stepped out from his hiding spot, confronted them in the living room, and rattled off the same story he'd given to the Oteros. But since Rader hadn't expected more than one person, he'd hadn't brought rope. Instead, the Bright siblings were tied up with bandannas and nylons from Kathryn's wardrobe. Kevin was led to Kathy's bedroom, where his hands were bound and his feet were fastened tightly to the bedpost. Rader then led Kathryn to the other bedroom, where he tied her to a chair and bound her ankles with stockings.

Lulling Kathryn into a false sense that she would survive this ordeal, Rader began rifling through her belongings, demanding to know where she kept her money. It was almost time, but the brother would have to be dealt with first.

If there is a hell, it's Dennis being forced to rifle through my undies drawer for all eternity!

Rader now knew how noisy a strangling could be, so he turned up the radio to keep Kathryn in suspense. She was none the wiser as Rader wrapped a nylon stocking around her brother's neck and began to pull, but the garments binding Kevin's feet snapped and Kevin charged his assailant. It wasn't enough. Quickly, Rader drew his .22 and shot Kevin before going back to Kathy, who was hysterical by this point. Rader tried calming her down by telling her that her brother was still alive, only wounded. As it turned out, this was the truth. When Rader went back to check on him, he discovered that Kevin had broken the tethers on his wrists as well. The young hero leapt off the ground and managed to wrest control of the gun from

Rader for a moment, but Rader managed to fire another shot, this time directly into Kevin's face.

Covered in sweat, Rader decided it was time to finish this project. He attempted to strangle Kathryn with a piece of cloth, but she had broken free from her bindings as well. Rader punched her in the face to try to regain control, but still she fought. That's when he produced his knife and chased her around the room, stabbing her again and again, until she finally collapsed. Then came a noise: even after a shot to the face, Kevin still had not died. The bullet had ricocheted off his teeth, and after he'd recovered from the shock of getting shot in the mouth, he'd run outside, yelling for help. Rader quickly escaped out the back door with some of Kathryn's clothes, having both failed and succeeded. When it came to realizing his fantasy, it was a disaster, but murder-wise, he was unfortunately successful. Police arrived minutes later to find Kathy lying in a pool of her own blood. Her larynx had been broken, so she was able to speak only two words before passing out: help me. She died four hours later.

This is when BTK became a full-blown monster, and with it, he got the confidence he needed to push his killing spree further and further. Can you imagine how many people he would have murdered if he'd had Eminem's "Lose Yourself"?

Poor woman, she deserved better than to die at the hands of this fat gym teacher-looking asshole.

Adrenaline racing, Rader drove to his parents' house, where he stashed his weapons in an old wooden box and hid his blood-soaked clothing and shoes inside their chicken coop along with what he'd taken from Kathryn's home. After securing his souvenirs, Rader went home to greet his wife upon her arrival from a long day at the VA hospital.

This is where you can win an argument if you play video games all day while your partner is at work. Just be like: "At least I am not hiding my murder souvenirs at my mommy's house!"

This is why it's so important to ask your partner, "How was your day, get into anything felonious?" every night!

Investigators on the scene of the Bright murder were hesitant to connect this near–double murder to the quadruple murder they had encountered only months before. In retrospect, their reasoning sounds naive at best. Even though both crimes were home invasions that involved the binding of multiple people, investigators hesitated because the tethers used were of a different variety and because the phone line hadn't been cut at the Bright residence. Somehow, it was more comforting to think that these two events were not connected in any way whatsoever.

Of course! No one wants to be dealing with Michael Myers! Either the actor *or* the murderer.

Being a cop is super easy when you don't acknowledge you have a serial killer on your hands.

In contrast to the Otero murders, however, the Bright scene produced a living witness. After he recovered from his injuries, Kevin Bright told police that the perpetrator was an average white man with a mustache. The only distinctive characteristic that Kevin could give was that the monster who had terrorized him and his sister had been pouring sweat for the duration of the crime. A sketch was circulated that Rader felt was uncomfortably close to his likeness, but not a single person suspected churchgoing good citizen Dennis Rader of the crime. It seemed as if Kathryn Bright's murder would join the Otero massacre as another brutal unsolved crime in Wichita. It wasn't until a sex offender—who had once been arrested for publicly having sex with a duck—was picked up for molesting a child at the library did cops get anything close to a break in either of these cases.

During his molestation interrogation, admitted duck-rapist Gary Sebring had begun giving hints that he and his brother Ernest may have been involved with the Otero murders. It was fairly obvious to police that Gary had nothing to do with the Otero case, but since that case was the biggest story of the year, media outlets erroneously reported that two plausible suspects were in custody.

He would rather be BTK than a famous duck fucker.

Wait, these cops had a serial killer *and* a duck fucker on their hands? Is there pure ethanol in the water supply of Wichita or something? How does this happen?

Upon hearing that someone else was taking credit for a crime he so expertly committed, Rader was indignant. He decided it was time for his alter ego to come out of hiding. Calling a tip line for the Otero murders at the *Wichita Eagle*, Rader spoke in a comically gruff voice and said that the man who killed the family had left a letter inside a textbook called *Applied Engineering Mechanics* on the second floor of the Wichita Public Library. Rader later claimed that he did this because he "wanted taxpayers not to spend endless dollars on false leads," but his true motivation was to show the city of Wichita his misplaced belief that he was an intelligent, sophisticated killer on the level of Jack the Ripper. It was the first communication in an idiotic cat-and-mouse game that would last for thirty years.

"I'm the only one in this town who fucks ducks!"

I guess BTK took that whole "fiscally conservative, socially liberal" cliché to the next level.

Detective Bernard Drowatzky of the Wichita Police Department was the first to reach the library. He walked to the second floor, opened the pages of the engineering textbook, and found a white envelope labeled with three words: Bill Thomas Killman. Inside was a misspelled, badly written, threatening screed outlining the Otero murders. It read, in part:

> I can't stop it so, the monster goes on, and hurt me as wall as society. Society can be thankfull that there are ways for people like me to relieve myself at time by day dreams of some victim being tortore and being mine. It a big complicated game my friend of the monster play putting victims number down, follow them, checking up on them waiting in the dark, waiting, waiting . . . the pressure is great and somt-times he run the game to his liking. Maybe you can stop him. I can't.
>
> He has already chosen his next victim or victims. I don't know who they are yet. The next day after I read the paper, I will Know, but it to late. Good luck hunting.
>
> YOURS, TRULY GUILTILY
>
> P.S. Since sex criminals do not change their MO or by nature cannot do so, I will not change mine. The code words for me will be . . . bind them, torture them, kill them, B.T.K., you see he at it again. They will be on the next victim.

Other sections of the letter detailed facts about the Otero case that were not known to the public, an intentional tip so police would know that it could only have been written by the killer. But with no way to trace the letter, the best response they could muster was to print a personal ad in the *Wichita Eagle* that said, "BTK Help is available." Paired with the ad was a phone number and a polite request that any calls made should be done before 10:00 p.m. Rader never called, as he had no interest in getting help, nor did the police help the public by letting them know that there was an honest-to-God serial killer operating within their city. Nevertheless, the Otero and Kathryn Bright murders were still big news. The highly publicized killings meant big business for local security companies, and who should get a job installing for one of the biggest in town other than Dennis Rader.

Serial killer legend has it that Rader used his position at ADT Security to locate victims or futz with systems he'd installed, but he was far too careful to directly mix business with pleasure. While he did stalk some women who used his services, no ADT customers became BTK victims. Many, however, did become projects in the intervening years between his fifth and sixth murders.

It has long been assumed that Rader paused his murder spree for three years due to the birth of his first child, Brian. In truth, fatherhood did nothing to mellow his desires. During the thirty years that Rader operated, he rarely stopped stalking potential victims. Interviews with Katherine Ramsland revealed that there was always an active project during the three-year interval between Kathryn Bright and his next victim. On March 17, 1977, Rader felt ready to unleash BTK once again.

Cut to BTK holding his limp dick in his hand, desperately shaking it so he could become even moderately hard.

In the weeks leading up to the murder, Dennis had initiated multiple projects to give himself options when the time came. On the day of decision, Rader settled on Project Blackout, so named because the potential victim, Cheryl Gilmour, was a regular at a local college bar with the same title. That morning, he dressed as a stereotypical police detective and loaded his "hit kit" with everything he needed: electrical tape, cord, a gun, plastic bags, and a photograph of a little boy. Preying on good intentions, the photo, combined with the detective's outfit and a story about a missing child, was going to be Rader's passkey.

I walked around with this same exact "hit kit" as a sketch comedian for fifteen years.

At the last second, however, Rader changed his mind and abandoned all of the work he'd done in scouting his next kill. Instead, he chose a neighbor who lived only two doors down from Cheryl Gilmour. Shirley Vian was home sick with the flu that day with her three children, Steven, Bud, and Stephanie. Steven had been sent next door to borrow a can of chicken soup from the neighbors when Rader stopped him, showed the photo, and asked if he'd seen the "missing boy." Steven said he hadn't and went home to his mother. Moments later, Rader knocked on Shirley's front door and gave the same story, but when he was invited inside to elaborate, he pulled a gun and told Shirley that he "had a problem with sexual fantasies." It was now her job, he said, to help him with that. All she had to do was cooperate while he tied her up and took pictures. Nobody would get hurt.

As I read this, the only thing giving me solace is the idea of Dennis in the corner of his jail cell scared shitless of his new celly who demands respect.

He then forced the three children into the bathroom, kept company by a few stray toys Rader tossed inside to keep them quiet. The children screamed for their mother as Rader took her to the bedroom and bound her forearms and calves with black electrical tape. To ensure no movement whatsoever, Rader further restrained her with cords around her wrists and ankles. Finally, he tied her feet to the metal head rail and, using the leftover rope, wrapped the cord around her neck. Terrified, she vomited. In a cruel moment of supposed kindness, Rader went to the kitchen and fetched a glass of water. The sympathy ended there, as he then ended Shirley Vian's life by placing a plastic bag over her head and strangling her with a rope. Rader then turned his attention to the children, still trapped in the bathroom and waiting for their mother to return. He'd decided the Otero massacre needed repeating. But just as he was about to open the door, the phone rang. Rader suddenly realized that he hadn't done his homework here at all—someone could walk through the door at any second. So instead of taking the little girl down to the basement as he'd planned, he stole two pairs of Shirley's underwear to add to his growing collection of trophies and strolled out the front door.

This cocktail shrimp-dicked piece of human trash makes Charlie Sheen seem like a reasonable dude.

Later, Rader used Shirley's clothing along with garments taken from other victims in a way that makes him unique in the annals of serial killer history. Whereas some killers take trophies to hold and caress in order to relive their crimes, Rader would wear the clothing of his victims and bind his arms and legs just as he did during his victim's murder, using himself as a stand-in.

As Rader cavorted in his own home draped in evidence, Wichita police were desperately trying to convince themselves that BTK had not returned. The existence of a serial killer in Wichita had not only been kept from the public but was being denied internally as well. Despite the evidence, nobody wanted to admit that such a thing was possible in their relatively small city, telling one another that these sorts of things only happened in places like Los Angeles or New York. It was only after the murder of twenty-five-year-old Nancy Fox in December 1977 that some detectives began to suspect they might have wasted years of potential investigative effort on wishful thinking.

Unlike the others, Nancy's murder went exactly as planned. Rader broke a window while Nancy was out, crawled through, and waited until she returned. Once she arrived, he restrained her by tying her up on her bed and told her, "I'm BTK. I'm a bad guy."

"I'm BTK. I'm a bitch."

Man, just cut to Razor Ramon being like "I'm the bad guy, pal" and then giving Dennis the Razor's Edge!

Nancy Fox met her end by strangulation with her own belt. After the murder, Rader searched her belongings for souvenirs and came away with jewelry, lingerie, and her driver's license. All were stored in one of his many hidey holes and used in later reenactments. Later, when commenting about using the lingerie of his victims in this manner, Rader said, "Leave it to a weird guy like me to do that."

Since Nancy lived alone, Rader knew that it might be days before anyone found the body. He couldn't wait that long to see his handiwork plastered across the front page of every newspaper in town, though, so using a pay phone the morning after the murder, he called police to report the homicide himself.

"Yes, 911, I'd like to report that a mustache-covered turd has just done something extremely shitty."

Detectives were now starting to see a pattern among the murders. Rader had cut Nancy Fox's phone line and had masturbated into her blue nightgown after the murder, which seemed to be directly in line with the Otero massacre. And yet, even with these similarities, many police were still not convinced that a serial killer was operating in Wichita, so the information was once again kept from the public.

It's a huge deal to open a serial killer investigation. You have to work across departments, and no one likes to do that. Trying to build the case for a court hearing is very difficult. Sadly, serial murder is a very hard crime to punish someone for.

Seriously, people still weren't convinced it was a serial killer? They're in more denial than my mother was when she tried to convince herself I wasn't smoking a bunch of weed throughout high school.

Inspired by his seeming invincibility, Rader decided to reach out to the press. He spent weeks writing a seven-line poem about the murder of Shirley Vian, still managing to misspell two words in the finished product before he sent it off for publication. His wife found an earlier draft, but he waved it off by saying he was working on a project about the BTK case for one of his classes at Wichita State. The final draft was submitted to the *Wichita Eagle* on February 1, printed on an index card with a child's rubber stamp set. This is what Rader sent for publication:

SHIRLEY LOCKS! SHIRLEY LOCKS
WILT THOU BE MINE?
THOU SHALT NOT SCREEM
NOR YET FEE THE LINE
BUT LAY ON THE CUSHION
AND THINK OF ME AND DEATH
AND HOW ITS GOING TO BE.
B.T.K.
POEM FOR FOX NEXT

He inspired me to write my own poem:

DENNIS RADER! DENNIS RADER?
ME THINKS THOU ART A DORK
HOW IS THE SALZBURRY STAKE
THAT YOU ARE EATING IN JAIL
YOU BALD DROOPY-NOSED FUCK
THANK U NEXT
POEM FOR SON OF SAM

To Rader's great annoyance, the poem was not published. Since the letter was received in February, the employees in the mail room assumed that it was a bizarre, misguided Valentine bound for the classifieds. Because no payment was included, the index card was unceremoniously tossed in the dead letter pile.

Undeterred, Rader sent another package to KAKE-TV instead because, as he later said, he had grown up watching Westerns on the Saturday morning program *KAKEland* and was sexually attracted to KAKE news anchor Susan Peters.

In this package, Rader made it plain and clear that they were receiving a communication from someone who should be taken seriously. Included were a pencil drawing of a woman bound and gagged, a two-page note complaining that the sender hadn't gained the notoriety of other serial killers, and a rip-off of the old folk song "O Death" called "OH! DEATH TO NANCY":

```
What is this taht I can see,
Cold icy hands taking hold of me,
for Death has come, you all can see.
Hell has open it,s gate to trick me.
Oh! Death, Oh! Death, can't you spare me, over for another
year!
I'll stuff your jaws till you can't talk
I'll blind your leg's till you can't walk
I'll tie your hands till you can't make a stand.
And finally I'll close your eyes so you can't see
I'll bring sexual death unto you for me.
```

He is a bargain-store Scott Weiland who was a bargain-store Eddie Vedder who is a bargain-store Kurt Cobain.

Attached to the end of the letter was another pathetic plea for notoriety:

```
How about some name for me, it's time: 7 down and many more
to go. I Like the following. How about you?

"THE B.T.K. STRANGLER," "WICHITA STRANGLER," "POETIC
STRANGLER," "THE BON DAGE STRANGLER" . . .
```

As ridiculous as the letter was, it was now undeniable that a serial killer stalked the streets of Wichita. It was February 1978, four years and one month after the Otero murders, when police finally unveiled the twisted world of BTK to the general public. Naturally, a task force was needed to both catch the killer and assuage the fears of the general public. Luckily, the Wichita Police already had a crack squad of detectives that had gained notoriety in the press. Colloquially, these men were known as the Hot Dog Squad. They were the best men Wichita had, and they were woefully out of their depth when it came to solving the BTK murders.

Meanwhile, Rader now had projects in half a dozen cities around Kansas, but he was getting reckless at home. Anytime his wife and child were out of the house, he would dress in either one of his victims' clothing or clothing he had stolen from other projects and watch his neighbors—or himself in the mirror—while performing autoerotic asphyxiation. Wearing grotesque masks of his own making, Rader even rigged a camera with a remote so he could take pictures of himself tied to chairs or standing, bound head to toe with nylon.

He could have just done this and not have been a serial killer. It's legal to have fetishes!

It wasn't too long before Rader's carefully hidden persona almost destroyed his life. One day, Paula came home unexpectedly as he was in the middle of what he called a "big bondage." She came close to leaving him, but he was able to convince her that he would never do anything like that in the house ever again. Life resumed as normal, and in 1978, the Raders welcomed their second child, Kerri, into their home. Rader's facade as a dedicated family man was only strengthened.

Oh yeah, keep having kids with him. That'll fix it. Always add more children.

Just reminder to everyone out there, friends are the family that you choose!

After the birth of his daughter, the BTK Strangler disappeared from the public eye for six years, but once again, Rader did not spend the intervening time just mowing the lawn and going to church. After Paula caught him in the throes of fantasy, he decided that the only safe place to practice his fetish would be at what he called his "motel parties." While out of town on trips for ADT, in lonely rented rooms around Kansas, he would use Nancy Fox's slip or Shirley Vian's underpants to satisfy himself. During stretches when he wasn't traveling for work, Rader would do his big bondage sessions in a shed attached to his home that he built specifically for this purpose.

If for whatever reason the shed wasn't safe when the urge struck, Rader would retreat to the back roads of Kansas for photo shoots in secluded areas, often wearing an expressionless harlequin mask to hide his face. But this, too, came with risks. During one such day trip, Rader suffered a sunburn that left obvious tan lines in the shape of the bra he'd worn during the shoot. But even if Paula had noticed them, it's doubtful she would have pressed the issue. Rader had turned into quite the family man since his daughter's birth, even becoming a Boy Scout leader when his son was old enough to join.

We have a lot of weird alone nights in hotel rooms, but normally that's when I eat strange meats and play video games. Those are *my* fantasies!

But in 1985, Rader decided to let Factor X loose upon the world once again. As a true crime fanboy, Rader knew the conventional wisdom about serial killers that said they were mostly loners who rarely, if ever, killed anyone they knew personally. He decided to buck that convention with Project Cookie.

Project Cookie is what I called sneaking into the kitchen at midnight when I was six years old.

Not unlike Project Cookie Puss, which Carvel had to cover up.

Project Cookie was Rader's name for the murder of his neighbor, Marine Hedge, who lived just six doors down in the Wichita suburb of Park City. Rader did not know her well—just enough to say hello—but he was intoxicated by the thought of exacting this plan.

Since this murder was close to home, it needed an airtight alibi. Rader chose a camping trip with his son's Boy Scout troop as cover.

As the first night around the campfire ended, Rader complained of a headache and slipped away from the other dads who were helping chaperone. He snuck back to his car, changed out of his Scout uniform, and drove to a bowling alley. There, he sloshed a little beer in his mouth and splashed some on his face as a part of his increasingly complicated ruse. After establishing himself as "intoxicated," Rader called a cab and took a ride back to Park City, asking the driver to let him out before they'd reached his destination so he could "sober up a bit" before arriving home. He then snuck over to Marine Hedge's house, cut the phone line, and broke in through the back door with a screwdriver.

Silently making his way to a closet, Rader waited for Marine to return home. But when she finally did, Rader once again had a wrench thrown into his plan, as Marine had a gentleman caller in tow. Remembering how much trouble a man could be, Rader remained in the closet and waited for him to leave. An hour later, the man left and Marine crawled into bed, only to be awoken by Rader crawling in with her. She screamed but he quickly silenced her, strangling her to death with his own bare hands.

After killing Marine, Rader followed through with his MO of tying up her arms and legs. With her body bound the way he liked it, he wrapped it in blankets and carried it to the trunk of Marine's own car. Rader then drove to the church where he'd served as a deacon for years and brought the body inside for a photo shoot. He'd planned ahead: black sheets had been stashed in advance for the express purpose of covering the windows to hide the camera's flash.

"Hey, Deacon Dennis, what are those tarps for?" "I'm gonna bring a dead body in here and take pictures of it!" "Ha! Deacon Dennis should be on *SNL*!"

Jesus Christ, he's like an even worse Terry Richardson.

Once the area was prepared, Rader laid Marine's dead body on the church's brown shag carpeting and took numerous shots with a stolen Polaroid. He carried it from room to room, positioning the limbs differently each time. The only place left sacred was the altar, as Rader said he "still had respect for some items in God's house."

Fuck you, Dennis Rader.

Following the macabre photo shoot, Rader loaded Marine's body back into the trunk of her car, drove it to a known dumping ground, and tossed it in a ditch. With his fantasy realized, he went back to the church, cleaned up, and returned to the Boy Scout campsite. Not a single person had noticed he'd left.

Rader's next murder would take place a year later. Project Piano was a twenty-eight-year-old single mother named Vicki Wegerle. Posing as a telephone repairman, Rader talked his way into Vicki's home on his lunch break one day. After pretending to inspect her phone, he pulled a gun. Vicki fought back, deeply scratching Rader's face in the process, but in the end, he strangled her with her own nylon stocking, then made sure to take a few Polaroids of the body posed in different positions before leaving. Since he didn't contact the police or the press about either Wegerle or Marine Hedge, neither was linked to BTK until years later. As far as the Wichita PD were concerned, if BTK didn't claim a murder, there was no reason to resurrect the nightmare.

Dennis should've gotten a job with the CIA naming operations for the Iran-Contra affair.

In 1989, two years after the murder of Vicki Wegerle, Rader lost his job at ADT and replaced it with a position as a field operations supervisor for the U.S. Census Bureau. Now armed with a legal excuse to knock on doors without invitation, he stalked more women and entered more homes than ever before. He estimated that in the period between the murders of his last two victims, he embarked on over thirty projects. None of these women were killed or attacked, but in each case, Rader stole items of clothing for motel parties he had while traveling for the Census. When that job ended, he celebrated by throwing a solo "office party" at the local Census headquarters, wrapping himself in a large plastic sheet while taking pictures.

So his version of "hooking up at the company Christmas party" would just be masturbating alone in the bathroom?

But as the nineties began, there was still a niggling need curled up in the back of Rader's brain. The previous decade had been a heyday for serial killers, with everyone from Richard Ramirez to Ted Bundy achieving celebrity status. Even unknown murderers such as the Green River Killer commanded headlines across the country.

Nobody, though, was talking about the BTK Strangler. He was unheard of outside of his native Wichita, and even then, people seemed to have forgotten about the bogeyman of the seventies. If BTK was going to be mentioned in the same breath as fabled killers like Jack the Ripper, he'd need to stage an encore performance.

The encore performance nobody wants! Kinda like when the Knack play "My Sharona" in concert for the fifth time.

In 1991, four years after the Vicki Wegerle murder, forty-six-year-old Rader chose sixty-two-year-old Dolores Davis as his next victim. Again, so he could use a Scouts trip as cover, he happily volunteered to chaperone the annual Dead of Winter campout. This second Boy Scout murder, however, was not as elaborate as the first. He simply snuck away, drove to his church, parked, and walked to Dolores Davis's backyard. Abandoning any sense of stealth, Rader hurled a cinder block through her sliding glass door and ambled inside. After locating and tying up his victim, he went to the kitchen and opened a few cereal boxes in what he thought was a clever commentary on his choice of hobby. He then returned to Dolores and strangled her with pantyhose as she begged for her life.

The craziest thing is, BTK's daughter still hopes her dad has a chance of going to heaven, because I guess God needs a human toilet for his bathroom.

Again, Rader left the house with the body, but instead of returning to the location of his first off-site photo shoot, he drove to a lake near the highway. He'd planned to pose the body and take more pictures, but daylight was coming, and if he wasn't there to greet the campers, his alibi would be shot. So he left the body at the lake and went back to the church, where he stashed some of Dolores' possessions in a hidey hole in the church's utility shed. Then he returned to the body, picked it up, and dumped the body under a bridge.

Nothing good happens under a bridge, other than the occasional inspiration for a great song about kicking heroin.

But the notion of a photo shoot with Dolores Davis wouldn't leave Dennis's head, so a few days later, even as the police were engaged in a concerted search for the missing senior citizen, Rader returned to Davis's resting place, bringing along one of the masks he'd used time and again in his personal bondage photos. He'd painted it with eyebrows and red lips, giving it just the slightest sheen of humanity, and laid it on the dead woman's face. He took a few pictures and then left the body there for the police to find. While detectives were arguing with one another over whether this murder belonged to BTK, Rader was using Davis's clothing for solo bondage parties. He'd return to these clothes many times over the years, often fondling them in his parents' basement when they were out of town, pairing the garments with a wig he'd stolen from a Boy Scout museum.

I don't know which is scarier, what BTK does in his parents' basement or the Boy Scout museum.

If you wanna be on the front lines of fighting pedophiles, just stake out the Boy Scout museum and you'll clean up!

Following this murder, Rader claims that the desire to kill went away, and for a time, it seemingly did. In 1994, he found a new outlet for his urge to control the lives of others. That year, Park City hired Dennis Rader as a compliance officer, a job that required him to catch stray dogs, enforce zoning rules, and write tickets for city ordinance violations. Rader took this as an opportunity to become a sanctioned bully, doling out citations to single mothers too busy to mow their lawns, or men who couldn't afford mechanics so they worked on their cars on their front lawns. He'd measure grass with a ruler and issue infractions if it was even a fraction of an inch too tall, and on multiple occasions, he put down dogs that were merely off-leash, not causing anyone trouble. One woman, Misty King, even moved away after a three-year campaign of harassment that culminated in the death of her beloved dog. This petty work satisfied Rader for only a short while—the urge to kill rose again at the turn of the century, when he began initiating new projects on the road between Park City and the dog shelter outside of town.

Seriously, he needs to be drowned in a tub of mayonnaise, because he's truly the worst kinda white guy!

Then, in 2001, Rader got spooked. The increasingly sophisticated science surrounding DNA was solving dozens of cold cases across America. When the long-sought Green River Killer was caught, Rader was afraid he would be next. After all, he'd left semen at two of his crime scenes, and Vicki Wegerle had taken a chunk out of his face as he was strangling her. Rader wanted to be known, but not punished. He had imagined dying as a free man, and only then would the world know that family man and Lutheran deacon Dennis Rader had been the BTK Strangler all along. So, rather than risk jail, in the spring of 2004, Rader threw one last motel party in Dodge City, Kansas, and began to pare his collection of souvenirs down to the basics; namely, the keepsakes from the ten times his most horrible fantasies had been realized.

He could've hosted a show on HGTV called *Downsizing: Serial Killer Edition*.

It seemed as if the BTK Strangler would indeed go quietly into the annals of true crime, a minor footnote in the world of unsolved serial murder. And had it not been for a Wichita lawyer named Robert Beattie, he might have. In early 2003, on the anniversary of the Otero murders, Beattie gave an interview about BTK to the *Wichita Eagle*. Beattie believed the people of Wichita had forgotten about the

BTK Strangler, so he was writing a book on the killings and the investigators who had spent decades working to break the case.

I don't understand how the people of Wichita forgot about ten murders! The only other noteworthy things happening there are a steampunk festival and the painting of a mural so big that it's listed in the Guinness World Records. You'd figure this would rank up there.

Rader was incensed. The mere suggestion that BTK had been forgotten was an insult to everything he had worked toward for the previous thirty years. If people didn't remember BTK, Dennis was going to remind them. Hoping to reenter the scene with a bang, Rader rummaged through one of his hidey holes and pulled out Vicki Wegerle's driver's license and the three post-murder Polaroids. The Wegerle murder had not been connected to the BTK Strangler in any way whatsoever, so the revelation that he was responsible would likely elicit the fear and reverence that Rader felt he deserved. Instead, the decision to make contact after years of silence would be the first wrap on the noose that Rader was tying for himself.

WHAT A FUCKING IDIOT.

The "noose" analogy sounds like something BTK would literally cum to, thinking about it.

In March 2004, Rader sent these items along with a letter to the *Wichita Eagle* in an envelope postmarked with the return name of Bill Thomas Killman and a symbol comprised of the letters *BTK*. Fortunately, the person opening the mail that day recognized his style and instead of throwing it in the crank pile again, contacted the police. This time, Wichita PD spoke directly to BTK through the media. Correctly deducing that this was all about ego, they held large press conferences in which BTK was the only focus to encourage him to keep sending information. They wanted to form a sort of relationship with the killer, so they chose seasoned homicide detective Ken Landwehr as the conduit.

RIGHT INTO THEIR HANDS, YOU MORON. What am I saying? I love a press conference.

Dennis Rader is so dumb, he snitched on himself!!

Landwehr had worked on the original 1984 BTK task force, known colloquially as the Ghostbusters, but had been reassigned three years later when there were no further breaks in the case. In the seventeen years since, a day hadn't gone by when Landwehr didn't think about BTK. In fact, the BTK case had haunted the entire department for decades. One Ghostbuster had even died a few years earlier with a BTK case file open on the nightstand beside his body. The brass may have biffed the bigger decisions, but the rank and file had never stopped searching. And now one of those men had the best shot anyone had ever had at solving the case.

Landwehr must've consumed more whiskey than Ernest Hemingway.

Over the next eleven months, Rader communicated with Landwehr through multiple channels, ranging from badly done Zodiac-style word puzzles he sent to KAKE-TV, to packages taped to street signs around town filled with letters recounting his crimes and graphic drawings with titles like "The Sexual Thrill Is My Bill." He even returned to his original method of leaving messages at the library while taking credit for crimes he didn't commit, all leading up to a threat to strike again:

> I have spotted a female that I think lives alone and/or is a spotted latch key kid. Just got to work out the details. I'm much older (not feeble) now and have to conditions myself carefully. Also my thinking process is not as sharp as it uses to be. Details-Details-Details!!! I think fall or winter would be just about right for the HIT. Got to do it this year or next! Number X, as time is running out for me.

This just shows that no matter what age you are, you can always get back in the game. I wish I hadn't used this moment to teach.

Rader was finally getting what he wanted. Each communication only increased his standing, both in his own mind and in the minds of the general public. The victory was made all the sweeter when he received both a commendation for ten years of service as a compliance officer and the vice presidency at Christ Lutheran Church.

"To Dennis Rader, here is an award for ten years of service. Please don't jizz on this or use it like an S&M ball gag like the last recipient, Pastor Richard 'Lover Boy' Tickles. Ten years of service and only twenty recorded incidents of you being a perverted piece of shit—that's half as many as our last recipient received. Pastor Tickles, now Reverend Tickles, can't wait to work with you on our missionary platform, 'TIE 'EM UP FOR JESUS.' Again, thank you for your service."

By October, Rader was so confident in his ability to evade authorities that he decided to commit what he secretly thought of as his "retirement murder." This was to be, as he put it, his opus. Right around the time that he was elevated to president of Christ Lutheran, Rader intended to create a crucifixion scene wherein his victim's body would be strung up with cables and eyebolts, then slathered with the semen he'd been saving for months in small containers in his family's freezer, next to the fish bait. Finally, as a coup de grâce, Rader planned to set the victim's house on fire. However, on the day he'd hoped to carry out what he was calling Project Boardwater, a work crew camped out on the victim's curb all day, so he abandoned the scheme.

Despite this failure, Rader continued communicating with the police, each transmission becoming more and more ornate. In December, he drew pubic hair on a doll, tied its hands behind its back, attached Nancy Fox's pristine twenty-seven-year-old driver's license to its ankle, and left it to be found by the authorities in Wichita's Murdock Park. About a month later, Rader drove his black Jeep Cherokee to the parking lot of a Home Depot, pulled up next to a truck, and dropped a Special K cereal box with the words "BOMB" and "BTK PRE—" written on the outside. Inside, he'd left a beaded necklace and a note warning that his inner sanctum was rigged to explode should they ever find it and try to enter. The owner of the truck, a Home Depot employee, thought it was a joke and threw it in the trash.

When Rader got no response to his clever "serial" box, he sent a postcard to the police, politely asking if they'd found it. Police asked everyone who worked at Home Depot if they'd seen anything strange, and sure enough, the employee who'd found the box was able to fish it out of the garbage. Surveillance footage from the parking lot was too grainy to make an ID, but cops now knew that BTK drove a black Jeep Cherokee.

It was at this point that Rader revealed his Achilles' heel: technology. He'd been playing this cat-and-mouse game for more than a year, and at well past fifty, he was exhausted. Every communication required him to buy all of the materials for his arts and crafts projects from different stores, meticulously wipe each item clean, and mail every package from a different location. Rader wanted to streamline the process, so he sent a note to the police asking a simple question:

> Can I communicate with Floppy and not be traced to a computer. Be honest. Under Miscellaneous Section, 494, (Rex, it will be OK), run it for a few days in case I'm out of town—etc. I will try a floppy for a test run some time in the near future—February or March.

Amazingly, Rader trusted the police to give him an honest answer, and when they gave him the A-OK in a classified ad, he was relieved. But since his home computer was on the fritz and his work computer was a little too risky, he drove to Christ Lutheran and used theirs, under the cover of official church business. Inserting a purple floppy disk he purchased at Walmart, he typed up a test file with instructions on how to communicate from then on and sent it to KSAS-TV with the return address "P. J. Fox," immensely proud of himself. Rader thought he had figured out a way to keep this little game going until he died. All it took was a quick click on the "Properties" field of the test file for it all to come crashing down.

Within seconds, police discovered that the disk had last been edited by a user named Dennis on a computer registered to Christ Lutheran Church right there in Wichita. A quick internet search gave them the address of Dennis Rader, President of Christ Lutheran and the proud owner of a black Jeep Cherokee. But while this evidence was indeed strong, it was still circumstantial. If they wanted to really nail BTK, they needed forensics. Fortunately, Rader's fears about the efficacy of DNA were about to come true. Semen found at two of the known BTK crime scenes were cross-referenced with a pap smear his daughter, Kerri, had undergone while she was a student at Kansas State University. Although the semen samples were old, the familial DNA was still enough of a match to tie Dennis Rader to at least two BTK crime scenes.

From the moment the results came back, Wichita police began typing up warrants, and on February 25, 2005—over thirty years after Dennis Rader's first murder—two hundred cops were waiting at the ready to finally take down the BTK Strangler. While other teams were preparing to storm Rader's house, church, and office, the lead detectives trapped him as he drove home for lunch and arrested him, without resistance, in his brown compliance officer uniform.

Rader spent the first few hours of his interrogation admiring this mysterious BTK fellow and trying to make friends with the police and visiting FBI agents, telling them that he, too, worked in law enforcement. It wasn't until they brought up the evidence discovered on the floppy disk that Rader finally admitted, "I'm BTK."

Rader plead guilty and confessed to each of his crimes in open court, sounding almost bored when talking about the murders themselves and botching the names of his victims. The only thing that seemed to elicit any sort of real emotion from Dennis Rader was talk of his fantasy life. For Rader, the fantasy was always what he'd liked best. He had no uncontrollable urge to kill, no mental illness to skew his worldview. Selfishly, he only wanted to bring his fantasies to the real world. It wasn't Factor X that drove him to kill; it was a lack of satisfaction.

After taking all of Rader's crimes into account, the judge sentenced the infamous BTK Strangler to ten consecutive life sentences. Rader took the sentence stoically; his legacy as the most depraved man to ever call Wichita home was now all but assured.

Reportedly, some of the police who had been hunting BTK for decades found themselves disappointed in this so-called monster. They had expected a beast—a minotaur, as Rader would say. Instead, they found a dumpy, bald, mustachioed middle-aged bully with an inflated sense of self-importance. Nobody lent Dennis Rader a shirt like an investigator did during Jeffrey Dahmer's trial, nor did he gain the misplaced respect of the judge like Ted Bundy had during his. Why not?

Because nobody likes Dennis Rader.

Aw, he's the Chris Rock of serial killers!

He's the Livia Soprano of serial killers.

DENNIS RADER'S COMPLAINT LETTER TO VICTORIA'S SECRET

To the upper management of the Wichita, Kansas, Victoria's Secret:

Madam,

I consider myself a man of quality, and as such, I have high standards for the establishments where I shop.

Up until last week, I was under the impression that your store—the Victoria's Secret at the Wichita-area outlet mall—was a high-quality establishment. I am sorry to say I have been thoroughly convinced otherwise by my recent experience.

Let me begin by saying that I consider myself an expert in undergarments—an aficionado, if you will. My interest began during my time serving in Vietnam, a country with no shortage of undergarments. So please know I take this subject very seriously.

On Saturday, April 4, I visited your store with the intention of buying a strappy lace thong for my wife, who is a woman and wears lace thongs.

I have no interest in women's "panties," but my wife, who is a woman, enjoys the silky feeling of a well-made lace thong against her skin. Many women I know enjoy this. I'm sure my wife, who is a woman, is not the only one.

Because I have very high standards for what goes on my wife's WOMANLY body, I took my time looking through your stock. Before I purchase an "intimate" product, I like to feel it. The face boasts the most sensitive skin on the body, so I proceeded to press the fabric against my face, administer a quick "sniff test," and rub the garment between my fingers.

I was bothering no one as I shopped. I carefully placed ALL of the undergarments that did not pass the "skin and sniff" test back in their place, and yet was still rudely approached several times by different employees who informed me that I was making many "customers" uncomfortable. The store manager confronted me at least three times.

I am a respectable churchgoing man and don't deserve to be followed around your store by middle-management stooges. That was the first insult: treating me, a respectable public employee, like a common thief. But the disrespect didn't end there.

While testing the quality of your hosiery by seeing how many times I could wrap it around my wrist (stretch and breathability are the two most reliable indicators of well-made hosiery, according to *Good Housekeeping*), the manager approached me again, this time requesting I quickly make my purchase and leave the store. Mind you, I had barely been in the store for two hours at this point, which was not nearly enough time to find the perfect pair of panties for my wife, who is a woman of quality.

The final insult occurred when I politely asked the store employee if I might try on a pair of undergarments, specifically the lace thong. To my utter surprise, "Elizabeth" said they didn't allow customers to try on "materials that cover our most sensitive parts." Meanwhile, I had been observing many young women enter and exit the fitting room with similar undergarments in their hands, and they were all allowed to try on their products before purchase.

You see, although she is a woman, my wife and I have similar body frames, and I know that if the panties fit me, they'd definitely fit her. Even though I was being met with opposition the entire time I was perusing the panties at your store, I crossed my fingers and purchased a pair, despite not being allowed the common courtesy of trying them on.

This culminated in one of the worst nights in my wife's life.

As soon as my wife put on the panties, she could tell something was wrong. My wife is a curvy woman and she is proud of her body, and I am proud of her, so you can imagine my horror when she struggled to pull the undergarment over her thighs, only to burst out of it as soon as it encompassed her groin area. And if that wasn't bad enough, as the thin fabric broke, the thong cut deep into my wife's rear end. I screamed in pain just thinking about what she must be going through.

Thankfully, I am a Boy Scout leader. I am trained to react in situations such as this and was able to cut them off.

Because of this event, I have not been back to your Wichita Victoria's Secret store, and have no plans to return. As a matter of fact, a perfectly fine Dress Barn opened about five miles from my house, so I'll be shopping there from now on. They have not prevented me from trying on their wares, nor have they scolded me for my quality checks.

I hope this letter helps the Victoria's Secret brand improve customer relations. Just because a man is in your store alone does not mean he should be treated like a criminal.

Sincerely,

Dennis Rader

P.S. Your best hosiery only wrapped around my wrist three times before showing signs of breaking. Pathetic.

CHAPTER 8

ANDREI CHIKATILO

THE RUSSIAN REGION OF ROSTOV HAS NEVER BEEN A PLACE of joy. When the eighties arrived and the Soviet Union began coming apart at the seams, its largest city, Rostov-on-Don, had a murder rate of almost one a day. This entire region, partly populated by a steady stream of transients, criminals, and runaways attracted to its relatively pleasant climate and low cost of living, was and still is one of the most crime-ridden areas in all of Russia. Simply put, Rostov was the perfect environment for an impotent supply clerk named Andrei Chikatilo to earn his place as one of the most savage serial killers to ever exist.

Between 1978 and 1989, Andrei Chikatilo slaughtered over fifty women and children in a bloodbath that far surpassed the brutality of any known American serial killer. That's not to say American killers weren't capable of such depravity. But when it came to Chikatilo, the total inaction and ignorance of the Soviet government allowed him to evolve into a cunning butcher far beyond anything America and the world at large had seen.

America gave the world Steph Curry, Brett Favre, and Bruce Springsteen, and Russia gave the world Anna Kournikova, Maria Sharapova, and Chikatilo . . . Now that I think about it, it's kind of a draw.

Chikatilo's skill was not the almost supernatural talent Bundy had for abduction, nor did he have the patience for stalking possessed by Dennis Rader. Chikatilo was little more than a vicious animal tacitly permitted to roam Rostov, killing for the sole pathetic goal of a sustained erection. Having somehow gotten his wires crossed in the worst way possible, the only way Chikatilo could reach that aroused state was by seeing blood born from suffering that he himself had inflicted. Like a wolf who circles a herd, waiting for a sick calf to fall away, Chikatilo would approach women and children in railway stations and public parks when they were at their most vulnerable, offering a drink to the more desperate women or an interesting lure to the children until finally one said yes. Once they were in a suitably secluded location, often an empty field or lonely forest, Chikatilo would strike with the ferocity of a starving, rabid animal, sometimes ripping his victims to shreds with his teeth.

When I first moved to Florida, I played basketball with kids five years younger than me. I crushed those children and they looked at me like I was Larry Bird. Jump shots, hook shots, I was DOMINATING IN THE PAINT. Sometimes your skills can appear more impressive when the bar is incredibly low. Like Andrei Chikatilo. This has nothing to do with killing to get an erection, but we are really looking to add levity to this chapter.

For almost a decade, the Soviet government largely ignored the fact that women and children were being butchered in remote fields in and around Rostov. The reason behind their hesitation was simple, if not maddening: in order to justify the suffering that most Russians endured during the Soviet era, Communism had to give the appearance of providing a superior life compared to other societies, namely that of the United States. Part of the myth sold to the Russian people was that serial killing and rampant crime were not Soviet problems. These types of troubles were uniquely American, products of a selfish, capitalist society.

Hey, Americans aren't selfish! We've given weapons to everyone around the world.

Because the Soviets refused to inform their citizens about the monster that stalked the region's railway stations, Chikatilo easily took advantage of a naive populace. After all, his method of approaching stranger after stranger was not necessarily odd behavior in the Soviet Union. Given that Soviets had to endure long lines to obtain everything from a loaf of bread to a new sweater, it was quite normal for citizens to strike up random conversations with one another to alleviate boredom. To the average person, Chikatilo was just another ennui-filled comrade.

Don't worry, I looked up the word *ennui* for you. It means "boredom."

It's nice that Communism fostered human connection. If anyone talked to me on the streets when I was living in NYC, I ASSUMED they were a serial killer because *who* talks to people?

BORN UNDER THE DARK SHROUD OF JOSEPH STALIN'S RULE in 1936, Andrei Chikatilo was the son of two Ukrainian field peasants, Anna and Roman Chikatilo. By Soviet standards, the Chikatilo family never starved, but according to Anna, a cousin of Chikatilo's fell victim to the rampant cannibalism that swept the Ukraine during the early thirties. While the reality of cannibalism frightened the young Chikatilo, the fact that people could be capable of such acts also fascinated him. Soon after, he wouldn't have to imagine what widespread carnage and misery was like. In 1941, Adolf Hitler invaded the Soviet Union and by September, Chikatilo's home country of Ukraine was officially occupied and controlled by the Nazis. The fear he felt was only compounded by the fact that his father had left home months earlier to fight on the front lines, meaning young Andrei and his mother were alone in witnessing the horrors of Nazi occupation.

See, this is when Chikatilo could've used his power to kill to murder Nazis, like the way Dexter kills serial killers.

Absolutely. And on some level, Chikatilo must have been jealous that he missed legal cannibalism.

Death was an ever-present reality for Andrei during those early years. Often, he would walk out from the hut he shared with his mother to see the bodies and stray limbs of his neighbors rotting on the ground. But to look at it from another perspective, millions of boys in the USSR saw similar horrors during the war, and to the best of our knowledge, didn't grow up to be serial killers. Chikatilo was different. While he did look upon these gruesome scenes with a certain amount of revulsion, he internalized what was happening around him to the point where it was no longer a horror. Eventually, the bloody savagery would be his ultimate aphrodisiac.

Yeah, when you live in Russia during World War II and you think it's super sexy, like 1960s Los Angeles, you've got a big problem!

To continue the pattern seen among many of these monsters, Chikatilo's mother was an absolute terror. The two shared a bed during the war, and young Andrei was a chronic bed wetter. Instead of trying to look at the underlying problems as to why her son couldn't hold his bladder throughout the night, she beat him every time he had an accident.

Oh, to be a fly on the wall in that wonderful room! It's gotta be pretty upsetting to wake up in Nazi-occupied Ukraine and ALSO in a pool of your son's beet-scented pee.

Hell for Chikatilo's mom would be seeing how many drunk college freshmen wet the bed every Saturday night.

School was no refuge from humiliation. Chikatilo was remembered by classmates as shy and introverted, the kind of boy who would fall into a puddle of tears if he forgot his pen. Puberty brought even further indignities. Before he hit his growth spurt, Andrei had been a fat little boy with noticeable breasts. Seizing upon the opportunity for mockery, the boys coopted a derogatory term for a dirty old woman and nicknamed Chikatilo "baba." Fittingly, "baba" is also the first name of Russia's bogeywoman: Baba Yaga. Living in an isolated mobile shack on chicken legs that wanders the woods, Baba Yaga has haunted the dreams of Russia's children for centuries. After his capture in 1992, Chikatilo would replace her.

Pretty sure this is what Pearl Jam's song "Jeremy" is all about.

What I wouldn't give for a taste of that sweet Baba Yaga milk. I bet it tastes like cigarettes.

Long before that came to pass, Chikatilo's psyche was growing more and more twisted. The root, perhaps, was a seemingly innocuous incident in a boy's bathroom. Although there are no specifics, Chikatilo was relentlessly teased for the odd shape of his foreskin after a boy glanced over at a urinal. While this certainly isn't the only incident involving Chikatilo's penis, it certainly begs the question as to whether this was the source of his later mentally induced impotence.

Oh, come on, AC, you gotta flip that and make fun of the dude for looking at your pecker at the urinal. This is where humor saves people from becoming a cannibal.

That's why I think Chikatilo would really benefit from my new invention, the Quadruple P: Portable Penis Privacy Protector. It's covered in trendy hip designs to distract the eye from the penis.

Despite the relentless teasing—or perhaps because of it—once he came of age, Chikatilo became a force to be reckoned with, a formidable foe on the Ukrainian playground. His nickname changed from Baba to Andrei Sila—Andrei the Strong. But Andrei was still an outsider. It seemed as if his only real friend was the USSR.

That's the closest thing to your only friend being the principal from *Uncle Buck*.

With a fervor that surprised even the adults around him, Chikatilo became a dedicated Stalinist, gobbling up every bit of Soviet Communist propaganda sent his way. The cognitive dissonance couldn't have been stronger: at the same time that he was worshipping Stalin, his family was surviving on cat grass and leaves as a direct result of Stalin's policies. Andrei didn't even taste bread until he was almost a teenager.

And you know it wasn't good bread. It had rat teeth in it for protein.

Even so, Chikatilo never lost faith. In secondary school, he became the editor for the school newspaper. He worked as the agitator of political information, acting as a young horn of the state to explain and interpret the news and make it sound as flattering as possible to the USSR.

To be fair, it could've been worse. He could've ended up like Roger Stone.

Much of this desperate overcompensation resulted from what had happened to Chikatilo's father during the war. Just weeks after leaving home in 1941, Roman Chikatilo was captured by the Nazis and spent almost the entirety of World War II as a POW. Taking a cue from the government, most citizens believed that a person who had any contact with the non-Soviet world had been ideologically infected, which went doubly so for soldiers who hadn't had enough honor to die for the motherland. Dead, Roman would have been a war hero. Alive and returned home, he was another worthless peasant and a great source of shame for his son Andrei.

It's like if Lieutenant Dan just stayed really sad.

Let me take this opportunity to bring up VA reform! We need to treat our soldiers like heroes if they live *or* die. That's my take!

Despite his status as an outsider, Andrei Chikatilo was a highly intelligent student. He received the highest marks possible on almost every test he took, and his near-photographic memory put him head and shoulders above every other student at the collective farm where he grew up. He believed he was bound for greater things, possibly as a politician who could lead the USSR to future glories. He was sent to Moscow to take the entrance exams for Russia's most prestigious universities, but since his parents were so destitute, at night he was forced to sleep on the benches of Moscow's Kazansky Railway Station. Chikatilo fared poorly on the exams due to lack of rest, but he convinced himself that he hadn't been accepted because his father had been a POW, as close to an enemy of the state as one could get without being thrown in the gulag.

Oh man, I should've used the "I slept on a park bench" excuse when I failed my tests!

He was so close to making something of his big-titted self but he got railroaded by the system and became bitter. Sounds straight out of a comedian's biography!

Chikatilo switched paths, instead opting to go for a communications engineering degree at a local technical school. There, he had his first real love affair at the age of nineteen, with a woman named Tatyana Narizha. He'd already had an afternoon tryst with his sister's friend a couple of years before, but that had consisted of nothing more than a confused embrace that resulted in Chikatilo ejaculating into his pants. His relationship with Tatyana was similarly embarrassing.

Every once in a while, you're gonna snowball your pants. That's a fact of life, folks!

They attempted sex twice, but each time, Chikatilo got bashful and couldn't even come close to an erection, much less intercourse. After getting his first job as a communications specialist in the Russian city of Nizhny Tagil, he attempted the act again with other girls but encountered the same issue. Andrei became obsessed with his own erections—or lack thereof—and soon was unable to think about anything else. His fixation almost drove him to suicide, but once again, he was saved by Mother Russia.

Maybe if they put a World War II documentary on, he'd be able to achieve an erection.

In 1957, Nikita Khrushchev, the country's new leader, ordered the people to host an international youth festival in Moscow to improve the Soviet Union's badly tarnished image. Chikatilo traveled for the festival and later said that the time spent in the presence of other young Communists was the happiest of his life. This happiness was unfortunately short-lived. Soon after his return to Nizhny Tagil, he was drafted into military service, where he served for three long years. It was there that Chikatilo would discover in just what way his sexual wires were crossed.

Somehow, the rumors of Chikatilo's impotence reached his unit and soon became everyone's favorite joke. He was humiliated, but even so, Chikatilo continued his

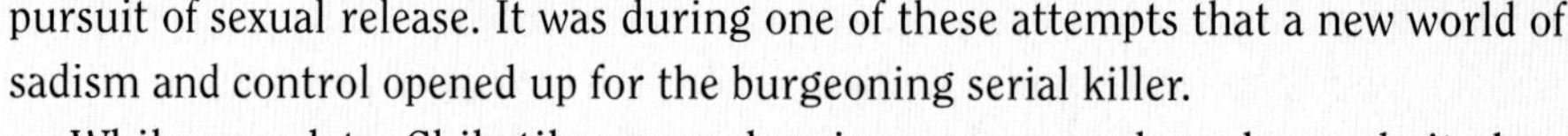

pursuit of sexual release. It was during one of these attempts that a new world of sadism and control opened up for the burgeoning serial killer.

While on a date, Chikatilo was embracing a woman when she made it clear that she was no longer interested. She tried pushing him away, but he decided not to let go. She began to struggle and he found that the harder she tried to get away, the more he enjoyed himself. The tension of holding a woman in his arms against her will gave Andrei a sensation he'd never felt and he quickly ejaculated. With this, Chikatilo had made his first conscious link between sex and violence.

Yikes! What an unfortunate way to know the turkey's done. This is going to be a very gross chapter.

Sounds like he could get a job producing at Kink.com.

After his military service, Chikatilo returned home to Ukraine and attempted another relationship, but he had the same results as with every previous bid for sex. Once again, word got around. The would-be lover had asked a few of her friends if they knew of any cures for impotence, and soon everyone in their village knew about Andrei's problem. Rather than live with these indignities, Chikatilo tried hanging himself but was saved at the last moment by his mother. Too ashamed to show his face anymore, he left Ukraine forever and crossed the border into Rostov, his family joining him a year later.

Here, Chikatilo finally discovered masturbation, and it wasn't long before he was a full-blown addict. Whenever the urge came, he would be compelled to ejaculate somewhere, anywhere, even if he was at work. While he was still the new guy at his job as a telephone engineer, Chikatilo began masturbating in the woods on his lunch break, thinking his fellow comrades couldn't see him. His lifelong shortsightedness betrayed him, however, prompting the group leader, just a few yards away, to shout, "Andrei goes into the woods to masturbate!"

He brought this on himself, just like how kids who eat boogers in class are known as "Booger Brian" until junior year of high school.

Wouldn't it be fun if Chikatilo leaves the office to masturbate in the woods and he interrupts the teddy bear picnic?

Chikatilo used the humiliation as an excuse to isolate himself further. He later said, "I always thought about [this incident] and suffered because I realized I was different from everyone else." Those differences were about to become even more stark.

I'm not going to say I don't know people who have masturbated at work. I do. But you have to put the blame on yourself if you get caught. This is not the movie *Idle Hands*—you can tell your fingers what to do.

At this time, most men in Russia married before the age of eighteen, but Chikatilo was pushing thirty. Worried that he might become a permanent bachelor, his sister set him up with a woman named Fayina from the nearby town of Novoshakhtinsk. Fayina mistook Chikatilo's shyness for gentleness and actually appreciated his request to wait for sex until marriage. It wasn't until their wedding night that she found out the real motivation behind this request.

What a fun time to be a woman this must have been.

Marital sex was an unpleasant chore in Chikatilo's eyes, an embarrassing failure repeated ad nauseam. The couple wanted children, but since Chikatilo could never get an erection, they had to resort to him masturbating onto Fayina's body and then pushing the semen into her with his fingers.

Nothing like a "hand-thrown" baby.

They call this "the ol' Tennessee Winnebago."

Surprisingly, the method worked, and by 1969 Andrei and Fayina had two children, Yuri and Lyudmila. That said, Chikatilo's growing family did nothing to quell the desires growing within him. The night he'd spent during his time in the army embracing a woman against her will left an indelible impression on Chikatilo's psyche. It was the seed for a garden of increasingly violent fantasies that all shared one central theme: sexual domination. He would make those fantasies a reality when he took a job teaching the Russian language at a boarding school in his wife's hometown of Novoshakhtinsk, deep in Rostov coal country.

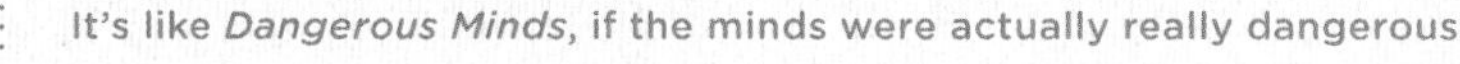

It's like *Dangerous Minds*, if the minds were actually really dangerous.

It must've been weird for those kids to learn only synonyms for murder.

Predictably, Chikatilo was a terrible teacher. Just as shy and introverted with his students as he was with everyone else, he could not control a classroom. Fellow teachers hated him as well, rightly pegging him as morose and sullen. He never discussed his sexual problems at work, but they soon manifested themselves in other ways. Chikatilo began showing up at the girl's dormitory at bedtime and more than once was seen with his hand in his pocket, clearly masturbating.

In America he could've said he was searching for loose change, but in Russia no one would believe he had change in his pocket.

This behavior soon escalated into full groping. While swimming in a river with his students during a school trip, Chikatilo swam over to a fifteen-year-old girl and began to fondle her. She naturally screamed in fear, which only increased his pleasure. He only stopped when other students swam over to investigate the noise. Although one would think this would result in the swift end of Chikatilo's teaching career, he suffered not a single consequence for his actions.

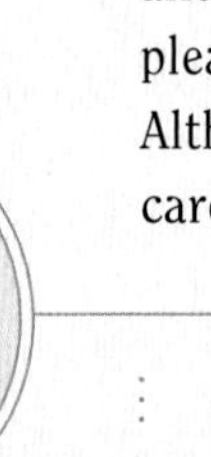

If only he'd worked for the Catholic Church—he would have been promoted.

In the Soviet system, if a subordinate was accused of wrongdoing, it was not just the perpetrator who would bear the brunt of the punishment; their supervisors would be roundly disciplined as well. While the Soviet Union had moved past Stalin's hellish gulags, they were by no means a distant memory, so Chikatilo went unpunished, his bosses turning a blind eye to the behavior. Furthermore, Soviet society was regressive, to say the least. When Chikatilo molested another student by repeatedly slapping her with a ruler on the small of her back until he ejaculated in his pants, the parents refused to report the incident for fear their daughter would be blamed for somehow inviting his behavior.

Meanwhile, Chikatilo had begun to shift his behavior out of the school. Trains and buses became frotteurism buffets for him, and at one point he forced his wife's niece to watch him masturbate in her bedroom. Fayina laughed off every incident, refusing to acknowledge that her husband had become a serious child molester.

Thank you, Marcus! From now on, I will see every bus as a "Frotteurism Buffet."

After years of this type of behavior, complaints had begun to pile up against Comrade Chikatilo, so the director at his school gave him a choice: resign or be fired. He chose to resign, but only under the condition that no mention of the incidents would show up on his record. They agreed, and as a result he was free to continue his behavior elsewhere. Had the director chosen to do the right thing no matter the consequences, Chikatilo would have shown up far earlier in the Rostov Ripper investigation.

And they say Russia isn't the land of the free.

In the parlance of Soviet Russia, Chikatilo was *blat*, meaning he knew how to maneuver the Communist system for his own personal gain. Soon after being dismissed from his position in Novoshakhtinsk, he picked up a job at a technical school in Shakhty that trained high school kids in the ways of mining.

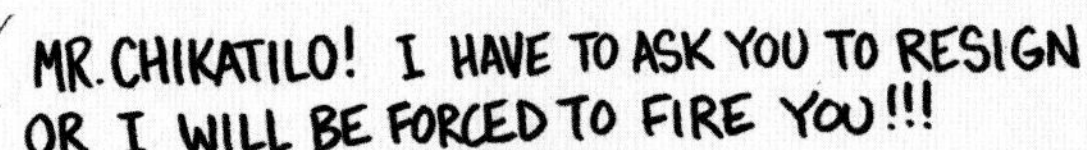

Holy shit, Russian Mining High School. Can you imagine this? Six hundred Russian orphans sitting on piles of coal instead of chairs. They would send the cheerleaders down the mine shaft to see if they died from methane. The valedictorian was voted "Most Likely to Get Black Lung." This is why the Russians are beating us right now—they made every child into a hardened rock slinger.

Here, Chikatilo demonstrated that he was a true master of bureaucracy. While other teachers struggled for years to obtain a nice home near the school, Chikatilo and his family were given one almost instantly. He was also able to buy a car—a rare luxury in the Soviet Union—though, according to rumors, he was eventually forced to give it away as a payoff to avoid a public molestation accusation.

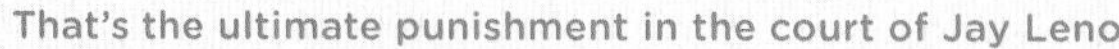

That's the ultimate punishment in the court of Jay Leno.

This is why it's smart to buy a car. It's a bribe that takes you to work.

Although life in the bureaucracy was good, Chikatilo began pulling away from his family. His two children became unruly as they approached adolescence, so Andrei simply began ignoring them, along with his wife. Then, in 1978, he had a brief affair with a woman named Tanya Petrosyan, but it ended as it always did after he repeatedly failed to perform in the bedroom. Chikatilo was beginning to learn that his only path to an erection was paved with depravity.

Chikatilo is a study in purposeful ignorance, both about his mind and his awareness of his relationship with others. You can feel all these lives dying at the root, all of them starving for lack of care and attention.

In autumn of that year, a fifteen-year-old boy named Sherbakov, who lived in the dorm Chikatilo supervised, woke up with his penis in Chikatilo's mouth. Andrei scurried away when the boy screamed, but he returned a few days later to try again. This time the boys were waiting and forced him out of their rooms permanently. Once again, nothing happened to Andrei Chikatilo, either professionally or at home. His wife tried to get him to see a psychiatrist for his increasing pathologies, but he refused, acting wounded that anyone but himself would see him as abnormal. To make matters worse, he was already working on his own cure for impotence that was rooted in the violent fantasies he'd been entertaining for years.

Not long after moving to Shakhty, Chikatilo bought himself a home away from home. This one-room shack on the edge of town was to be a sexual laboratory of sorts. Here, in a barely furnished hut with no running water, Chikatilo would experiment with different sexual practices, trying to find something to alleviate the embarrassment that had been following him for years. Unfortunately, he found it exactly where he thought he would: in violence.

The first visitors to Andrei's new abode were desperate young women. Lured by the promise of food or drink, Chikatilo would convince them to perform sexual acts beyond anything he would ever ask his wife to do. But the women were too easy for what Chikatilo wanted, too compliant. He wanted complete domination. He found this by preying on little girls.

Remember what I said about this being a very gross chapter? It might be a very, VERY gross chapter.

At first, most of the girls who Chikatilo approached on the street quickly sensed that something was amiss and ran away. But as he targeted more and more prospective victims, he began to refine his approach. Eventually he was able to lure

two six-year-old girls to his hut, where he assaulted each before letting them go. Lena Zakotnova would not be so lucky.

At only nine years old, Lena wasn't particularly worried when Andrei approached her as he was walking home from work one afternoon. She mentioned that she needed to use the bathroom, so he kindly offered his own. The moment they entered the shack, however, Chikatilo's demeanor changed. Turning into a monster out of a nightmare, he attacked the little girl and attempted to rape her, but his familiar affliction prevented him from doing so. Becoming enraged, he tried to force his flaccid penis inside her vagina, breaking her hymen in the process. The girl began to bleed and, upon seeing that, Chikatilo had the strongest, most satisfying orgasm of his life. It only made him want more.

Pulling a knife from his pocket, Chikatilo thrust it into Lena's stomach. Upon looking into her eyes and hearing her screams, he now found that the only thing that excited him more than blood was anguish. As the little girl bled out on the floor, Chikatilo realized he now knew the cost of his own personal impotence cure: a single human life. It would be two more years before he would seek it again.

> There were several ways he could have turned around and stopped doing this, but this fucker followed the crooked impulses of his body straight into murder.

Immediately following the killing, Chikatilo was struck with remorse and panic. He quickly disposed of the body by stuffing it in a sack and throwing it into the Grushevka River, but he'd made a mistake before even leaving his property: he left the light burning in his shack all night long. A neighbor, seeing Andrei shuttling young girls in and out of the hut for weeks, had long since sussed out that it was a house of secrets. After news of the little girl's disappearance spread, the neighbor notified police about what he'd seen and Chikatilo became the main suspect. Inexplicably, though, Fayina provided him with an alibi, claiming he'd been home all evening.

> She straight lied for him. He didn't deserve the loyalty of a mob wife.

As a consequence, police dropped Chikatilo as a suspect and focused their attention on a neighbor named Aleksandr Kravchenko. He wasn't an unreasonable suspect; years earlier, he'd been convicted of killing a little girl in Crimea, but escaped the executioner's pistol because he'd been under eighteen when the crime was committed. Police swiftly arrested him for Lena Zakotnova's murder, and after one Soviet-style interrogation, Kravchenko confessed. He recanted by the time the charge made its way to court, but his wife testified that he had confessed to her as well. Kravchenko was executed in 1984 for Andrei Chikatilo's first killing. And he wouldn't be the last to be punished in Chikatilo's place. For the next twelve years, Andrei would remain unknown to Soviet authorities, continuing his murder spree without abatement.

Despite being a suspect in a child murder and a known pedophile who orally raped a boy in his charge, Chikatilo kept his job for another two years before they finally told him to leave—and once again, he was able to do so without a single mark on his record.

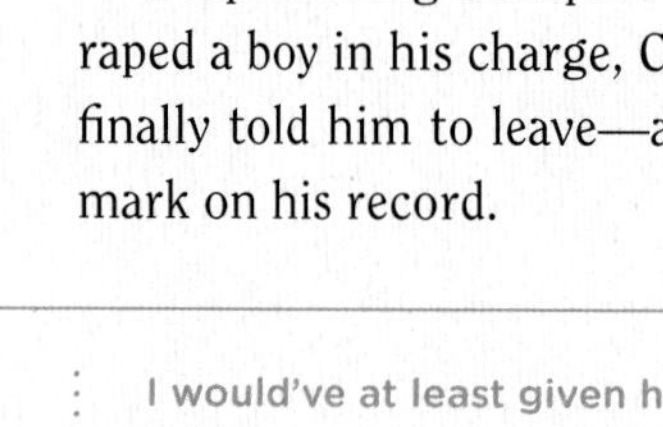

> I would've at least given him double-secret probation.

Tiring of close calls, Chikatilo left the education field. He was hired in the specifically Soviet position of supply clerk. In this profession, Andrei was tasked with traveling the country for the sole purpose of ensuring that industrial materials made it from one factory to another by persuading factory managers to release said supplies to the necessary locations.

> One of my dad's last assignments when he was working for Wackenhut Security was to drive to various Wackenhut details and make sure the guys were wearing the Wackenhut hats. That was the entire job. Eastern European men are built for jobs that sound like they came out of a Chekhov story.

It certainly wasn't as prestigious as being a teacher, but the supply clerk job opened up a whole new realm of possibilities when it came to killing. Suddenly, Chikatilo had freedom of movement. But like many serial murderers, when he decided to murder again, he did it close to home.

It's like the Milo and Otis story, minus the cute animals and with murder.

Chikatilo is doing the *Diners, Drive-Ins and Dives* serial killer tour of Russia, and he couldn't have done it without his brotha from anotha mother.

WE'RE CHECKING OUT RUSSIA'S FAVORITE BORSCHT, URANIUM FIELDS, AND MURDER SHEDS WITH MY BUDDY ANDREI!

FLAVORTUNKT

Two years after the murder of Lena Zakotnova, Chikatilo spotted fifteen-year-old Larisa Tkachenko at a bus stop, on her way to join friends for the annual tradition of helping out on local farms during harvest season. As she waited, Chikatilo approached her and eventually talked her into taking a walk with him. Ostensibly, they were going to drop by a place that loosely translates to what is called a Relaxation Station. Made completely of concrete, these complexes of cafés and recreational facilities also doubled as a good place for casual sexual encounters.

If it is really a Relaxation Station, they better have at least a dozen recliners or I would complain to the manager.

Both parties were game—Soviet Russia stated "sexual maturity" as the only requirement for legal intercourse—but as Andrei and Larisa were walking along a lonely pathway along the Don River, Chikatilo grabbed the girl and pushed her to the ground. When she tried to scream, he grabbed a handful of dirt and filled her mouth with it. He began choking and punching her, but as he'd left the house with no intent to kill that day, he had no knife. Instead, he got his blood by ripping her skin with his teeth. Chikatilo ejaculated as she died, then undressed the dead body and bit one of the nipples off her corpse.

CHECK, PLEASE!

Instead of the paranoia and panic that he'd felt after his last murder, Chikatilo felt a kind of euphoric delirium. Holding his victim's clothes in his hands, he ran circles around the body for twenty minutes. He had suspected it after his first murder, but now he knew for certain: there was no sexual pleasure in his life that did not come from the agony of others. Eight months later, he would rape and kill again, taking things even further.

The murder is obviously horrific, but what really scares me is him doing the Mexican hat dance around the corpse. It's the same feeling I had when imagining Ed Gein dancing in a field in his mother's skin. Serial killers shouldn't dance!

In June 1982, Chikatilo approached thirteen-year-old Lyuba Biryuk as she was returning home from the food collective. He'd been following her, waiting for the right moment. Once they were on a path that was reasonably hidden from the main road by a row of bushes, he forced her to the ground and ripped off her clothes. He attempted rape, but couldn't get an erection. Enraged, he pulled out his knife and stabbed her over thirty times. By the time he was done, he had gouged both eyes from their sockets, then he covered her corpse with leaves and tossed her clothes into the woods. Her body was not found for another two weeks.

Exhilarated by this slaying, Chikatilo embraced the full abandon of merciless serial killing. The murders came swift and steady over the next decade, especially after Chikatilo began using his business trips as a cover for his crimes. By August of that year, he'd expanded to boys, killing Oleg Pozhidaev on a business trip to Adygei. The savagery increased as well. In December, Chikatilo lured a ten-year-old girl into a cornfield on the outskirts of his old town of Novoshakhtinsk and stabbed her over fifty times, ripping open her torso from neck to pelvis before pulling out her bowels and uterus.

Chikatilo reminds me of Bundy and Ramirez because of his sheer brutality. His rage against society because of his failed sexuality is expressed in a werewolf-like destruction of the body. It becomes an expression of his dark hate toward the world.

By July 1983, Chikatilo had expanded to adult women, killing twenty-four-year-old Lyudmila Kushuba. Teenage boys were the next group to feel Andrei's wrath; fifteen-year-old Sergey Kuzmin was found just a mile away from another of his victims. Yet despite the brutality of these killings, the public had not been warned. That's not to say authorities were ignoring the murders altogether. In the early spring of 1983, a task force was officially launched, named for the most common locations where the murders occurred: Operation Forest Path. Ten investigators were assigned to solve what they thought was a string of four murders (although Chikatilo had killed eight by this point), but they neglected to tell the public, partly because they believed the sheer viciousness of the murders would cause a panic. Multiple stab wounds was one thing, but it was thought that the Russian people wouldn't be able to handle the news that one of their comrades had been gouging the eyes from the skulls of their children.

What's weird is that I think Russians are the exact type of people who would be able to handle this news. Cannibalism happened regularly there for like ten years. The Russians are hard-core!

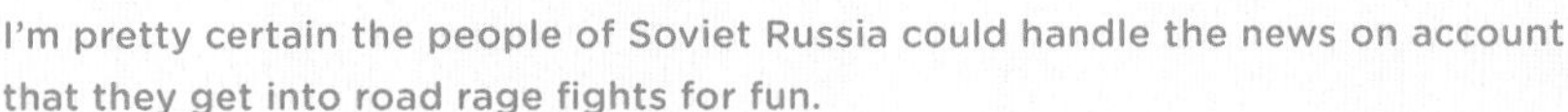

I'm pretty certain the people of Soviet Russia could handle the news on account that they get into road rage fights for fun.

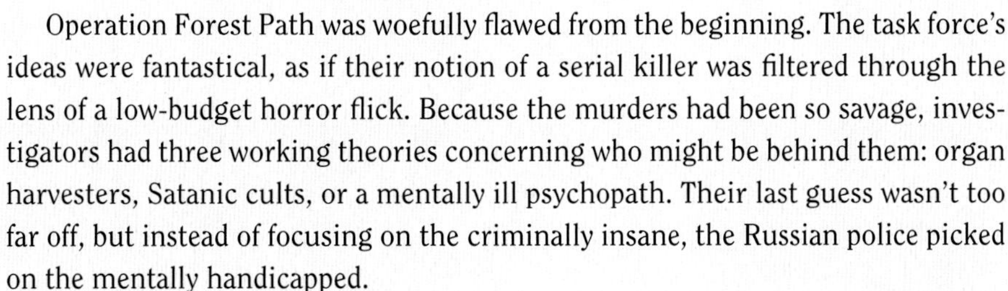

Operation Forest Path was woefully flawed from the beginning. The task force's ideas were fantastical, as if their notion of a serial killer was filtered through the lens of a low-budget horror flick. Because the murders had been so savage, investigators had three working theories concerning who might be behind them: organ harvesters, Satanic cults, or a mentally ill psychopath. Their last guess wasn't too far off, but instead of focusing on the criminally insane, the Russian police picked on the mentally handicapped.

I like the idea that there were so many organ harvesters or Satanic cults they'd be like, "It's probably one of the supervillains we have in every town in Russia."

Their first suspects were two men named Kalenik and Shaburov. Residents at a hostel for the mentally handicapped, the pair had been arrested for attempting to steal a car.

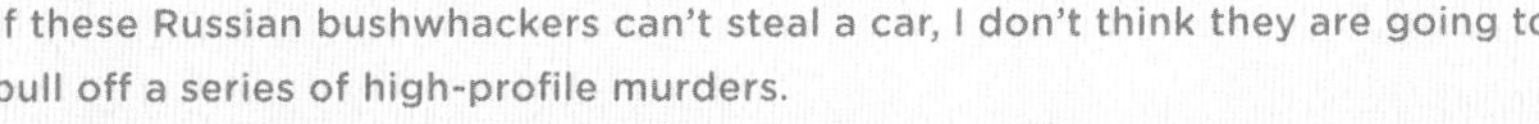

If these Russian bushwhackers can't steal a car, I don't think they are going to pull off a series of high-profile murders.

Desperate to solve the four murders and sensing a sudden opportunity, investigators began interrogating the two men about the bodies. Before long, both had confessed to raping and killing several women and children in the Rostov region. Investigators took these confessions as fact, as it was reasoned that a mentally handicapped person would not have the imagination necessary to invent such a story.

The pair stayed in custody for months, even when fourteen-year-old Sergey Markov was stabbed seventy times, eviscerated, and castrated. But instead of admitting that they might be on the wrong track with the mentally handicapped perpetrator theory, police instead arrested two more men from the same hostel, quickly obtaining two more confessions. The low-hanging fruit was proving to be irresistible, and while the authorities were wasting precious time and resources trying to claim these incidents were resolved, Chikatilo murdered seventeen-year-old Natalya Shalapinina. Not content with mere stabs or eye gouges with this one, he cut her nose and upper lip from her face before slicing a finger off her left hand.

As Andrei's gruesome experiments with the human body escalated, his private life began to unravel. Murder now filled his every thought and, as a result, his work suffered. When seventy meters of linoleum flooring went missing from his job, Chikatilo was held responsible. Though he'd had nothing to do with the possible theft or accidental loss of the linoleum, instead of dealing with the problem, he simply stopped showing up for work. Seeing this as an opportunity to pursue murder full-time, Chikatilo temporarily abandoned his family and laid low, sleeping in railway stations when he wasn't looking for victims. His only companion was a murder bag not unlike Dennis Rader's hit kit. Filled with knives, hammers, rope, and a change of clothes, it was a constant companion on Chikatilo's murder sprees.

When I was fired from my office job, it was one of the best things to ever happen to me! So, again, another very appropriate comparison of my life to Andrei Chikatilo's.

From Joseph McCarthy to BTK to Chikatilo, only sociopaths carry bags with them wherever they go.

On the same day that formal charges were brought against Chikatilo for theft of state property, he killed forty-four-year-old Marta Ryabyenko in the very park where he had murdered another woman a month prior. Yet he still was no closer to being a suspect for the growing number of serial murders in his community.

What was scarier at the time: being confronted by a serial killer or being prosecuted by the Russian government?

Hold on a second. There's no investigation into the rape and murder of the women, but no one in Russia gets away with linoleum theft? Nope, not in Chernenko's USSR!

For the murders of Marta Ryabyenko and Natalya Shalapinina, police charged yet another mentally handicapped man after forcing a confession. This time, however, a public awareness of Chikatilo had begun to surface. After the murder of ten-year-old Dima Ptashnikov, a woman claimed that she'd seen the young boy walking away from the housing estate where he lived with a six-foot-tall stranger between fifty and fifty-five years old who was wearing glasses and carrying a bag. She said he limped slightly and dragged one leg behind him. This described Chikatilo perfectly, as a blood vessel issue in one of his legs made it difficult for him to walk.

He's got clots like Kissel!

But for the police, this tip wasn't worth investigating. It was easier to accept that a horde of psychopathic mentally handicapped monsters had descended upon Rostov than to spend time and resources searching for an average-looking citizen with a limp.

THAT'S the remake of *CHUD* the world needs.

Ya know, it's just nice the U.S. and USSR have so much in common when it comes to arresting innocent people.

Meanwhile, Chikatilo was about to commit his first and only double murder. He had bumped into his former lover Tanya Petrosyan in the Shakhty train station. She'd just left her husband and was there with her young daughter, Sveta. Immediately, Chikatilo felt a deep desire to murder them both. Since he was acquainted with Petrosyan, his approach took a more delicate touch than usual: he suggested they all go on a picnic a few days later, swearing Tanya to secrecy under the guise of hiding the rendezvous from his wife.

I would rather have Bear Grylls take me camping in an alligator swamp than go on a picnic with this maniac.

No, Kissel, you would be totally safe with Bear Grylls! But can you imagine the delicious spread Chikatilo must have offered for lunch?

When the day of the picnic came, Chikatilo laid down a blanket and set up a scene for what Tanya thought would be a nice day out, possibly with a bit of romance. Chikatilo sent the little girl off into the woods to play, and soon afterward, he and Tanya were both nude. When she began teasing him for still having the same problem he'd during their first affair, Chikatilo reached into his bag, pulled out a kitchen knife, and plunged it into the side of her head. When she screamed, he grabbed his hammer and finished the job.

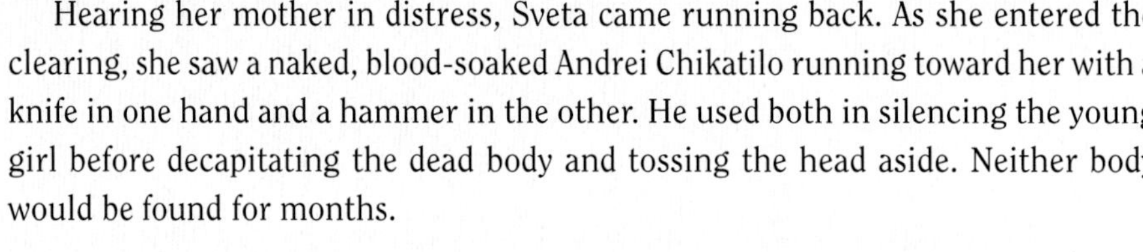

Hearing her mother in distress, Sveta came running back. As she entered the clearing, she saw a naked, blood-soaked Andrei Chikatilo running toward her with a knife in one hand and a hammer in the other. He used both in silencing the young girl before decapitating the dead body and tossing the head aside. Neither body would be found for months.

Can I scream? Aahhhhhhh! This is a horror movie.

Soon after, Chikatilo returned to his family and managed to get another job in Rostov-on-Don, this time at a factory with the verbose name of the Sevkavenergoavtomatika. Now that his work was centered in Rostov proper, two hours from his home in Shakhty, he had a valid excuse for ditching his wife and children for days at a time. The anonymity of Rostov-on-Don also gave him the sense that he could shed the skin of a respectable family man. As such, Chikatilo began his most prolific killing spree in the summer of 1984, murdering ten people between the ages of ten and twenty-two.

Again, he is still managing to KEEP A JOB while all this shit was going on. For many serial killers, the precious balance between their surface lives and their "real pursuits" is crucial for the crimes to continue. Somebody's gotta pay the bills! But Chikatilo is a little different than some of the other killers we cover in this book. He "settled down," but this socialization allowed him to slip into berserker mode.

After this summertime rampage, the Soviet government had no choice but to admit to the public that a murderer roamed Rostov. The admission, however, lost its impact after being filtered through the trap of Communist superiority. After the body of eleven-year-old Sasha Chepel was found strangled, castrated, and missing its eyes, Soviet officials responded with a rambling article in the local newspaper stating that while Chepel's murder was tragic, Communism had still drastically reduced the crime rate. According to this op-ed, not only did the people have nothing to fear, but they should, in fact, be thankful for what the state was providing them.

I love these Russian clapbacks. "You should be thankful he cut his penis off and didn't let it go to WASTE 👏 ON 👏 THAT 👏 CORPSE 👏."

Somewhere the White House press secretary just got jealous of their incredible political spin.

Meanwhile, top-level Soviet investigators were at odds with local police as to who was actually responsible for the rash of killings. It was becoming clear to some that these murders were the work of one man. By police reckoning, the count had reached twenty-three by September 1984; the real number was thirty-two. But when investigators traveled from Moscow to Rostov to see how the local authorities were handling the situation, they discovered a jail full of mentally handicapped individuals who had since recanted every single confession.

Tragically, Chikatilo was almost captured in the middle of his 1984 murder spree through old-fashioned shoe-leather detective work, but he was set free through a bizarre stroke of what could appropriately be described as serial killer luck. Soon after the murder of twenty-four-year-old Irina Luchinskaya in Aviators Park in Rostov-on-Don, a police inspector named Alexsandr Zanasovski noticed Chikatilo approaching over a dozen women in the course of an hour in the Rostov railway station. He only smiled at them or spoke a few words, not going any further because none had invited him to extend the conversation. After exhausting the supply of women there, he left and tried the same thing at the bus stop. Curious about the suspicious behavior, Zanasovski asked Chikatilo to come with him to the police post for a routine check. When asked what he'd been doing, Chikatilo said that he was waiting for his bus home and was merely bored. He was allowed to go free, but Zanasovski remembered him.

He did the subway romance move, where you proposition women for twelve hours a day until one falls for your routine!

About a week later, Zanosovski returned to the Rostov railway station and again watched as Chikatilo spent hours approaching woman after woman without success. Eventually, at around 3:00 a.m., he found a teenager in a brown suit sitting on a bench. After a short conversation, the girl laid her head in Chikatilo's lap and he

covered her with his jacket. After she presumably fumbled around with his limp penis for two hours, she left and Chikatilo was once again taken in for questioning.

Really great of the cop to just watch her play the spaghetti game with Chikatilo for a full TWO HOURS.

Even at a glance, Chikatilo seemed to be a slam-dunk suspect. When they searched the bag he constantly carried, they found an eight-inch kitchen knife with a tip obviously bent from a stabbing incident, plus lengths of rope and a jar of Vaseline. Furthermore, it was discovered that Chikatilo had lived in the town of Shakhty, where many of the murders had taken place. The case was soon passed to the Forest Path task force, who discovered that Chikatilo had been questioned in the murder of Lena Zakotnova six years prior. The seeming coup de grâce came when they found that his shoe size matched perfectly with a print found near the body of Dima Ptashnikov.

And that's the end of the chapter. Thank you, guys, for reading.

However, Chikatilo evidently had the luck of the devil on his side. When his blood was tested, investigators found that he was type A, but the sperm found at multiple murder scenes was type AB. Although Soviet police didn't know it at the time, it's possible, in rare cases, for a man's blood and semen types to be different. Since that scientific discovery was still a few years in the future, that's where the investigation into Andrei Chikatilo, serial murderer, ended in 1984.

Damn! He was literally saved by the cum in the seat of his pants.

That said, in the course of all of this, police did discover the long-standing linoleum charge that Chikatilo had skipped out on serving. He was sentenced to a year of corrective labor, but the judge took into account that he'd just spent four months being investigated as Russia's worst serial killer and was cleared, so he was set free after a ruling of time served.

Only in Russia does being investigated as a serial killer make your sentence more lenient.

What followed was a full year of relative quiet. Spooked by his brush with the executioner's pistol, Chikatilo laid low again, working as an engineer at the Elektrovozostroitelny factory, whatever that may be, in the town of Novocherkassk. He was just as unpopular here as he had been at every other job he'd held, and a deep depression fell over Chikatilo. At one point, he dug his own grave in a local cemetery in a pathetic lead-up to a suicide attempt, but he changed his mind and left the hole and shovel as they were.

So Wednesday Addams of him.

If they'd had Instagram during this time period, people would have really liked Chikatilo's bleakness.

The miseries of daily life piled up for Chikatilo, with meaningless fights at home and the lack of respect from his coworkers further fueling his rage. His only real outlet was missing, and not even his close call with the police and inevitable execution was able to quell his desires. So when he was sent on a business trip to Moscow during the 1985 Goodwill Games, Chikatilo let the animal inside loose once again.

chikachikabang53

2 likes

chikachikabang53 #bigmood

Eighteen-year-old Natalya Pokhlistova had approached Chikatilo on the train near the Moscow airport, asking if he had anything to drink. He did, he said, but only if she agreed to disembark and find someplace secluded to "relax." They got off at the next stop, and Chikatilo failed to get an erection as he always did. Feeling the old rage returning, he pulled out a knife and stabbed Natalya thirty-eight times before strangling her to death.

Chikatilo struck again a week later, murdering eighteen-year-old Irina Gulyayeva. Then he waited another two years before killing again.

Only once before his first and second arrests did people come close to knowing the truth about Andrei Chikatilo. His daughter was in the middle of a divorce and, as a result, was sometimes living in an apartment in Shakhty that served as a sort of in-between dwelling. Chikatilo knew exactly when his daughter was there, so, deciding to see how far he could push his limits, he brought a sixteen-year-old runaway named Tatyana Ryzhova back to the apartment. Again—and I'm getting just as tired of writing this as you are of reading it—Chikatilo failed to get an erection.

Not me, buddy, I love it!

But instead of derision, Chikatilo found himself confronted with a teenage girl screaming that she was owed five hundred rubles for her time. To silence her, Chikatilo fatally stabbed Tatyana in the mouth. He then removed the limbs and head from her torso, cleaned up the blood with a mop, and used a sledge he found outside to drag the pile of remains through the snow. His mission was nearly derailed when the sledge got caught on a set of railway tracks, but was saved when a stranger appeared and helped him carry the dismembered remains of the sixteen-year-old over the hitch. As soon as the stranger was gone, Chikatilo gathered himself and stuffed the corpse into a set of large pipes near the railway station, where it was discovered nine days later.

This gives new meaning to "It was when you see only one set of footprints . . . it was then that I carried you."

While Chikatilo wasn't exposed as a direct result of this murder, the proximity of the body to a transportation hub gave investigators a possible location for where their killer was picking up victims. Desperate for a lead, local authorities began staking out the Shakhty station, using policewomen in short skirts as lures while policemen hid in piles of leaves on the outskirts, ready to make a move. Chikatilo didn't take the bait and, ultimately, the focus on the train station distracted authorities from seeing the bigger picture.

He continued on, undeterred. In August 1989, Chikatilo approached a ten-year-old named Alyosha Khobotov in Shakhty. After a short conversation, the boy revealed that he was a horror movie aficionado. Chikatilo remarked that this was a wonderful coincidence as he just happened to have a large collection at home.

Bloody Footprints in the Sand

"When you only see one set of footprints, it was then that I carried your lifeless body."

Aahhhhhhh!!!

The two were walking to a secluded area when Chikatilo was suddenly struck with the memory of the grave he'd dug for himself two years prior. Thinking that this would be the perfect burial spot for Alyosha, he took the gamble that no one had refilled the hole and told the boy that they should take a shortcut to his house through the cemetery. Sure enough, the hole was still there, complete with the shovel he had used to dig it. Picking up the spade, he looked at the now-terrified boy and struck him. Then, as his victim lay on the ground, he bent down, bared his teeth, and ripped the boy's tongue out of his mouth. He then took out his knife, emasculated the boy, and tossed the severed member into the open grave before rolling the rest of his body in as well. Alyosha Khobotov wasn't found until Chikatilo himself led police to the grave years later.

As Chikatilo was becoming more and more inhuman, the Soviet Union was softening. When Mikhail Gorbachev took control of the Soviet Union in 1985, he instituted a policy known as *Glasnost*, or "openness." Under this directive, information about the inner workings of the Soviet Union were revealed to the public at a shocking pace. And as Gorbachev's admission of the horrors committed by Stalin during his reign made worldwide news, the local press in Rostov was finally free to speak of the bloody terror that had been the stuff of rumor for the previous decade. As a result, the head of the investigation finally alerted citizens that a maniacal killer lived in their midst, but tragically, the Russian police were completely new to this sort of thing, and the reveal was handled poorly. In trying to warn and comfort people, they ended up telling Andrei Chikatilo exactly where the largest police presences were, giving him a virtual map of the safest areas in which to avoid capture.

The cops created a WAZE for him!

Consequently, Chikatilo managed to escalate both in the number of his victims and the ruthlessness of his attacks. He murdered eight people in 1990 alone, sometimes cutting out the uteruses of his victims to use like a hellish bubble gum, later saying, "I did not want to bite them as much as chew them. They were so beautiful and elastic."

He was not just escalating because he could; for him, it had become a necessity. Simply killing a person gave Chikatilo little pleasure. If he truly wanted the rush, the murder had to be absolutely depraved. For example, in October of that year, Chikatilo killed a mentally handicapped teenager named Vadim Gromov by biting out his tongue while he was still alive, and finishing him off with multiple stabs to the skull. He followed that by cutting off the boy's genitals before returning home and placing the knife back among his family's cutlery.

Although it seemed like the nightmare would never end, the Soviets eventually caught Andrei Chikatilo by employing much the same tactic they used to win World War II. Swarming every railway station in Rostov with plainclothes officers, they threw as many bodies as they had at the problem until someone finally came up with a lucky break. But also similar to World War II, the victory didn't come without bloodshed.

In November, a police officer named Igor Rybakov spotted Chikatilo walking toward the Donleskhoz station in Rostov-on-Don covered in mud, with a red substance streaked on his cheek. Despite the extra police presence at the station, Chikatilo had managed to slip through their net with twenty-two-year-old Svetlana Korostik, whom he had just murdered in the woods.

Chikatilo's appearance was suspicious, but the officer thought that it was possible he had been out picking mushrooms, a popular pastime in the area. The only thing that gave him pause was that Chikatilo was wearing a suit, which was obviously a ridiculous thing to wear for such an activity. Rybakov approached Chikatilo and asked for his documents. During questioning, Chikatilo reminded the officer that a heavy rain had swept through Rostov earlier that evening. He said he'd been caught in the squall. Since a muddy suit alone wasn't enough to take him in, Chikatilo was once again let go. The officer made a note about the encounter and left it on his supervisor's desk, but it held no real significance until two weeks later when Svetlana Korostik's body was found with her arms tied behind her back, sans genitals, tongue, and nipples. Once the approximate time of death was established, the man in the muddy suit became top priority.

But several bushels of mushrooms were still missing from the area, so the Case of the Pilfered Porcinis remained open. Someone had to be picking those goddamn mushrooms . . . and they were gonna find out who! This week on Funghi PD . . .

Nothing like a police captain demanding officers find him the man in the muddy suit! Sounds like a Hardy Boys mystery.

The report from two weeks earlier was reexamined, and, as luck would have it, an officer named Mikhail Fetisov recognized Chikatilo's name from his 1984 arrest. While the evidence they had gathered in his previous arrests had all been circumstantial, this time they'd obtained Chikatilo's travel schedule from his employer and soon found that his business trips coincided with multiple murders around Rostov. They'd also noticed that the murders abruptly stopped after Chikatilo's arrest, and continued only after a suitable cooling-off period had occurred.

While these facts were certainly getting them closer to conclusively proving that Chikatilo was their man, there was still the matter of his blood type. Fortunately, science had been kind to the investigation in the intervening years. A Japanese study had discovered that it was theoretically possible for a man to have different blood and sperm types, though no known cases had been discovered yet. At the very least, it provided a little hope, but in order to make the charges truly stick, officers wanted to see Chikatilo fully incriminate himself.

This is when they called in Dick Tracy to get a confession just like he did from Mumbles!

For days, they followed their suspect, observing him talk to person after person but failing to get anyone to follow him to a second location. This dangerous game almost saw Chikatilo walk away with a young boy he was chatting up on a train; it was only the arrival of more passengers that prevented Chikatilo from slipping away with another victim. After that near-tragedy, it was decided that risking one more murder probably wasn't the best idea, so Andrei Chikatilo was arrested without incident outside a café in the town of Novocherkassk on November 20, 1990.

Thankfully, the Japanese study had been correct. Chikatilo's sperm was tested and found to be AB, connecting it to multiple murder scenes. After days of interrogation, he finally burst into tears and confessed. Eventually he would admit to fifty-three murders, leading police to undiscovered bodies with startling accuracy. Every single murder was recounted according to Chikatilo's uncanny recall, a wasted photographic memory useful only as a slideshow of some of the most heinous crimes committed in a country already known for widespread tragedy.

Once the high and relief of confession abated, Chikatilo realized he would undoubtedly be put to death for his crimes. He feigned madness, claiming that he had suffered from fifty-three cases of temporary insanity over which he had no control. The long pause after his 1984 arrest demonstrably proved that to be a bald-faced lie, but it was the killer's sole lifeline going into trial.

Held in a cage for his own protection, Chikatilo appeared in court with a shaved head, giving him the appearance of a vicious alien creature. It took three full days just to read the charges. Soon realizing that he had no chance, Chikatilo began acting out during his trial, yelling out at inopportune times, singing the Soviet anthem "The Internationale," and refusing to answer questions. The height of his chicanery came when he pulled his limp penis from his pants and waved it at the court, saying, "Look at this useless thing. What do you think I could do with that?" a stunt he repeated on the last day of his trial.

What's interesting is I heard Steve Guttenberg did the same thing in his audition for *Police Academy*. It's all about right place, right time.

This does seem like something Richard Dreyfuss would've done at trial.

Aw, Kissel, he would have been hard!

Chikatilo's feeble insanity gambit predictably failed. On October 15, 1992, Andrei Chikatilo was sentenced to death. As the audience cheered, he sneered and repeatedly shouted, "Swindler!" He stopped only when a guard gladly grabbed him by the throat. A year and a half later, Chikatilo was unceremoniously executed in the Soviet style, with a single pistol shot behind the ear.

For being so inhumane and cold, the Soviet style of execution is actually the most painless. At least they don't rely on a corrections officer pretending to be a chemist to inject a prisoner with Tide bleach.

It was later discovered that Chikatilo was not the only serial killer operating during the eighties in the Soviet Union. Igor Chernat, the Evil Spirit of Kaukjarvi, murdered thirteen people and sold their belongings afterward on the black market. Vasiliy Kulik raped over thirty children and elderly women between 1984 and 1986, killing thirteen. Aleksey Sukletin, aka the Alligator, killed and cannibalized seven young girls. On and on the list goes: the Bataysk Maniac (aka Chikatilo's Double), the Urals Strangler, the Gatchina Psychopath. And these are just the ones that the former Soviet Union came to acknowledge. Still, it pales in comparison to what we've experienced here in the United States.

The joke regularly bandied about the internet is that America has had so many serial killers that we're the only country with a separate article on the "Serial Killers by Country" Wikipedia page, which was true until 2019. But the assumption that the U.S. has the most serial killers is only given credence when we consider that we know who our serial killers are. In other words, you have to capture them to know their names. It very well could be that we have more than anyone else, but as the case of Andrei Chikatilo illustrates, it could just be that we, with few exceptions, pay more attention to our bogeymen.

We write books about them!

Well, thank you for this, Marcus. I'm not going to sleep for the rest of the week, but it was fascinating information!

CURRICULUM DEVELOPMENT PLAN

Content Area	Comprehensive Serial Killing	**Grade Level**	8th Grade
Course Name/Course	Teacher: Andrei Chikatilo		

Standard	**Grade Level Expectations**	**GLE Code**
Child Luring	Evaluate the newest trends in kids' entertainment and know the phrasing they use, develop an understanding of what types of candies they like best, and master driving a van with no windows.	SK09-GR.8-S.2-GLE.1
Train Riding	Hide in plain sight, and have the ability to appear to be heading to a destination other than a graveyard to bury a victim.	SK09-GR.8-S.4-GLE.3
Murder	Know how to pack a "kill kit," improve knife skills and aim with a firearm, move fast while appearing to walk, quickly dig a grave, and acquire the ability to act like a humble old grandpa or grandma.	SK09-GR.8-S.4-GLE.5
Covering Up Crimes	Know the best bleach solution to scour even the harshest bloodstains, burn a body with ease, clean a crime scene with lemon zest, and explain to a significant other why you've been gone for so long.	SK09-GR.8-S.4-GLE.2

Critical Thinking and Reasoning:
Thinking Deeply, Thinking Differently, Unlocking Your True Potential to Kill
Information Literacy:
Untangling the Web of Lies Set Forward by the Establishment
Collaboration
Working Together, Learning Together, Murdering Together
Self-Direction
Own Your Learning, Kill Your Enemies, Fuck Your Child Corpses
Invention
Creating Solutions to Cover Up Mass Murder

The USSR Academic Standards describes what learners should know and be able to do as they develop proficiency in education. The utilization of knowledge and skills to enhance physical, mental, emotional, and social well-being will be supported in each unit through the standard areas of Physical and Personal Wellness, Emotional and Social Wellness, and Prevention and Risk Management.

Unit Titles	**Length of Unit/Contact**	**Unit Numbers/Sequences**
Child Relations	6–8 Weeks	**1**
Understanding Mass Transit	6–8 Weeks	**2**
Knife-Sharpening Skills	6–8 Weeks	**3**
Thinking Critically About People	6–8 Weeks	**4**

Generalizations	Guiding Questions	
My Students Will Understand That . . .	**Factual**	**Conceptual**
They are superior to others	They are actually extremely average people	Convince them their faults are because of other people
It's OK to take whatever you want	The world is a cold, selfish place	Convince them that if they don't do it, someone else will
Quickly reaching orgasm in public is possible	It's not easy to do so without touching yourself, but it is accomplishable if you psychologically remove yourself from humanity and ignore social mores	Crack open the true potential of the human mind

Critical Content	Key Skills:
My students will KNOW . . .	**My students will be able to (DO) . . .**
How to find, stalk, approach, charm, and kill whoever is the best victim	Hunt, stalk, and kill a victim of their choice

Critical Language: includes the Academic and Technical vocabulary, semantics, and discourse that are particular to and necessary for accessing a given discipline.	
Academic Vocabulary:	Liquidator, manslayer, murderer, spree killer, limp dick
Technical Vocabulary:	Homicidal maniac, sociopathic tendencies, erectile dysfunction

PORNO TAPES
RECIPES
TO SERVE MAN
HUMAN ANATOMY
BONES
Chef BOYARDICK'S
UNCUT MINI RAVIOLIS
tomN. 19

CHAPTER 9

JEFFREY DAHMER

JEFFREY DAHMER WAS OUR GENERATION'S SERIAL KILLER. Discovered in 1991 in a Milwaukee apartment filled with the dismembered body parts of over a dozen men, Dahmer became an instant celebrity, for better or worse. The three of us were only preteens when Dahmer was convicted, but it's safe to say that most Americans, even the children, knew Dahmer's name, especially after he was murdered in prison. On my playground, Dahmer became a character in a game simply called Serial Killers, where he was the only real-life person to join Freddy Krueger, Jason Voorhees, and Michael Myers in a mock-stabbing free-for-all between me and my friends. Dahmer had joined the ranks of slasher legend, and our ten-year-old brains didn't know the difference. In essence, we, along with thousands of other young horror fans who confused fact with fiction, thought he was cool.

I was introduced to Dahmer from my local news as I was waiting to watch *SNL*, because nothing says palate cleanser like the lunch lady song. The early nineties are known for the Super Soaker, HyperColor shirts, and Dahmer.

Jeffrey Dahmer was the subject of many a joke we shared as kids. In the midnineties we had a whole stable of true crime characters that were perfect fodder for inappropriate things to talk about in school. Amy Fisher, Lorena Bobbitt, and O. J. Simpson helped fill our hallways with laughter, but Dahmer was the icing on the cake. Also the "cream of sum yung gai" jokes always got a laugh.

As I grew older and learned the facts behind Dahmer's killings, though, I, along with everyone else my age who grew up with the crimes, realized that not only was murder very real, but the victims involved were human beings with lives and stories of their own. And yet, the perception of Dahmer did not change to something like revulsion. The details were still shocking—who wouldn't recoil at the deaths of seventeen men, some butchered and partially eaten—but the blow was softened by a seemingly relatable story: a young boy is emotionally abandoned by his parents in the midst of their own struggles and finds comfort in the darker things in life. The relation naturally ends when the murders began, but many an outcast could relate to Dahmer's subsequent inability to connect with other human beings.

But there might be an additional reason why so many people, including us, key into Dahmer's personality. In a way, people have a desire to relate to serial killers so they might understand them. No sane person is going to find themselves connecting with the inhumanity of Andrei Chikatilo or Richard Chase's homicidal dysmorphic delusions. But every person who's ever felt like an outsider knows what it's like to be lonely, and loneliness was Dahmer's defining characteristic. He didn't murder because he enjoyed the act; he actually had to drink to the point of blackout in order to remove his sense of right and wrong. Rather, Jeffrey Dahmer murdered because he didn't want people to leave.

It's also why people love bragging about how sad they are on Twitter.

In this, Jeffrey Dahmer was a selfish monster, no different from the more reviled killers like Ted Bundy and Dennis Rader who similarly saw others as nothing more than playthings. The only difference is that Dahmer perceived victims as lovers. Put differently, a man who murders seventeen men in a drunken stupor because he won't deal with his own hang-ups is not deserving of our misplaced youthful sympathy.

Yeah, I grew up feeling lonely as well, but I just listened to Pearl Jam's *Ten* and Nirvana's *MTV Unplugged* on loop!

Dahmer was as manipulative and calculating as the other killers we've covered in this book, demonstrating a keen understanding of how to evade capture. The vast majority of his victims were Black men, not because Dahmer was exclusively attracted to the type, but because he knew that police were much less likely to investigate their disappearances. In this, he was absolutely correct, harkening back to the "less dead" theory we discussed in Gacy's case. When you add gay and poor to that victim profile, as many of Dahmer's victims were, you've got the perfect trifecta of investigative apathy.

Let's just say the Milwaukee cops were more biased than local Green Bay Packer radio announcers.

This shows that Dahmer was perfectly aware of what he was doing, and was a deceptively able predator. He had to get drunk to commit murder as a way of disconnecting his conscious brain from his crimes, but the rest of it was entirely planned.

To be fair, Jeffrey Dahmer surely had his fair share of mental problems. Diagnosed with everything from schizophrenia to borderline personality disorder, Dahmer certainly wasn't well by any metric. But his refusal to take responsibility for his own demons is more than enough to remove any and all sympathies for the man who defined for the Millennial generation what a serial killer was.

THE FIRST CHILD OF A LOVELESS MARRIAGE ON THE BRINK of collapse, Jeffrey Dahmer came into this world on May 21, 1960. His parents, Joyce and Lionel, were wildly incompatible, a fire-and-ice mixture only made worse by the horrible nausea and discomfort brought by Joyce's pregnancy. She never fully recovered from the postpartum depression she suffered following Jeffrey's birth, a fact that she was never shy about mentioning to him.

A good way to make sure your son makes you sad later in life is to start his life by telling him how sad his birth made you. To wit: your lifestyle is my sadstyle.

Ironically, and at odds with the expected behavior of a burgeoning serial killer, young Jeffrey Dahmer was a lover of animals, able to handle a goldfish and a turtle at the tender age of eighteen months. Even as a toddler, Jeffrey found animals easier to deal with than humans. He'd had problems with shyness from the time of nursery school, never quite figuring out how to play with the other children.

Like Christopher Robin! I believe Christopher Robin was also responsible for seventeen murders.

His detachment grew in 1964 when he was forced to endure a hernia operation. Just like fellow serial killer Joseph Kallinger, the intense pain that Dahmer suffered during the procedure changed him forever. The pain was so excruciating that he believed for a time that the doctors had completely removed his genitals in the process of fixing his affliction. Brian Masters, author of *The Shrine of Jeffrey Dahmer,* speculated in his 1993 book that this operation was the beginning of Dahmer's fixation with what existed inside a human body.

Honestly, how scary would it be to a kid if you were afraid of bones, and then one day you found out YOU WERE MADE OF GODDAMN BONES!?

This curiosity was bolstered the next year when Dahmer discovered a radiation research center that experimented on farm animals on the outskirts of Ames, Iowa, where his father was studying for a PhD in chemistry. Dahmer watched and wondered about the mysteries of a cow's innards as men wearing arm-length rubber gloves shoved their hands inside its anus to take readings.

They would be so surprised to reach up inside these cows and be like, "Here's the problem . . . there's a bowling pin stuck in here."

True fact: shoving a hand in a cow's butt is how farmers were able to tell how long the winter would be.

Soon after, Dahmer came across a cache of bones in the crawl space of his family's home that would escalate his obsession even more. There, in the dark, he found the bare skeletons of rats. Eternally amused with his new toys, he called them his fiddlesticks. Before long, Jeffrey had logically deduced that inside every animal is a whole new set of fiddlesticks, ready to be harvested. But he also had a softer side: upon discovering an abandoned baby hawk in his yard, he named it Dusty before nursing it back to health.

Although young Dahmer was noticeably pendulating from kindness to creep show, his parents couldn't have cared less. His mother was falling deeper into depression, partly due to her own predilections toward the affliction, but mostly because her husband had become completely absorbed with his PhD program. Joyce ignored her child, losing herself in a torrent of tranquilizers, while Lionel ignored both of them. Jeffrey was left to fend for himself.

Aw, like Littlefoot from *Land Before Time*.

I would be pretty distant with that little creep as well. Or I would try to send him to one of those archaeology summer camps they send rich kids to.

Comparatively, it was still a safe environment. No psychopathic Vietnam veteran cousins were waiting in the wings to warp Jeffrey's mind, no known molestation occurred. In fact, with proper direction, Dahmer might have made a perfectly competent pathologist or coroner. Instead, he was left to develop into a bad day at work for the Milwaukee medical examiner.

It NEVER turns constructive. Unless it's David Lynch. He's the only working artist I know of who came from a background of sucking on roadkill.

When the Dahmer family moved to Doylestown, Ohio, in 1966, Jeffrey grew more and more withdrawn. Joyce became pregnant again soon after, and Dahmer hoped that the birth of a baby brother might provide him with a companion. Instead, the second pregnancy made his mother's occasional cloud of depression a permanent fixture in the Dahmer household. A year later, the family moved to Bath Township, Ohio, where Jeffrey would live out the rest of his formative years, and retreat further into his increasingly twisted imagination.

It's so nice for Jeff to have a sibling, so if by some miracle the brother dies of childhood flu or polio or a car accident, he can get ahold of some real fiddlesticks. Human fiddlesticks!

It was called Bath Township because they actually sold President Taft the tub he got stuck in.

While Jeffrey was wholly uninterested in the typical activities of a young boy, he managed to make one close friend in Bath in David Borsolv. Bringing David into his confidence, Dahmer shared a favorite game of his own devising: Infinity Land. In Infinity Land, men represented by sticks would be made to inch closer and closer together until one of them, apparently overcome by nothing more than the presence of the other, would disappear into a vortex of nothingness. It was an impressive display of intelligence and imagination for a boy who was not yet ten, but the sense of alienation radiating from this game is palpable.

Oh, that's not so bad; I had more imaginary friends than the girl from *Drop Dead Fred*!

Jeffrey's intelligence soon began to extend itself into the world of the macabre. One night after dinner, he asked his father what would happen if they were to soak the leftover chicken bones in bleach. Lionel, impressed with his son's curiosity and jumping at the chance to share his love of chemistry, walked him through the

process step by step. Soon after, Lionel gifted his son an introductory chemistry set, hoping to encourage a scientific mind. Instead, young Dahmer used it only to test the effects of caustic chemicals on insects and dead animals.

A well-placed old-school chemistry set will turn any twelve-year-old into a Nazi scientist.

That's why I didn't pay attention in school—so they couldn't corrupt me.

As Dahmer approached adolescence, what started as small experiments had turned into a full-fledged collection of specimens. A shed near his home became a Mütter Museum of his own design, adorned with the acid-burned corpses of various woodland creatures stripped completely of their flesh. Next to the shed was a graveyard complete with headstones decorated with the skulls of the animals buried within, many of them found already dead on the road. Young Jeffrey would scoop the bodies off the pavement with his bare hands, bring them back to his shed, and dissect the rotting corpses just to see what was inside.

His father gave an almost resigned approval to this behavior, as the dead seemed to be the only things that kept his son's interest. Otherwise, he was seen as a polite but ultimately apathetic child. It wasn't until Jeffrey discovered alcohol at the age of fourteen that he began to show any signs of coming out of his shell. He found that although drinking didn't necessarily make him happy, it certainly made him a hair less miserable. Chasing that feeling for the rest of his life, he entered high school as a low-functioning alcoholic, often getting through the days by bringing a bit of scotch or gin into the classroom.

These are the opening scenes of the new CW Show *Edgar Allan Poe: The Middle School Years*.

School can be more boring than a U2 concert—sometimes ya need a nip!

After alcohol was introduced into the mix, Dahmer's "experiments" began taking on a darker tone. In one instance, he decapitated a dead dog he'd found on the side of the road, removed all the skin and flesh from the skull, and then displayed it on a pole in the middle of the woods. But something besides his willingness to get his hands even dirtier with animal carcasses had also begun to crystallize. From a young age, Jeffrey Dahmer had known deep down that he was gay. He and a friend had done some innocent experimentation before Dahmer had reached adolescence, but when he reached an age when he felt the need to go further, that urge manifested itself in a display of bone-chilling voyeurism.

Soon after hitting puberty, Dahmer started spending every afternoon after school sitting in the bushes, watching as a blissfully ignorant jogger ran past. Dahmer knew he felt sexually attracted to this man, but instead of the normal fantasies a boy might have about an unattainable object of desire, his sex drive took them to a place of darkness. He dreamed up a vague fantasy of the jogger lying perfectly still so Dahmer could explore his body for however long he liked. What made this desire abnormal was that he planned to make it actually happen. Knowing he couldn't just flag down a stranger and make a casual proposition, he prepared to knock the man unconscious and drag the body into the woods. Luckily for the jogger, on the day that Dahmer sat waiting with a baseball bat in his hands, he'd taken the afternoon off. Jeffrey never tried again, but the fantasy stuck.

See, this is why I take every day off from jogging! The human skin tent a sociopath could make from my flesh would be bigger than Kanye's ego!

This fantasy was part of Jeffrey's secret inner life, something he kept tamped down. Some of the kids at school had stumbled across his shack of horrors in the woods, but as high school progressed, he gained more of a reputation as an alcoholic oddball willing to do anything for a laugh than a potentially dangerous misanthrope. Feeding off the attention that he could get from a bizarre act, Dahmer would bleat in the hallways, fake seizures during class, or do impressions of his mother's cerebral palsy–inflicted interior decorator. Jeffrey was so well known for these antics at Revere High School that this sort of behavior became known among certain kids as "doing a Dahmer."

Remove the word *Dahmer* and you describe Henry and me in high school.

This is entering into high school royalty. There's the guy/girl who's good at sports, the guy/girl who gets good grades but can still drink beer, the leads of all the high school plays, the "class clowns" who are often in trouble, and then the most unique position of all: weirdos who do funny shit for attention.

Even with this dubious distinction, Dahmer managed to score a date to the prom with a girl named Bridget Geiger. Predictably, the date did not go well. Jeffrey technically behaved himself but was completely disinterested in dancing with her, or even having a picture taken. He left halfway through the dance to grab a burger but was stopped at the door by the chaperones. When Bridget returned to Dahmer's car after prom was over, she had to sweep aside the hamburger wrappers.

That's the coolest high school story of any of the killers we've covered. Go your own way, baby! Burger up!

This was called "pulling a Spicoli," from *Fast Times at Ridgemont High*.

Meanwhile, the marriage of Lionel and Joyce Dahmer was mercifully coming to an end, albeit eighteen years too late. The final indignity came when Joyce slept with another man while she was in another state attending her father's funeral. Although the welfare of Jeffrey's younger brother, David, became the main point of contention in the vicious divorce that followed, Jeffrey himself was nothing more than faint background noise. He'd recently turned eighteen and, as it had been for most of his life, was left to figure things out on his own.

He was finally off into Infinity Land. It seems like his real dream was to become invisible.

He coped by drinking. A teacher remembered finding a solitary Dahmer on Christmas Day 1977 wandering around Bath, three cans into a twelve-beer drunk. His sense of abandonment deepened when his father, still living at home even during the divorce, got in the family's station wagon and left town.

This is how I spent at least three Christmases in my twenties, while I was struggling doing comedy. And they were some of the best Christmases I ever had.

Since Dahmer was nothing more than an amusing curiosity to the kids in high school, he was mostly left alone with his thoughts and fantasies. The chance to make them a reality came when, in the summer of 1978, his mother and brother went to visit relatives in Chippewa Falls, leaving Jeffrey alone in the house while he waited to attend Ohio State.

I can feel for him here. The structure of going to school every day and being forced to talk with other people gave him something he could anchor to. As soon as that was gone, he was left swinging in the wind, with free time to delve deeper into his dark fantasies.

Small side note: Chippewa Falls is the home of Leinenkugel's beer. It's not the best, but it'll do the trick!

Aw, I love a Leiny!

That summer, Dahmer fantasized about picking up a hitchhiker. The nineteen-year-old kid who unluckily fulfilled that fantasy was named Steven Hicks. He'd been in Akron for a rock concert and was hitching his way back home to make it in time for his father's birthday party. Standing shirtless on the side of the road with his thumb sticking out, Hicks must have seemed like a gift from God to Dahmer, who slowly pulled over. Hicks hopped in quickly, no doubt relieved that someone his own age had decided to stop. He probably felt even luckier when Dahmer invited him back to his house for a few beers and a little weed.

NEVER GO TO A SECOND LOCATION.

The two of them drank and smoked for hours. Jeffrey felt as if they were connecting, but when Hicks stood and said they'd better get on the road, Dahmer was struck with a feeling somewhere between rage and longing. As he put it simply years later, "The guy wanted to leave but I didn't want him to leave."

This is the opposite thought that every single bouncer had about Dahmer at last call.

Dahmer told Hicks that it was fine if they had to go, but he needed to grab something from the cellar before they headed out. What Dahmer needed to grab was an eight-inch barbell. He walked over to Hicks, raised the weapon, and smashed it down on his head twice. When Dahmer discovered that Hicks was still alive, he strangled his new friend to death. Still in the fog of fantasy, Dahmer undressed the body and caressed it before masturbating on the corpse. Only after the sexual haze had disappeared did he realize what he'd done.

Similar to when I get super stoned and realize all the Domino's I just ate.

Seized by fear and regret, Dahmer dragged the body outside to the crawl space beneath the house and left it there overnight. The next day, he returned to the body as if it were just another pile of roadkill. Using a long knife, he removed the arms, legs, and head before slitting open the belly, and at long last Dahmer saw what was inside a man with his own eyes. The parts were then shoved into plastic garbage bags and relegated to different corners of the crawl space, as if separating them would mitigate what he'd done. One as experienced in the ways of corpses as he was should have known that decomposition would come quickly in the hot June sun, but perhaps that was part of the point. He let the bags of flesh rot for days, allowing the stink to rise through the floorboards of the Dahmer home.

A lot of spooky candle opportunities here.

Between the beer and the corpses, Dahmer's body must've smelled worse than the mansion in *Nothing But Trouble*.

Finally, after a few days of living on top of the remains, Jeffrey decided it was time to get rid of the evidence. He slammed a few beers for courage, loaded the bags of decomposing flesh into the back seat of his car, and began driving toward a ravine for disposal.

He'd only gotten a few miles down the road before seeing police lights in his rearview mirror. He'd been tagging the line so the officer suspected he might be drunk. But as Dahmer passed every sobriety test with flying colors, the officer, Richard Munsey, started to notice a rank smell coming from Jeffrey's car. Shining a light into the back seat, Munsey asked Dahmer what he was transporting. Dahmer explained that it was nothing more sinister than plain old garbage, and that he'd decided to drive out to the dump in the middle of the night because he couldn't sleep.

This sounds like the worst UberPool ever!

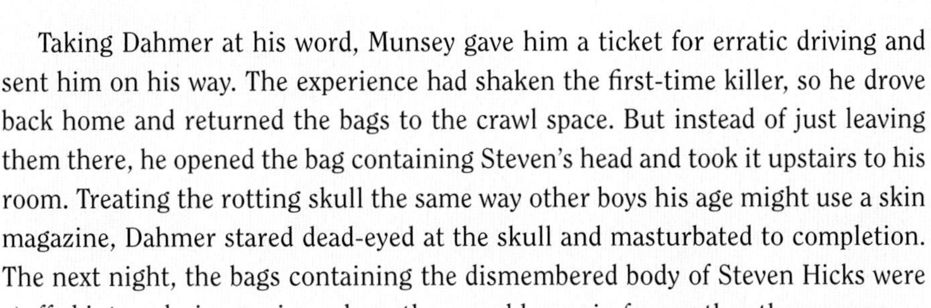

The officer was like, "Well, you're a creepy loser, but so am I! You get on out of here—I'm gonna go watch people through their bedroom windows, and if they stop me, I'll arrest them."

Taking Dahmer at his word, Munsey gave him a ticket for erratic driving and sent him on his way. The experience had shaken the first-time killer, so he drove back home and returned the bags to the crawl space. But instead of just leaving them there, he opened the bag containing Steven's head and took it upstairs to his room. Treating the rotting skull the same way other boys his age might use a skin magazine, Dahmer stared dead-eyed at the skull and masturbated to completion. The next night, the bags containing the dismembered body of Steven Hicks were stuffed into a drainage pipe, where they would remain for another three years.

In August, Lionel returned to his former home to find his son completely alone in a pile of his own filth, surrounded by empty beer cans. Outraged that his ex-wife had abandoned Jeffrey for months, Lionel moved back into the house and brought along his new girlfriend, Shari Jordan. The two of them kept an eye on Jeffrey until he began a short and undistinguished half semester at Ohio State.

Ohio State: Home of Jeffrey Dahmer, R. L. Stine, and Art Schlichter!!!

Dahmer's college roommates remember him as a hard-drinking weirdo who laid on the top bunk incessantly singing "I Am the Walrus" by The Beatles, downing whiskey straight from the bottle. The only times he left the dorm during the day were to buy more booze or sell blood for drinking money. Naturally, he was a bit of a buzzkill at parties, so the boys usually neglected to bring him along. That said, he still wanted in on the fun. One night, his roommates returned to find all their furniture stacked in the corner, pizza slathered on their walls, as punishment for leaving him behind. Their lucky break from the world of Dahmer came when he dropped out of school after just two months to join the army.

I had two roommates in a row like this in college. One guy used to call us into the living room and then he'd pee onto the tops of his feet, and then there was another guy who made "gooseberry wine." There should be a separate dorm on every campus that's just for potential serial killers.

All I'm gonna say is, if we'd had Dahmer in Vietnam, we might have won the dang thing!

Fittingly, Dahmer became a medic, training at Fort Sam Houston in San Antonio, where he was taught the ins and outs of human anatomy. By June 1979, he was on his way to Baumholder in West Germany. It wasn't long before he'd earned the distinction of being the drunkest soldier in his squad.

That's hard to do!

He was like Foster Brooks surrounded by rib cages.

Although alcohol wasn't allowed in the barracks, Dahmer hid a minibar in a small briefcase, complete with a martini shaker. While the rest of the men went drinking together, he would spend his weekends drinking alone, either during long, meandering walks or while lying in his bunk, listening to Black Sabbath on his Walkman and sometimes weeping over what he'd done to Steven Hicks.

He had an entire bar in a suitcase? Is this a story line from *Bosom Buddies*?

From the naked eye, Dahmer looks like a recently divorced dad trying to find a way to see his family again.

Dahmer didn't last long enough in the army to generate more of a reputation than for being a whiskey-soaked wretch who, at his best, said nothing, and at his worst, got belligerent when he drank too much, hurling racial slurs at his fellow soldiers. The irony of his time there came when he failed at being a medic and told his commanding officer a half-truth that he couldn't stand the sight of blood. Paired with the drinking, Dahmer's inability or unwillingness to perform his duties earned him a dismissal, so he returned to Ohio.

You CAN get fired from the army!

Unable to help himself, when Dahmer returned home he revisited the site where he'd dumped Steven Hicks's body. After peeling off and disposing of the remaining rotting flesh, he crushed the bones into manageable pieces. Then he walked to a ledge behind his house and, in an act that was almost ritualistic, spun in a circle and scattered the broken bones in a macabre halo.

The strangest thing about this is that the whole time, he was singing, "The hills are alive with the sound of music"!

I'd love to see a slow-motion video of it set to "I Believe I Can Fly."

Seeking a fresh start after his discharge from the army, in 1981 Dahmer decided to go down to Florida to try his hand at beach life. He lived in a motel and worked in a fast-food shack on Miami Beach, drinking away his earnings at the local bars. When he was evicted from the motel, he camped out on the beach for months.

The subplot to every single Jimmy Buffet song.

Eventually, Dahmer was lured back to Ohio at the behest of his parents, but it did nothing to curb his drinking. On an October night in 1981, he ambled into the lounge of a Ramada Inn carrying a bottle of vodka and was told to leave. He became belligerent, and after a brief scuffle with the police, Dahmer was arrested for a multitude of offenses and ultimately fined sixty dollars.

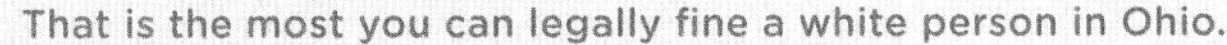

That is the most you can legally fine a white person in Ohio.

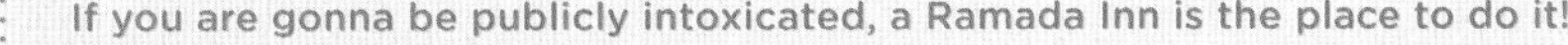

If you are gonna be publicly intoxicated, a Ramada Inn is the place to do it!

Following that incident, Dahmer was sent by his parents to live in his grandmother's basement in West Allis, Wisconsin, just outside Milwaukee. They had hoped that the presence of a loving relative would stem Jeffrey's increasingly self-destructive behavior, but moving him to a private basement close to a major metropolitan center was probably the worst thing they could have done.

That basement must've smelled worse than Gérard Depardieu's breath after a cheese and wine bender.

After moving in with Catherine Dahmer, Jeffrey behaved himself for years, although there were a couple of small hiccups. Lending support to the assumption that he'd lied about his blood aversion to get out of army service, Dahmer started working at Milwaukee Blood Plasma Inc. Out of curiosity, he once took a vial of blood home with him after work and tried drinking it, but found he didn't like the taste.

"I wanted strawberry-flavored! What is this, carpenter nails??"

Relatable. This is kinda like how I used to bring a pizza home when I worked at Pizza Hut.

The other kerfuffle came at the Wisconsin State Fair, when Dahmer drank to excess and urinated in front of approximately twenty-five people while leaning against a planter. He was fined only twenty-five dollars for this drunken mishap, but shortly thereafter lost his job at Milwaukee Blood Plasma Inc for showing up either hungover or flat-out drunk multiple times.

Following that, Jeffrey entered a two-year period of sobriety, prayer, and unemployment. Reading the Bible almost daily, he decided to privately chastise himself not for being a homicidal necrophiliac, but for being gay. The predictable self-imposed guilt trips kept the killing at bay for some time, but prayer and shame were only stopgap measures.

Christianity only helps, it never hurts. I am certain the crushing shame of the super-hetero eyeballs of Jesus Christ made his life a living hell.

The Bible is so full of blood and guts, Dahmer probably read it with the same enthusiasm I had when I used to read *Penthouse Forum*.

Paradoxically, when Dahmer wasn't praying, he was masturbating while thinking about the bodies of dead men. On average, he would pleasure himself at least four times a day, sometimes reaching as many as twelve sessions. But he found that the more he masturbated, the less punch his fantasies packed. The basic need for human companionship, even if it was as skewed as Dahmer's, was getting stronger, but his hang-ups kept him either in the basement or a church pew.

Is that too many times to masturbate? Whatever helps you not kill somebody is good in my book. Of course, it didn't help him, and now I'm thinking about what Dahmer's face must've looked like as he orgasmed. I put that image into your head from my head. You're welcome.

Dahmer tried curbing his habits in other odd ways. One day in 1984, three years before his second murder, as he was aimlessly wandering the streets he saw a mannequin in a store window. Feeling deep in his gut that this might be the answer to his prayers, Dahmer hid inside the store as it closed and only emerged when all the lights had been turned off. Sneaking up to the window display, he zipped a sleeping bag over his new plaything and carried it home.

Jeffrey spent weeks experimenting with the oversize doll, pretending it was a real person. He talked to it, dressed it, undressed it, masturbated onto it. The only reason he got rid of the mannequin was because his grandmother had found it in his closet and he was embarrassed. She hadn't shamed him for it; in fact, no one in Dahmer's family ever shamed him for his sexuality. When his father discovered that his son was gay, he only asked Jeffrey why he hadn't told him sooner. His mother, who was working at an AIDS clinic in Fresno when Jeffrey came out to her, gave him nothing but love and reassurance. While societal pressures certainly played a role, Dahmer's murderous urges weren't caused by his inability to accept his sexuality. It's fair to say that the only bearing his sexuality had on his crimes was in determining the gender of his victims, just as Ted Bundy's heterosexuality led him to choose exclusively female victims.

During this period, there *had* been one relatively bright spot in Dahmer's life. His long drought of unemployment was broken when he got a job as a mixer on the overnight shift at the Ambrosia Chocolate factory, earning nine dollars an hour. He'd hold the job until the end of his killing spree.

THERE'S BOOONES IN THE CHOCOLATE!!

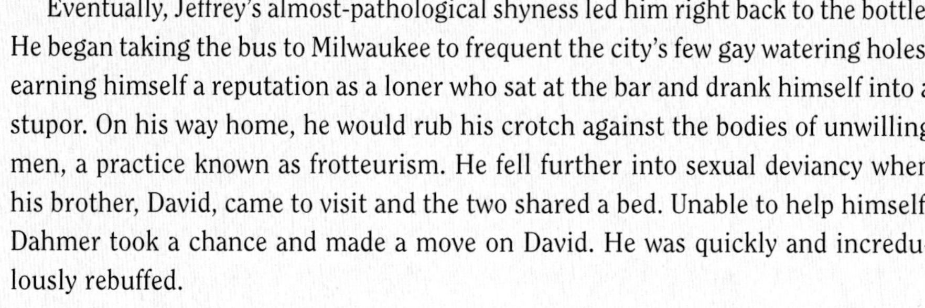

Eventually, Jeffrey's almost-pathological shyness led him right back to the bottle. He began taking the bus to Milwaukee to frequent the city's few gay watering holes, earning himself a reputation as a loner who sat at the bar and drank himself into a stupor. On his way home, he would rub his crotch against the bodies of unwilling men, a practice known as frotteurism. He fell further into sexual deviancy when his brother, David, came to visit and the two shared a bed. Unable to help himself, Dahmer took a chance and made a move on David. He was quickly and incredulously rebuffed.

Dahmer really would've loved the strange family trends so prevalent on Pornhub right now.

It wasn't until Dahmer discovered the bathhouses of Milwaukee that he found a suitable hunting ground for his urges. His favorite one, appropriately called Club Bath, was outfitted with a coffee bar, a TV lounge, saunas, Jacuzzis, and private rooms for anonymous gay hookups. Dahmer met plenty of willing and able men but found that he had no desire whatsoever to give as good as he got. He saw his partners as nothing more than vehicles for his own pleasure and would get annoyed when they asked for even a little reciprocation. Then, in 1986, he found the scumbag's shortcut to getting exactly what he wanted: Halcion.

Struck with an idea for a way to treat men exactly how he wanted, Dahmer told his doctor that his internal body clock was having trouble resetting from working overnights at Ambrosia Chocolate, and from that single visit, Jeffrey was suddenly flush with sleeping pills. He'd stuff some into his pockets before leaving for Club Bath, where he'd mix them into drinks bought for other customers. Once he saw his potential victim getting woozy, he would usher him to a private room and assault him. The other patrons reported Dahmer, but it wasn't until he caused an overdose that resulted in a coma that his membership at Club Bath was revoked. Due to the sensitive nature of the establishment, the police were never called.

This is where homophobia actually helped Dahmer. The owners of the bar couldn't bring the law into this situation whatsoever. They had no protection by authority—they had to protect themselves and their community like it was Deadwood.

Permanently barred from the gay wonderland that was Club Bath, Dahmer moved on to Milwaukee's Club 219 and began drugging men there before taking them to a flophouse called the Ambassador Hotel. Once inside, he would masturbate onto the unconscious men and then press his ear to their chest or stomach to hear their innards work. However, Dahmer's eternal problem was that he knew these men would eventually wake up and leave. He needed something more.

Dahmer listened to guts moving around like it was the most morbid white-noise machine in the world. I'd love to find a sleep aid app that has a music track called "FOOD MOVING THROUGH INTESTINES."

Taking yet another step back to murder, Dahmer attempted to go the Gein route and procure a corpse from a graveyard. He pored over the obituaries for a suitable candidate before settling on an eighteen-year-old boy. After attending the boy's funeral, he followed the procession to the graveyard and, from a distance, watched where the body was buried. A few days later, he returned and tried to dig up the corpse, but discovered that Wisconsin soil freezes fast in the wintertime. Abandoning the plan, Dahmer began letting his urges run wild.

As the only person from Wisconsin here, I would like to clarify that not everyone is a grave robber! Some of us are just comedians.

In September 1986, Dahmer was arrested for drunkenly masturbating at two twelve-year-old boys on the banks of the Kinnickinnic River. While this wasn't Dahmer's first arrest, it was his first serious offense. To the authorities, though, he framed this incident as nothing more than a misunderstanding. He said he'd been having a few lonely, miserable beers in the park, then went to relieve himself. Thinking he was alone, he figured he'd might as well masturbate. The kids unfortunately stumbled upon the scene, and it all went downhill from there.

He used the "meddling kids" defense in real life!

If you're masturbating and there's the potential that a twelve-year-old could "stumble" onto the scene, I'm just gonna say stop.

For the charge of lewd and lascivious behavior, Dahmer was given a suspended one-year sentence and was ordered to undergo counseling. He refused to speak to his counselor, possibly out of fear of admitting his prior transgressions, but she was able to get him to talk just enough to come to this conclusion: "[There is] no doubt at this time that he is a Schizoid Personality Disorder who may show marked paranoid tendencies. He is definitely SPOOKY!"

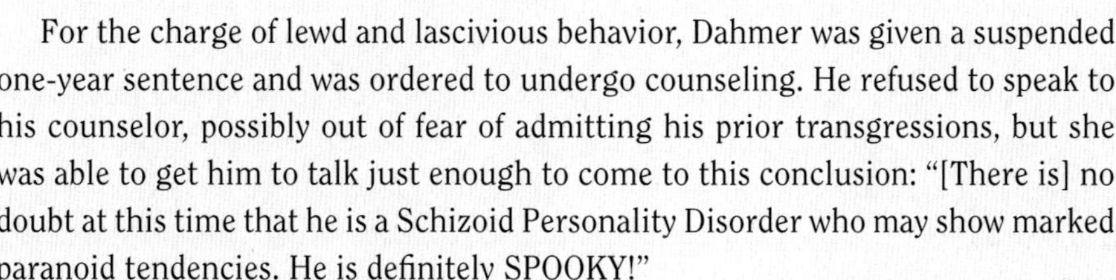

Did she seriously write *spooky* like this was a review for Halloween Horror Nights?

Ha ha! Was this counselor the mean girl from *Hey, Arnold!*?

A second counselor who saw Jeffrey gave a somewhat more measured analysis. She said that his deviant behavior would continue in some form, and without an intervention of some sort, his behavior would escalate to sadism. While Dahmer was certainly no sadist, the prediction of escalation was spot-on. On September 15, 1987, Dahmer would kill again.

Steven Tuomi met Dahmer on September 15, 1987, at 219 Club. Playing the same tune he had for months, Dahmer spiked Tuomi's drink and took him back to the Ambassador Hotel, where he sexually assaulted him after he passed out. Dahmer claims that he remembers Tuomi being just fine when he went to sleep, but when the morning came, there was nothing more than a corpse lying next to him. In reality, Dahmer had beaten Tuomi to death, caving in his chest with his bare hands. He'd savaged his victim so badly that Dahmer's own arms and hands were black and blue with bruises.

After the initial panic had subsided, Dahmer dragged Tuomi's body to a closet and then walked to the Grand Avenue mall. There, Dahmer purchased a large suitcase on wheels and returned to the Ambassador, where he roughly shoved Steven Tuomi's body inside it and wheeled it back down to the street. Hailing a cab, he directed the driver to his grandmother's home in West Allis. Once there, he pulled the suitcase into his basement room and went to sleep. The body remained there for another week, decomposing in the suitcase, before Dahmer gave it another look.

In college I would visit home with dirty laundry so I wouldn't have to do it at the dorms. This . . . is different.

After days of letting the corpse lie in wait, Dahmer started his vile dissection. He began by decapitating the body, then continued by slicing the belly open to remove the organs. Next, he cut the flesh away from the body in small chunks that he disposed of along with the organs in a series of garbage bags. Then he wrapped the bones in a sheet and smashed them into smaller pieces with a sledgehammer. All in all, the dismemberment took two hours. The finished product was placed on the curb for garbage collection, and to this day, no trace of Steven Tuomi's body has ever been found.

But Dahmer was unable to let go completely. Bereft of any other kind of trophy, he decided to keep the head, at least for a little while. He boiled it in a powerful household detergent called Soilex to separate the flesh and brain from the skull, then bleached it to give it a nice shine. Just as it had been with Steven Hicks, his victim's head became nothing more than a masturbation tool. The skull lasted two weeks before the bleach ate away at the bone. When it became too brittle, Dahmer smashed and tossed it.

However, he'd been sloppy in his cleanup job. Months later, his grandmother noticed a distinct smell coming from the basement and called Lionel over to see if he could suss out the source. After very little searching, Lionel came upon the obvious culprit: a piece of human flesh had missed its date with the garbage collector and had turned into a black, slimy residue. Jeffrey's excuse was that he had merely been continuing his childhood hobby of de-fleshing dead animals. His father passively accepted the story, although he did imply that Jeffrey should consider moving on from this particular hobby if he wanted to be a functioning member of society. Jeffrey had no interest in anything of the sort.

At this point, if I was Jeff's dad, I would be pretty hesitant to criticize him. "Hey, son, I mentioned one word of what you're like to my friends at work, and they told me to burn you at the stake. You think you could not be a creepazoid for two weeks so I can feel good again?"

To be fair, "My son has rotting flesh in his room; what do I do?" is rarely a question answered in parenting books.

About a month later, Dahmer spotted fourteen-year-old James Doxtator outside of Club 219. Doxtator was one of many boys who were too young to enter the club and instead cruised for older men at the bus stop located just outside its door. To Dahmer, he was an easy target. Doxtator readily agreed to Dahmer's offer of fifty dollars to spend the night, and the two took the bus back to West Allis.

After fooling around for a few hours, at 4:00 a.m. Doxtator stood up and said it was about time for him to head home. Feigning assistance, Dahmer mixed his young guest an Irish coffee for the road and surreptitiously slipped five crushed sleeping pills into the cup. Doxtator was asleep in his lap within minutes.

Knowing that he couldn't have a young boy asleep in his room when his grandmother woke up for church, Dahmer lifted James's head from his lap and strangled him to death before shoving the body in the fruit closet. He then went upstairs and casually ate breakfast with Catherine. Once she left, he brought the body to the upstairs bedroom and spoke to it as if a soul was still inside. Soon growing tired of that, he had anal sex with the corpse, his first of many acts of necrophilia.

This time, the body stayed in the basement with Dahmer for a week. When Catherine again complained of the smell, he disposed of Doxtator's body the same way he'd gotten rid of the previous victim's, again saving the head. Two months later, his probation ended. It had done nothing to curb his killing—four days after, he killed again.

I don't remember any of these scenes from *Grandma's Boy*.

Dahmer met twenty-three-year-old Richard Guerrero outside of the Phoenix Bar, another gay hangout, and repeated his encounter with James Doxtator almost to the letter. The only difference was that Dahmer skipped the skull-bleaching step. While that certainly saved the bone from brittleness, the stench of decay became much more noticeable. But Dahmer was finding that he didn't particularly care.

Literally a pig in shit.

Dahmer would not kill the next man he brought home, a fortuitous turn of events for the victim. Twenty-three-year-old Ronald Flowers Jr. woke up in the middle of a field near Dahmer's home after going there with him following an encounter at Club 219. After sexually assaulting his victim, Jeffrey had gotten cold feet and had dragged Flowers out there himself. Flowers reported the incident to the police, which resulted in a cursory investigation, but since the story couldn't be proven, they refused to charge Dahmer.

They still had the view of "Gay sex? Ew!" They thought gay men were deviants and purposely didn't try to understand, let alone accept, their lifestyle.

Because there was an investigation, Catherine Dahmer had been grilled by the police. While the strange visitors, noises, and smells had been tolerable, this was too much for her to handle. She kicked her grandson out, which, of course, he took as another personal abandonment. So after packing up his meager belongings and the skull of Richard Guerrero, Jeffrey briefly moved to Milwaukee proper. His newfound independence would last less than forty-eight hours.

Cut to him packing up all his polished skulls in a duffel bag: "I hate you, Grandma!"

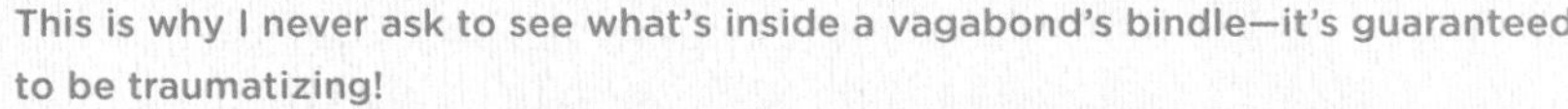

This is why I never ask to see what's inside a vagabond's bindle—it's guaranteed to be traumatizing!

The day after he moved into his new apartment, Dahmer spotted thirteen-year-old Somsack Sinthasomphone walking home from school. He approached the boy and started a conversation about a new Polaroid camera he'd just bought. Dahmer casually mentioned that he'd been offering prospective models fifty bucks a session for photo shoots, but nobody had taken him up on the offer. Not knowing what he was getting himself into, the teenager jumped at the easy money.

I was paid one hundred dollars for pictures of my hairy chest and then had sausages eaten off of me, but this was for television and I was over eighteen, so it wasn't a crime, just a sad life choice I made.

Once they were back at Dahmer's apartment, he gave the boy Halcion-laced coffee and told him to take off his shirt, claiming that it would make for a better photo. Smartly, Sinthasomphone only sipped his drink. Dahmer then made a move and began fondling him. But when he brought his mouth into the mix, Sinthasomphone groggily grabbed his bag and hurriedly stumbled out the door. The next day, Dahmer was arrested at the Ambrosia Chocolate factory and charged with second-degree sexual assault and enticing a child for immoral purposes.

Very specific crime. So specific it makes me shudder to think how many times it had to happen before it became a very specific *official* crime.

But it wasn't the prospect of prison time for the Sinthasomphone assault that was filling Dahmer with dread as he waited to make bail—it was the skull of Richard Guerrero. Fortunately for Jeffrey, he had hidden it well. Police executed a search warrant on his apartment but only confiscated the Polaroid, the photos he'd taken of Sinthasomphone, and his sleeping pills.

The maddening part of this whole saga is that it didn't keep Dahmer from getting more pills. After being released on bail, he went straight to his doctor's office and refilled his Halcion prescription without incident. It was the fourteenth refill and many more were to come, as pills were as essential to Jeffrey Dahmer as a .44 Bulldog was to the Son of Sam.

The doctor just figured Jeff was really, really, really tired but couldn't sleep? Think of all the sugar at the chocolate factory—that has to hurt the sleep cycle!

Armed with more pills and back in his grandmother's house after falsely promising her he'd clean up his act, Dahmer chose Anthony Sears as his next victim. He lured the aspiring model to his home from the popular gay bar La Cage aux Folles with the promise of a photo shoot, pictures, drinks, and no-strings-attached sex. Sears would not survive the night.

PUN ALERT: The modeling industry is cutthroat. I'm sorry!

After drugging his victim, Dahmer laid his head on Anthony's chest and listened to his heartbeat. While this was something he had done for a sexual thrill since childhood, he had begun using the practice in a practical way as well. By that point, he had drugged enough men to know when someone was coming out of their Halcion-induced coma, so he would wait until he heard the telltale short, sharp breaths to end their lives through strangulation.

Dahmer is truly the ultimate example of a product killer. As such, he did not take pleasure in ending a life; it was only a means to an end. He wanted a pliant body that he could totally dominate without any consideration for that person's wants or needs.

Dahmer killed Sears the night before Easter Sunday, giving himself plenty of extra time with the body while his grandmother attended the extended services. He brought the corpse to the upstairs bathroom and dismembered it in the tub with precision. Instead of just saving the head, Dahmer kept his victim's genitals as well. Knowing that such a fleshy member would decompose fairly quickly, he called a local taxidermist and asked for a few tricks of the trade for preserving animal remains. The taxidermist replied that acetone would work just fine for an amateur such as himself, so Dahmer bought a ten-gallon bucket from Ace Hardware, filled it with a jug of acetone and some water, and soaked Sears's head and genitals in it on the floor of his bedroom closet for a week. Then, after removing them and drying them off, Dahmer applied makeup to both to make them look more lifelike for his masturbation sessions. When the head mummified, Dahmer removed the dried scalp and used that for a masturbation aid too.

Ack! And I thought the Fleshlight was a bit extreme.

Dahmer spent a week with Sears's body parts before he suddenly remembered that, once his trial came around, he was probably going to go to jail for the sexual assault rap. But parting with his new toys had become unthinkable. About Sears, Dahmer said, "Him I liked especially well." So, in the lead-up to the trial, instead of disposing of the evidence, he stored the head and genitals in a cosmetics case that he stowed at the bottom of his locker at Ambrosia Chocolate.

Oh good! Right next to the extremely porous vats of chocolate! Mmmm! So much fun!

He's a creepier night shift worker than Martin from *The Human Centipede 2*!

It turned out Dahmer's instincts were correct. In May 1989, he was easily found guilty of second-degree sexual assault. Once again, he was full of contrition at his sentencing, blaming his isolation and severe depression, but the assistant DA in charge of prosecuting the case wasn't hearing it. Taking his past offenses into account and seeing Dahmer for exactly what he was, she called for a sentence of five years. The judge was not so clear-eyed. He sentenced Dahmer to just one year in a work-release program, so he could still make his night shifts at Ambrosia, and five years' probation.

"You are guilty of sexual assault, but look at how sad you are!!! I sentence you to a night in on the couch watching *Mad About You*, and one thousand hugs."

The only slight comeuppance Dahmer received during this time period was when he himself was drugged at Club 219 while on Thanksgiving leave from prison. After going home with a bearded, long-haired stranger, Dahmer was surprised to wake up suspended from hooks, with his legs bound and his hands tied behind his back. The stranger sodomized Dahmer with a candle until Jeffrey screamed loud enough to be let go.

Wisconsin, the land of so many serial killers, they begin to kill each other. Can you imagine the egg on that other guy's face? And by egg, I mean blood!

What the hell was going on in the 1980s?!?!?!

Because of the lenient sentence, Dahmer's father, Lionel, tried getting the court to listen to sense. He wrote a plea to the judge, begging him to force his son to undergo treatment for his alcoholism, but the petition was ignored. Dahmer was released from prison on March 2, 1990. Less than two weeks later, he retrieved his cosmetic case from his work locker and moved into unit 213 at the Oxford Apartments in Milwaukee. Twelve people would die by his hands within these walls.

He was just starting his career as a serial killer! All of this happened before he even really got going!

Choosing the Oxford Apartments was no accident on Dahmer's part. While being the only white man in a poor Black neighborhood certainly made him stand out, it also provided a kind of protection. Milwaukee is a highly segregated city, and while Jeffrey may have seemed shifty in a white neighborhood, police officers working Black neighborhoods saw him as an almost-comforting presence, something familiar. He was never going to be the target of an investigation at Oxford Apartments; rather, the man whose first decoration in his new home was the spray-painted skull of a murder victim became someone to protect.

If you're a college sociology professor, please teach a course about white privilege in the context of Jeffrey Dahmer!

The first man to meet his end at the hands of Jeffrey Dahmer in unit 213 was Raymond Lamont Smith. Lured to the apartment with the promise of a fifty-dollar bill, Dahmer spiked Smith's drink and strangled him on the floor. With no possibility of Grandma Dahmer walking in, he could now do whatever he wanted with the body. He placed the corpse on his table, maneuvering it into various positions. When he finally got it into one he liked, Dahmer ran out and bought another Polaroid camera to capture the moment.

And then he had ice cream for dinner and pizza for breakfast! The ultimate bachelor life.

I've said a thousand times . . . if you know someone with a Polaroid, they ARE A SERIAL KILLER!

But Dahmer found that living in an apartment also had its drawbacks. Disposal became his number-one problem. Instead of having the wide-open space of his grandmother's cellar and the ease of curbside garbage service, he had to be content with dissecting Smith's body in the bathroom and disposing of it in-house.

Once the body was suitably dismembered, Dahmer boiled the various parts in an eighty-gallon kettle filled with water and Soilex to separate flesh from bone, then rinsed the bones in the sink to remove the last bits of meat. The skeleton was then soaked in a large trash can filled with water and acid for a week. When he finally opened the lid, he found that it had turned into a black slush that was easily flushed down the toilet. The only thing he kept was the skull, which he spray-painted and placed right next to the skull of Anthony Sears. His collection was again growing.

As someone who lives in an apartment building, I'm never going to trust my neighbors again!

Dahmer's next possible victim, however, turned the tables on him. Dahmer confused his own drink with the one meant for his guest and ended up passed out on his couch. When he awoke, all of his clothes were gone and he was three hundred dollars lighter.

This is scene four on the serial killers blooper tape, right after Son Of Sam finding out his milk was expired and Charles Manson falling out of his dune buggy.

Eddie Smith was not so lucky. Dahmer met him at the Phoenix Bar and killed him the night before the 1990 Milwaukee Gay Pride Parade. For this victim, Dahmer bought a freezer and placed the skeleton inside, hoping to preserve it. When he found that skeletons don't hold together without connective tissue, he acidified the remains. Eddie Smith's skull received an even more macabre end. Dahmer had placed it in the oven to dry it out, but the heat caused pressure to build and the skull exploded. Dahmer later lamented that he felt "rotten" about this murder in particular. He had regretted killing Eddie, yes, as he'd regretted killing every man he murdered, but that's not why he felt particularly guilty in this case. For him, without a trophy, the entire thing had been a waste.

Aw, this is like when a cake fails to rise on *The Great British Bake Off*.

Try writing a pilot that doesn't get picked up!

That rotten feeling became more outwardly noticeable during a visit with his probation officer. Jeffrey had been seeing her weekly since his release from prison, and in general, his behavior was odd enough to warrant a note that he needed extreme supervision. After Smith's murder, however, Dahmer was so distraught that she strongly recommended a home check. But since Dahmer lived in a crime-ridden neighborhood, nobody ever came. Ten more lives would be lost as a result of this negligence.

This truly makes me more angry than Nicolas Cage in *The Wicker Man* . . . NOT THE BEES!

His next victim, teenager Luis Pinet, was picked up outside another gay bar where Dahmer offered him two hundred dollars for nude photos and a hookup. The two ended up hanging out all night, taking photos and having sex, but Dahmer was distraught to find that he was out of sleeping pills. Pinet lived through that night and returned the next when promised more money for another session. Not willing to wait for pills, Dahmer improvised his plan of attack. As Pinet posed in bed while *The Exorcist III* played in the background (Jeffrey's favorite movie), Dahmer brought out a rubber mallet that he'd bought earlier that day at an army surplus store. Echoing his first murder, he smacked Pinet in the head with his new weapon, but Pinet didn't lose consciousness and reacted with anger. Jeffrey tried backtracking, saying he was afraid Pinet was going to leave without giving him what he wanted.

Pinet left, but sadly for him came back ten minutes later to ask if he could at least have a couple bucks for a bus ride home for his trouble. Dahmer figured he'd give it one more go and attempted to strangle the teenager, but Pinet was too strong. So instead of killing him, Dahmer walked Pinet to the bus stop and paid for a taxi home, threatening to murder him if he ever told anyone what happened.

And that concludes the weirdest episode of *Blind Date* ever.

Pinet did not keep his promise to stay quiet. He was taken to the hospital by his parents as soon as he got home and, while there, gave police Dahmer's description and exact address. Given that he was on probation, Dahmer should have gone to jail immediately, but that didn't happen. Pinet filed a false imprisonment complaint, but no follow-up was done. As far as the Milwaukee police were concerned, this had just been an icky homosexual lover's quarrel that had gotten out of hand. It didn't seem to matter that the victim was only fifteen years old.

In the middle of all this, Dahmer had been falling deeper into his own unique brand of depression, but he found something to lift his spirits: fish. Dazzled by the humanlike eyes of a puffer fish, Dahmer bought a tropical tank in 1990 and became an enthusiast. While his apartment was covered in mysterious brown stains and empty Bud cans, his fish tank was always immaculate, even as he fell further into depravity and bloodshed.

Nemo must've been pretty traumatized watching all these severed penises getting sucked on every night.

Dahmer's next victim was Ernest Miller. In town from Chicago, Ernest was lured back to unit 213 by a fifty-dollar bill. When they entered the apartment, Dahmer discovered he was running low on sleeping pills, but he still had two to spare. But rather than risk losing another confrontation as he had with Luis Pinet, Dahmer drugged Ernest Miller before slitting his jugular with a knife.

Dahmer was becoming more comfortable with killing despite feeling more guilt for doing it. After decapitating Ernest, Dahmer kissed the head, spoke with it, and apologized for his transgressions. He was about to transgress even further.

Can't wait for you to tell us how, Marcus!

After removing the limbs from the torso, Dahmer cut it into two sections and boiled each in Soilex for two hours. Afterward, he cleaned the bones with a light bleaching solution and spread them out on newspaper on his bedroom floor. Returning to the limbs, he sliced meat from the thighs and arms and stored it in the freezer for later. The cannibalism was about to begin.

Hey, Marcus, would you say, "And that's when the cannibalism *started*?"

He said the thing in the other chapter. This time Marcus is being classy.

He started with Ernest Miller's bicep. Using an adaptable grill placed over his gas stove, Dahmer would sear the flesh of his victims on both sides and eat it with mushrooms and onions. His motivation was the same as UK cannibal Dennis Nilsen's: both engaged in cannibalism so their victims would become permanent parts of them.

Dining upon the bodies while looking at Polaroids of the corpses pre-butchery, Dahmer would relive the experiences and then masturbate. However, he only ate the men he considered to be perfect specimens. Most of his victims were used purely as sex objects, although one was deemed useless even for that.

Dahmer met twenty-two-year-old David Thomas outside a gay bar called C'est La Vie and brought him home. After drugging him almost out of habit, he was suddenly struck with the thought that he wasn't particularly attracted to the man passed out in front of him. Dahmer killed him and dismembered his corpse anyway, not because it gave him a thrill but because he thought that Thomas might be angry when he woke up. In other words, Dahmer murdered this victim purely to avoid confrontation.

I guarantee he's more upset to be dead, bro!

For whatever reason, this murder seemed to throw Jeffrey off his game. Five months passed without another kill, though it hadn't been for lack of trying—Dahmer just couldn't get anyone to come back to his apartment. He was only able to break his dry spell by taking advantage of a struggling Marquette University student named Curtis Straughter.

It seems like this next murder could have been avoided if college was more affordable!

Straughter had just been fired from his job and was willing to do anything to make it to the next semester. Dahmer offered him the same cash-for-sex trade as he had with his other victims, but he was getting more aggressive. Instead of waiting until the college student was passed out, Dahmer strangled him with a leather strap while Straughter was performing oral sex. Afterward, as he dismembered the body, he plunged his hands into Straughter's intestines, feeling the viscera. He then placed his penis inside the guts and ejaculated into them. Once he was done, he decapitated the corpse, cleaned the skull, and placed it next to the other three.

His depravity was escalating. Between early April and late July 1991, he would murder seven men, furthering his experimentation into places never before seen in even the darkest recesses of serial killer lore. Ironically, though, the driving force that sent him down that road was in keeping his victims alive.

Dahmer had grown weary of killing people and having nothing left but the skull. After all, when it came to his motivations, the actual murder wasn't the point. Dahmer was what is known as a product killer: the goal was the body at the end. But as the murders continued, he began to wonder how much more satisfying a living, breathing person who was there only to satisfy his needs might be. The question was how it could be done. There were no guidebooks or medical journals concerning such a taboo subject, so Dahmer was forced to experiment. It began with nineteen-year-old Errol Lindsey.

You know what, Marcus? I am really glad there are no guidebooks for this kind of behavior. What kind of fuckery would we have to deal with if there were several textbooks for "How to Make an Undead Sex Slave That Don't Stink!"

Seems like Dahmer went to the same medical school as the demented doctor from *Re-Animator*.

Dahmer and Lindsey had casually met in broad daylight while the teenager was out getting a key made. Lindsey wasn't gay, but he agreed to try homosexual sex when Dahmer offered him a good amount of cash. The drugged drink came quickly thereafter, and Lindsey was soon out cold on Dahmer's couch. But instead of murdering him like he'd done with all his other victims, Jeffrey pulled out a new purchase and used it to drill a hole in his skull. Penetrating just far enough to reach the brain, Dahmer then used the cavity to inject a small amount of hydrochloric acid with a marinating injector. Somehow he thought this would turn the boy into a sex zombie of some sort, a slave who would do his bidding until the body eventually expired.

If it had actually worked, Dahmer would've had to deal with real relationship stuff.

Instead of turning into a zombie, Lindsey just woke up confused, complaining of a headache and asking for the time. Knowing he'd failed, Dahmer drugged him again and strangled him to death. But his experimentation wasn't done. He proceeded to flay the skin from Lindsey's corpse in one large piece with a small paring knife, later commenting in his confession that it was just like skinning a chicken. The skin lasted only three weeks before it began to disintegrate, so Dahmer disposed of it by flushing the entire thing down the toilet. But he had other problems besides the longevity of his trophies. People were starting to notice the smell.

Huh? No way!

You know what would fix that? Some Joop! Ever use Joop?! It's a cologne from the nineties that was like deer repellent, but for friends.

At first, most people with apartments on Dahmer's floor assumed the smell was coming from a completely different apartment where someone had been strangled during a one-off murder, but it continued to linger even after that body was carted away. Dahmer managed to get rid of some of his remains by crushing bones as he'd done before or throwing away shreds of flesh a few at a time in garbage bags, but the effort was Sisyphean to say the least.

Eventually, the building manager, Sopa Princewill, confronted Dahmer about the stench that was obviously coming from his apartment. Calmly and coolly, he explained that some meat in his freezer had spoiled. When the smell worsened, he claimed that some of his fish had died. Sopa didn't press the issue further. As a result, Dahmer felt more comfortable keeping whole bodies for longer periods of time. His next victim, Tony Hughes, rotted in his bedroom for days before Dahmer began the disposal process. He'd been enjoying the company.

In May of 1991, Dahmer left Hughes's body in his apartment and went wandering around Milwaukee's Grand Avenue area. He hadn't been looking for a victim that day, but there was something about fourteen-year-old Konerak Sinthasomphone that he couldn't resist. Impulsively, he offered the boy fifty dollars for photos and eventually he agreed. But Konerak should have known better. By some horrific cosmic coincidence, Konerak Sinthasomphone was the younger brother of Somsack, the boy Dahmer was currently on probation for molesting. He was falling into the same trap that had almost gotten his brother killed, but he would not be as lucky.

These must be some handsome boys! Is that not what I'm supposed to take from this?

Once Dahmer had taken the boy back to his apartment and drugged him, the drill made a return. Taking careful aim, he bored a small hole into the top of the skull, then once again injected pure hydrochloric acid into the cavity. However, this activity had made Dahmer thirsty. He got up to get another beer but found he'd just drunk the last one. But instead of just going out for another sixer, Dahmer left Sinthasomphone passed out on his couch while having a few rounds at a bar on Twenty-Seventh and Kilbourn. While he was gone, a disoriented and naked Konerak wandered out into the streets.

Three girls named Nicole Childress, Sandra Smith, and Tina Spivey were the first to try to help the dazed young boy. They'd noticed that in addition to being unclothed and out of sorts, his buttocks were stained with patches of blood. Obviously, something was terribly wrong. But as they were trying to assist him, Dahmer rounded the corner. He immediately took charge, grabbing Konerak by the elbow and saying he'd take care of the situation from there. When Konerak resisted, Dahmer put him in a headlock and started walking him away. However, the conflict had caused such a scene that both the fire department and the police arrived before he could get him off the street.

Whew, and this is where the story must end!

This should be where this chapter ends.

Okay, I stand corrected.

A quick background check would have told police that the person who was manhandling a naked fourteen-year-old boy was a registered sex offender who was currently on probation. What's more, they would have discovered that said offense involved this fourteen-year-old boy's older brother. But when the police began questioning Dahmer, he was calm. He told them that although Konerak looked young, he was actually his twenty-year-old boyfriend who sometimes lost control when he had too much to drink.

"He's forty but he looks fourteen. He has the Benjamin Button thing, or is it Jack? Robin Williams committed suicide and you expect me to remember which of these movies is right to help me get this woozy boy back in my room?!"

The girls who had found Konerak couldn't believe what they were hearing. At the very least, the boy was obviously nowhere near twenty years old. What was more, he was clearly in distress. But while Dahmer was spoken to in the courteous tone of an equal, the girls were told to "shut the hell up" and go on home. Wanting to avoid further confrontation with the police, they obeyed and relayed the story to an adult. The police were called but the girls were told that Konerak was definitely not a child and their assistance was not needed.

After apologizing profusely for all the trouble his boyfriend had caused, Dahmer returned to his apartment accompanied by three officers and Sinthasomphone. As Konerak sat on the couch, confused and terrified but unable to speak, the police poked around Jeffrey's apartment. Had they opened the bedroom door more than a crack, they would have found the dead body of Anthony Hughes. As it was, they only joked that it smelled like someone had taken a dump in the middle of the apartment and left. Then they called in the incident, laughingly reporting that they had returned an intoxicated naked Asian male to his sober boyfriend, ending the communication by saying they'd be back at the station any minute for a delousing.

I think it's safe to assume these bigoted cops are currently living in a nursing home yelling about how the government is using aluminum to create transgender folks.

By the time the cops were back in their squad car and making their little jokes, Dahmer was already injecting more acid into Konerak's brain. It was almost instantly fatal. His and Anthony Hughes's torsos were acidified together, their severed heads stored in the fridge for later processing.

While many of Dahmer's victims were ignored or forgotten by the police at the time of their disappearances, Milwaukee's gay community was all too aware that people had started to go missing. Many tried reporting these disappearances, but again found that none of their accounts were taken seriously or investigated in the slightest.

Meanwhile, it was becoming obvious to Dahmer that hydrochloric acid wasn't the way to go if he wanted to keep his sex zombies alive for more than a few hours. So when he drilled a hole in the head of his next victim a little over a week later, he tried using boiling water instead. It was also an idiotic idea, but the victim did survive a bit longer. He shuffled around the apartment for six hours, confused but still somewhat lucid. Dahmer thought himself to be an alchemist of the body, able to convert the lead of human interaction into a golden heaven of pure pleasure. But when he left for work and returned ten hours later, he found he'd killed this one as well.

Someone got a bit overconfident. Jeff was not an alchemist. He was an alcoholic psychopath.

If you come home to find you accidentally killed another person, I think it's time to reevaluate your life choices.

For Dahmer, though, this one was not going to be a total waste. By this time in his career, he'd become a fairly skilled butcher of humans. Later, during his confession, he said that for that last month of freedom, man flesh was his only source of meat.

But there was still only so much that Dahmer could store in the fridge. By July 1991, ten men had been killed in an apartment that wasn't very big to begin with. Now it was overflowing with the rotting gore of his victims. The dead fish excuse was no longer holding with the building manager and Dahmer was facing down an eviction notice. In a last-ditch effort to solve the problem, he bought a fifty-seven-gallon blue barrel and an industrial amount of hydrochloric acid. This vat, kept in Dahmer's bedroom, would act as a soaking tub to dissolve the body parts of some of his last victims.

This motherfucker needs OxiClean! That dead cokehead Billy Mays had been using it to hide the evidence of his own bodies. That's why he always showed viewers how to clean up human blood.

But because Dahmer was spending so much time on his outside hobby, his work began to suffer. Ambrosia Chocolate had put up with a lot from Jeffrey Dahmer during his six years of employment, and his constant tardiness, missed shifts, and perpetual cloud of stench eventually led to the pink slip. He was fired in July 1991 and went out that very night to look for a victim. He met Oliver Lacy near Twenty-Seventh and Kilbourn, took him home, and had sex with his corpse after killing him. Lacy's heart was placed on a dish and put in the fridge for later consumption, while his skeleton was slated to be part of a shrine that Dahmer had been dreaming about for years.

He finally rediscovered his passion. Next thing he has to do is visit Italy, dance with strangers, and eat a bunch of carbs.

I still can't believe this dude had a murder shrine like Jason Voorhees in a damn apartment!

In this monument to his own depravity, Dahmer hoped to construct an altar of sorts on the black table where he usually took postmortem Polaroids of his victims. Their skulls—ten in Jeffrey's sketch of the finished product—would be flanked by the complete skeletons of Ernest Miller and Oliver Lacy. The altar would be tastefully lit by two extending blue globe lights and, to keep it special, the whole scene would be hidden behind an opaque black shower curtain. Dahmer claimed that he believed this altar would be a power center that would help him with social situations and financial burdens, but in reality, he was building nothing more than the world's most macabre masturbation station.

Dahmer's reign of terror came to an end before he was able to complete construction, but not before one more killing. Four days after the murder of Oliver Lacy, Dahmer targeted a family man named Joseph Bradehoft who had come to Milwaukee from Minnesota to find a job to support his wife and kids—yet another struggling soul for Jeffrey to take advantage of. Out after one cocktail, Dahmer lured Bradehoft home and strangled him with a strap. He disposed of the body two days later, when maggots began crawling out of the eye sockets.

Bradehoft's head would join four others in the fridge, all waiting until Dahmer reached his magic number to begin construction on the altar. The body, however, remained in the bathtub with the decapitated corpse of Oliver Lacy. Dahmer had begun showering with them.

That is one disgusting Irish Spring commercial.

Somehow, the stench of two full rotting bodies didn't prevent him from luring one more man into his apartment, though Tracy Edwards almost turned around the moment Jeffrey opened his door. The thirty-two-year-old had agreed to come over for a beer, but once the social obligation had been met, Tracy commented that it was about time for him to go. Those were the magic words that turned Jeffrey Dahmer from a smelly weirdo into a full-blown monster. Just as Tracy made the remark, Dahmer slapped a handcuff around his wrist, pushed the tip of a knife into Tracy's chest, and told him he'd die if he didn't do exactly as asked. Having once again run out of pills, he kept Edwards awake and in abject terror for over four hours.

Dahmer led Tracy to the bedroom, where he immediately noticed the unmistakable stench of death emanating from the mysterious blue barrel. He'd already noticed a few odd pictures of just men's torsos hanging in the living room, but on the walls of the bedroom he saw Polaroid after Polaroid of severed heads, butchered human meat, and disembodied limbs. Some were freshly killed; others had been half-eaten by hydrochloric acid. But despite all that, all Dahmer wanted to do with Tracy in the bedroom was watch *The Exorcist III* and drink.

Jeff just got fired; he's trying to relax! "I've spent time in many houses like this, but it's always at the homes of special effects artists so I'm pretty numb to severed heads." But I would definitely ask what he was working on next to get a feel if he's in show business or if I'm about to be charcuterie.

Once the movie was over, Dahmer told Edwards what he had planned: he was going to cut out his heart and eat it, but first he wanted to get a few photos of him while he was still alive. However, when Dahmer turned to grab the camera, Edwards punched him in the face, kicked him in the stomach, and ran out the door still handcuffed. The first people he ran into upon reaching the street were two cops named Robert Rauth and Rolf Mueller.

Possibly wanting to keep his homosexual rendezvous gone bad a secret, Tracy Edwards wasn't interested in getting his assailant arrested. All he wanted was the key to the handcuffs. Had Dahmer been in possession of said key, it's likely he would have gotten away with it once again. But when the cops knocked on his door asking for it, he jokingly said that the only way to get Tracy out of the cuffs would be to cut off his hands. Unbeknownst to the cops, there was some truth to that joke: it was how Dahmer had always removed them previously.

Comedy is so respected in the Midwest that Dahmer literally got away with murder by using jokes! Not even Fatty Arbuckle was able to pull that off.

Resigned to his fate but hoping he might pull off one more escape, Dahmer invited the officers inside to search for the key. Within seconds, Mueller noticed the stench and spotted the Polaroids hanging in the bedroom, and it didn't take him long to realize they'd been taken in the very room where he was standing. Mueller immediately called to his partner to arrest Dahmer, and though Jeffrey came close to escaping through the front door, he wasn't fast enough. Officer Robert Rauth wrestled Jeffrey Dahmer to the floor and handcuffed him, putting an end to a serial killing spree that Milwaukee police weren't even aware existed.

Cue the polka music, 'cuz it's time to celebrate!

What followed was a worldwide media event the likes of which Wisconsin hadn't seen since the days of Ed Gein. TV stations broadcast images of men in hazmat suits removing the now-iconic blue barrel from Dahmer's apartment building as reporters gave subtle hints at the horrors still being discovered inside. Besides the ungodly amount of loose flesh and severed heads, investigators also found an aluminum kettle filled with hands and genitalia. While most of Dahmer's victims were Black, one of the penises had been painted with foundation to look as though it belonged to a white man. And in the middle of it all was a tattered copy of the King James Bible.

There's a lot to unpack here.

Seriously, the crucifixion of Christ was probably more erotic to him than the Barbi Twins are to a carnie.

Over the course of sixty hours of interviews, Dahmer unburdened his soul and told his entire story, starting with the killing of Steven Hicks in 1978. He laid all seventeen murders bare, giving excruciating details about each one in an attempt to identify every victim and, in some twisted way, atone for the deep pain he'd caused the community. He was later quoted as saying, "Because I created this horror . . . it only makes sense that I do everything to put an end to it, a complete end to it."

His attempts at atonement in the confession box were not accepted by the community. He had rightly become a symbol of Milwaukee's race problem when it came to fair policing, illuminating the difference between how cases were handled. It was the opinion of many in the Black and South Asian communities that had a person of either race had moved into a white neighborhood and started eating folks, the body count would have stopped long before it reached seventeen. Furthermore, most of the Milwaukee PD looked a lot like Dahmer; in 1991, 80.4 percent of Milwaukee police officers were white, despite the fact that over half of the city's population was comprised of people of color.

In a small sign that there might be consequences for the racist behavior that had enabled Dahmer to kill four additional men despite having evidence of his wrongdoing before their murders, the two officers involved in returning Konerak Sinthasomphone to his eventual killer were suspended pending an investigation after a journalist uncovered the tale. Typically, police soon formed rank, and the officers were not only reinstated but named Officers of the Year by the Milwaukee Police Union.

Eventually, Dahmer was charged with twelve counts of murder, as five of his victims could not be identified. He tried the insanity defense, but his early-eighties hiatus proved to a jury that he had the ability to stop—he just didn't want to. After a three-week trial, Jeffrey Dahmer was sentenced to fifteen consecutive terms of life imprisonment.

Dahmer seemed not long for this world after his arrival in prison. The first attempt on his life came a little over a year into his sentence, when another prisoner tried slitting his throat with a sharpened toothbrush during a church service. Courting death, Jeffrey refused special protection and was placed back into the general population.

I feel like he wanted to die. He knew what mayhem he'd caused, and every inch of his face read like a man waiting for the end. Being murdered in jail was true penance for his ghoulish actions. He acted like a true Catholic boy.

Four months later, a schizophrenic named Christopher Scarver, who believed he was the son of God, brought Dahmer's killing career full circle, caving in his skull with a twenty-inch metal bar in the weight room while they were on a cleaning detail. After his death, an urban legend began to circulate that Dahmer had been fatally sodomized with a broom handle. While the legend has a touch of homophobia, it also has a kernel of truth. Jeffrey Dahmer wasn't the only person that Christopher Scarver murdered that day. He'd also killed another inmate on the cleaning detail named Jesse Anderson using what else but the legendary broom handle.

Admittedly, when we recorded our series on Jeffrey Dahmer many years ago, our sympathy for him had not yet vanished. While we may have no longer thought of his crimes as "cool" like we had when we were children, the need to connect on some level to the horrific men and women we cover each week still existed. However, after ten years of studying, writing, and talking about serial killers, we now know that it isn't the killers that we needed to connect to—it was our fellow humans. It's our task to shine the light on these monsters to possibly make the world a lighter place for those who have to deal with darkness every day of their lives. People like Jeffrey Dahmer don't need nor deserve that light. You, dear reader, do.

It is a sad fact to consider that if Jeffrey Dahmer had received help during his lonely teen years, he could have been on a decidedly less murderous track. But ultimately, the responsibility for his mental health and his subsequent crimes was his own. It is not his fault that the smell of decay aroused him more than the love of a good man, nor is it his fault that his various mental disorders helped to propel that desire into the act of murder. But just like everyone else, it was Dahmer's responsibility to care for those abnormalities. Because he didn't, seventeen men died ugly, senseless deaths and never saw the light of day again.

A THANK-YOU LETTER FROM DAHMER'S NEIGHBOR THERESA

Hello Jeffrey,

I wanted to thank you for having my husband and I over for lunch last week. Herbert has not stopped talking about the sausages you served; he gets ravenous when he thinks about them! As a matter of fact, he asked me to request the recipe, but I reminded him you said it was "a secret family recipe." And trust me, I understand keeping it a secret because if it got out how good your sausages are, you'd have every Sam, Dick, and Harry knocking down your door to get just a bite of one.

This is more than just a thank-you: I wanted to invite you to our annual family reunion at Lakeshore State Park. My family has heard so much about you and I'm sure they'd love your homemade sausages just as much as I did. The way you stuffed the sausage with Wisconsin cheddar was genius! I believe you said you just "stuffed the cheese into the head" which I thought was a creative way of saying "end" of the sausage link, or perhaps you meant "head cheese," a savory snack Herbert and I tried while at the Milwaukee Summer Fest last year. You've mentioned your affinity for brain before, so I'm sure an adventurous eater like you would love it. In fact, you should sell your meats at the fest next year. My mouth is salivating right now just thinking about the moistness of your sausage dripping down my chin. Mmmmmm! Your mother would be proud of you!

So, regarding the family reunion, feel free to bring whatever you like. I also really enjoyed the "calf fries" you served as a side. I'm still laughing about how you described them as having the texture of a wet football. You are too much! I'm just so happy you feel comfortable enough around us to open up about your sexuality. As we've said a hundred times before, this apartment complex is a no-judgment zone. I mean, if I judged all my neighbors, I'd have no friends at all!

Oh, just one more thing. I know you were a little embarrassed about the smell overtaking your apartment. Of course, I know it's not your fault—the fish tank you have is immaculately clean. I'm sure you're right that it's coming from the old pipes running through the building. I was doing a little research at Walmart and I found this amazing Glade PlugIn scent that I think would work great! It's called Angel Whispers. I think it would do a perfect job of masking the smell that's making you so insecure. I apologize if I shouldn't have mentioned it, you just seemed so nervous when talking about it. I wanted to reassure you that it doesn't bother me at all!

I hope your week is full of fun and hopefully more great sausages!

P.S. If you ever need to borrow my makeup again, just give me a ring. I, of all people, understand the gift of a good full-coverage foundation.

Your Neighbor from Apt. 187,

Theresa

ACKNOWLEDGMENTS

MARCUS PARKS: Adoring thanks to Carolina, who read everything I wrote before anyone and supported and encouraged me during the hardest times; monumental thanks to research assistant Annie Powers, who made it possible for us to write this book and still put out the podcast every week; gigantic thanks to our editor, Kate Napolitano, who taught me how to actually write a book; appreciative thanks to my parents, Bill and Billie Parks, and my brothers, Thomas and Charlie, for always believing in me no matter how dumb the thing I was doing seemed to be; and overdue thanks to Kay Adkisson, who gave me my first encouragement while introducing *Slaughterhouse Five*, *On the Road*, *East of Eden*, and, most of all, *In Cold Blood* into my world.

HENRY ZEBROWSKI: I'd like to thank my wife and partner, Natalie Jean, for her endless support and read-over help. She has better eyeballs—and everything else—than me. I'd like to thank the librarian at the Queens Library at Woodhaven for showing me where the paranormal and occult section was, even though I was nine. This book would not have been written without Spring-Heel'd Jack Coffee—thanks for the beans. I'd also like to thank Philip K. Dick, Frank Herbert, Kurt Vonnegut, and Ursula K. Le Guin for showing me what good authors are and how ideas can make a lifetime. One day I hope not to suck.

BEN KISSEL: Thanks to John and Carmen Grossman. Without your support I would never have been able to pursue my dreams in entertainment. Special shout-out to Bengt and Laura Kissel for giving birth to me. Thanks for always laughing at my jokes, Mom! Also, to my wonderful brothers, Erich, Chris, and Michael, thanks for helping shape who I've become as a person. Thanks to my boy Puffin for all the cuddles and to Brooke Rogers for her incredible help on my essays! I endlessly appreciate all of you! And lastly, to everyone who's been told by others they'll never make it in this crazy life—everything I do is for you. Keep on truckin' and Hail Yourself!

INDEX

A

B

C

D

E

F

G

H

I

J

K

L

M

N

O

P

R

S

T

U

V

W

Y

Z